Llewellyn's 2009

Green Living Guide

Cover design by Ellen Dahl
Editing by Ed Day

You can order annuals and books from *New Worlds*, Llewellyn's catalog. To request a free copy call toll-free: 1-877-NEW WRLD, or order online by visiting our Web site at http: / / subscriptions.llewellyn.com

ISBN: 978-0-7387-1336-6

Llewellyn Worldwide
2143 Wooddale Drive
Woodbury, MN 55125-2989

Models on the interior pages are used for illustrative purposes only and may not endorse or represent the book's subject.

Printed in the United States of America on recycled paper comprised of 15 percent post-consumer waste.

Table of Contents

Transit & Travel

On the Home Front

About the 2009 Green Living Guide

Recycle more. Drive less. Turn off the lights when you leave the room. Bring a reusable mug to the coffee shop. These days, tips to be more environmentally friendly seem ubiquitous. That's why instead of bombarding you with redundant and prescriptive how-to lists, *Llewellyn's 2009 Green Living Guide* looks at energy-saving efforts where the rubber meets the road. The twenty-two in-depth articles largely describe the personal side of environmentalism from an array of perspectives—writers ranging from experts to end-users.

Hopefully, of course, there is useful information within this collection of original essays that readers can integrate into their lives, but it's doubtful every example can be followed. Not everyone can start an ecotourism business, raise chickens or honeybees, or ride a bike to work, but everyone can appreciate the effort.

As the title suggests, this is the first in a series of annual Green Living Guides. While this guide to the ever-changing green world will never be comprehensive, our goal is to provide insight into the lesser-known niches in green living. In the meantime, enjoy this year's stories.

Lifestyles

www.indexopen.com

My Green Wedding

by Joshua Houdek

A few puffy white clouds dotted the sky, breaking up the bright late-afternoon sun. From the bluff where Kristi and I would soon take our vows, I took a deep breath and looked out over the lake below. We were lucky. The farm supervisor told us this was the best weekend they'd had all summer. Curious weather patterns had brought drought to much of the Midwest, but some recent rains helped green things up just in time. In a few hours, we would be married in a beautiful wedding that would have an immense impact on our lives, but fortunately, not on our environment.

Kristi and I have known each other for over eight years. We bought a house in the city so we could use our feet, our bikes, and mass transit to get to where we work and play. Our 101-year-old home is small and cozy. We had an energy audit last year and sealed up all the cracks where the cold Minnesota winter air was sneaking into our home. Our rain barrel and native-plant garden keeps most of the storm runoff on our lot and out of the nearby Mississippi River. We of course reduce, reuse, and recycle—and we compost, too. Needless to say, Kristi and I are taking steps to shrink our footprint on the planet.

Pat O'Loughlin of Sandhill Photography

Joshua and Kristi planned a wedding celebration that was in tune with their values.

One evening, after a long weekend of tackling backlogged house chores, we sunk into our lawn chairs on the patio. It was there in our very own backyard that we finally decided to tie the knot.

Newly engaged, we were excited to let our friends and family know of our big decision. We have a lot of friends and we come from fairly large families. Kristi and I soon decided we wanted all of these folks to be part of our wedding day. When we started putting together our guest list, we became a bit concerned.

The average wedding generates 14.5 tons of carbon dioxide—that's two times more than the average person creates over an entire year. The question quickly surfaced: How do we wed our environmental values with hosting a huge event that will bring together, feed, and entertain nearly 250 people?

The answer took a little research and some extra planning. Weddings, as you may have heard, take a lot of planning. But planning our "green wedding" wasn't too difficult, and we learned a lot along the way. We got a great start by using tips from Sierra Club's "Green Life" blog by Jennifer Hattam. (Check it out at www.sierraclub.org/greenwedding). Our green wedding mantra is the same as our everyday mantra: reduce, reuse, recycle, and compost. In that order.

The Ring

Many engagements begin with a ring. Kristi and I decided to forgo the traditional engagement diamond for a variety of reasons—mainly because Kristi simply didn't feel the need to wear a big rock on her left ring finger. The bumper sticker adage "live simply, so others may simply live" rings quite true when one considers the impact of precious metal mining on society and the environment. "Blood diamonds," those that are mined in war zones and fund conflicts, fortunately, are avoidable.

If the bride-to-be has her heart set on a diamond, you can opt for one created in a lab. If you choose one that comes out of the earth, be sure it's certified as "conflict-free" under the Kimberley Process, an ongoing effort to reform diamond mining in Africa. Diamonds mined in peaceful regions such as Canada or Australia can be a more responsible alternative as well. Check out Amnesty International's buyer's guide and quiz your jeweler about your diamond's origins.

The most sustainable and sentimental wedding or engagement ring is vintage. A family heirloom can be passed on to your beloved, or its gold can be melted down and refashioned into a new custom piece. An antique ring is another "reuse" option. If you don't find anything vintage, think "recycled." Kristi and I found 100 percent reclaimed, recycled, ecologically responsible gold wedding bands at http://GreenKarat.com.

Transportation

Once we took care of the ring, we moved on to address the aspect of our wedding that typically has the greatest impact on the environment: location, location, location. Determining where any big event is to be held has a direct effect on the distance and mode of travel required of attendees. In fact, transportation typically accounts for individuals' biggest impact on the environment. If we all decided to just stay put, we could solve global warming!

So how do you gather together all your friends and family without generating a smokestack's worth of carbon monoxide, carbon dioxide, and a host of other pollutants?

Think cool. Set the tone for your wedding day by choosing a cool location. Cool venues are sustainable venues. Support a cause you believe in, such as an organic garden, farm, or restaurant, an art gallery, or a green-roofed/LEED-certified building. Think about a venue so cool you won't need to worry about the expense and waste of decorating it for a one-time event. Outdoor settings are a natural fit for a green wedding. And don't forget to inquire if they offer comprehensive recycling facilities and, ideally, composting too.

Think convenience. A green location is a convenient location. Choose one close and easy to get to for the majority of your guests. This minimizes travel impacts. Kristi and I got married at an organic farm on the outskirts of Minneapolis, since most of our guests lived in Minnesota. Although most of our guests needed to drive, we encouraged carpooling and we eliminated the need to travel between the ceremony site and the reception by holding them at the same location.

Think mass transit. Another option is to provide eco-friendly transportation to, or between, venue(s). The most environmentally friendly method of getting a bunch of people from point A to B is via public transit. Consider getting hitched in a venue located along a bus or train line. (We considered this, but went with the tradeoff of the natural farm setting). With transit, you can cut the emissions of each and every traveling guest by up to 90 percent! Did you know a full rail car removes 200 cars from the road, and a full bus removes 60 cars? That's a breath of fresh air—and something to think about when planning a green wedding, or any event for that matter.

Unfortunately, not every wedding venue is serviced by transit. When the closest train or bus stop is miles away, consider buying carbon offsets to compensate for your guests' travel impacts—or ask them to do this for you (and them and the planet) as your wedding gift. We could not afford to buy carbon offsets for everyone, so we provided the Web site on the invitation so guests could do so on their own. Carbon offsets mitigate the environmental impact of travel by first calculating the pollution generated from a specific trip—whether it be via plane, train, or automobile. The offset company then takes the credits you purchased and invests in programs such as tree planting projects to help reduce the amount of carbon dioxide in the atmosphere.

Invitations

Ring: Check. Location: Check. Then it became time to get the word out! We knew our wedding invitation would be the first impression guests received of our special day. The "greenest" invite is electronic. Online invitation Web sites, blogs, and e-mail allow you to go paperless—a convenient means of letting people know about bachelor/ette parties, the rehearsal dinner, directions, links to carbon offset Web sites and gift registry (I'll touch on this later).

But Grandpa, Auntie Beth, and too many of our other aging relatives still are not quite computer savvy. Call us old-fashioned, but Kristi and I wanted something tangible for our wedding announcements—something to put on the refrigerator. We found recycled paper with 100 percent post-consumer content to do the trick. Although we opted for elegant simplicity and a design printed with colorful soy ink, there are many options available. A great way to save postage, paper, and money is to use postcards instead of cards with envelopes for RSVPs and thank-you cards. Use a union print shop and opt for chlorine-free paper printed with soy-based inks. Sustainable, tree-free paper options abound: hemp, banana stalk, bamboo, knaf, organic cotton—or even elephant dung! Whatever you decide, you might want to pick up some extra for your guest book, place cards, etc.

But again, don't forget the first *R*. Reduce unnecessary printing whenever you can. Besides parents or grandparents, who really saves wedding programs anyway? We also avoided the hassle and expense of place cards by simply making a roster of guests and their table assignments. This system worked out just fine—even with 250 people.

While working on our invitations, we needed to decide about gifts. Like many couples, Kristi and I have lived on our own or with roommates for many years and have accumulated lots of household stuff. When we got together, we realized we had "doubles" of a lot of items. After all, who really needs two toasters? We didn't need more material goods for our home. We asked our guests to make a donation in our name to an environmental organization or to our 101-year-old home's fix-up fund. Jennifer Hattam of the Sierra Club offers several more creative ideas for eco-friendly gift giving: Register with the "I Do Foundation" or another website that gives a percentage of gift purchases to your chosen cause. Register with stores that sell local, fair-trade, handmade, organic, or other eco-friendly products like Branch, Gaiam, Greenfeet, GreenSage, Ten Thousand Villages, UncommonGoods, VivaTerra, or Patagonia. Another idea is to create a custom wish list of "green" gifts like a fresh-produce subscription to a local Community Supported Agriculture (CSA) farm, organic linens, park and museum passes, gift certificates to organic restaurants, and subscriptions to green publications or memberships in green causes.

Attire

Once we settled on our invitations and gift registry, next came the big challenge for Kristi—what to wear? We decided to have a very casual wedding, so the dress decision wasn't as hard for Kristi as it is perhaps for some brides. The second *R* is important here: Reuse. Getting married in something that can be worn more than once and not relegated to a box in the back of the closet is key. Kristi picked out a simple floral sundress that she could wear again and again. My wardrobe needed updating, so I found a nice shirt and pants that I've worn numerous times since our wedding day. It's a cool feeling to button into the same shirt in which you were married.

The green options for wedding attire are endless. Like a ring, you can go vintage with a dress or gown from grandma, a hip consignment shop, or something borrowed from a stylish friend. Or find clothes for the bride, groom, and wedding party that are sweatshop free and crafted of "green" threads. Think hemp, bamboo, or certified organic cotton, silk, or wool. Most importantly, think "Reuse."

Decorations

Reusing wedding décor is sometimes a bit more of a challenge. Here's where your location comes back into play. No need to go overboard. The first "R," Reduce, is king when it comes to decorations. An outdoor wedding may need little to no extra decorations. If the setting is indoors, remember that once a room is filled with people, decorations get absorbed into the scene and often go unnoticed. We simply picked up some flowers from our local farmers' market. Kristi's beautiful organic bouquet was locally grown on a farm just 10 miles from where we live. We complemented it with a few cuttings from our own native plant garden. Black-eyed Susans, a native wildflower with bright, beautiful yellow blooms, were at their prime for our August wedding.

We grappled over our table centerpieces. Candles or live potted plants? At first, I opted for the latter. Plants clean the air and guests can take them home. After purchasing our first home, I found myself getting into gardening. I wanted to have native wildflower centerpieces on our tables, but time and expenses prompted a compromise on this aspect of the wedding. Candles were just easier and they certainly set the right tone for an evening of dining and dancing. Choose beeswax or soy-based candles over those made with paraffin, a petroleum byproduct. For a natural effect, you can decorate with branches, dried grasses, grains, greens, berries, and stones. Of course be mindful of where you obtain these items. At the end of the day, donate your décor to a nursing home, hospice, church, or hospital.

Although centerpieces took a while for us to figure out, tablecloths were easy. This is where Kristi's friends and fellow volunteers from Global Citizens Network (http://globalcitizens.org) came into play. Textiles and cloth make ideal souvenirs after working on a sustainable development project in places like Guatemala, Kenya, and Nepal. They represent the intricate weave of cultural exchange that takes place between volunteers and the host community. For a colorful pattern of table coverings at our wedding, we borrowed these special fabrics collected from friends from their travels all over the world.

If you're looking for tablecloths that match or don't have access to an international rainbow of textiles that fits your theme, renting fine linens is the way to go, rather than using disposables.

Food

Think global, act local. Contrary to worldly tablecloths, our menu was just the opposite. Food shipped from a farm or factory thousands of miles away from your kitchen table burns a lot of fossil fuels. Not to mention working conditions and environmental protections often go unregulated in many developing countries. So the food Kristi and

I offered at our wedding was the same we try to eat every day—based in local, organic, and seasonal goodness. We had the luxury of using whatever caterer we wanted at our venue, so we found a women-owned, neighborhood business called "Chowgirls" that prepares delicious grub with a strong emphasis on the environment. The marriage of a vegetarian and an omnivore resulted in a carte du jour of veggie burgers and Italian sausage. The sausage was a big compromise from a much greener, all vegetarian or vegan menu. We did, however, find hand-packed sausage links from a local co-op that were certified organic, free range, and cruelty-free.

To accompany our casual BBQ dinner, we quenched our thirst with Finnegans, a locally brewed beer that operates as a nonprofit and donates all of its profits to fighting poverty. Etica, our fair-trade wine selection, was an excellent complement to our meal. What surprised me was neither the wine nor the beer we chose was any more expensive than comparable selections. And in case you didn't know, be advised you can go organic with wine, beer, and spirits as well. We washed down our dessert cupcakes with organic, fair trade, shade-grown, and bicycle-delivered Peace Coffee. Mmmmm.

A healthy, organic menu is one thing, but dealing with waste is another. At the end of your wedding, don't be left holding the "garbage" bag. Kristi and I diverted over 150 pounds of "waste" from going to the landfill by doing some simple advance planning. Our wedding was a zero-waste event. What do I mean by this? Eureka Recycling defines it as "designing and managing materials and resources in ways that conserve and recover them." Our wedding conserved resources by maximizing recycling and minimizing waste.

Maximizing recycling is a no-brainer for a green wedding. Make sure it is easy and convenient for your guests to do their part by ensuring an ample amount of well-marked recycling containers. Minimize waste by renting glassware, dishware, and linens instead of using

Pat O'Loughlin of Sandhill Photography

Here comes the bride—in a sundress that can be worn over and over again.

disposables. If this is too impractical, but composting is available, go the biodegradable route like Kristi and I did. Our guests dined with 100 percent biodegradable, compostable cornstarch utensils and unbleached paper plates and napkins. They enjoyed fine wine from clear, plastic-like cups made of glucose from corn and potatoes. Our guests sipped coffee with their dessert from cups made of bagasse, a byproduct of the sugarcane refining process.

At the end of the day, food scraps went to feeding the farm's pigs, the biodegradable dishware and flower arrangements either went home with guests or went to the local composting facility. Glass wine bottles and aluminum cans went to the recycling plant. Long after the event was over, we saved paper and chemicals by getting digital proofs of our wedding photos. We didn't use single-use cameras and gathered our friends' digital photos online in a free photo-sharing group we set up. Presto! Zero waste. No garbage to the local landfill.

Powering It All

On a global scale, the greatest contributor to global warming is energy production. Why power your wedding with energy from dirty coal plants when you can get it from clean, renewable sources? Kristi and I amplified our vows to our friends and family via a solar-powered sound system. The same solar-charged batteries ran the band's music and sound equipment for the reception. We rented the portable solar power system from a local nonprofit, the Minnesota Renewable Energy Society. If you can't get your hands on a solar panel or wind turbine, consider purchasing a renewable energy certificate, which invests in renewable electricity development. Go to http://eere.energy.gov for more information. Regardless of how your wedding is powered, brainstorm ways to reduce and conserve energy. For example, no lights need to be switched on if you hold your outdoor wedding during the daytime.

Accommodations

Kristi and I enjoy the outdoors so we decided to share one of our favorite pastimes with our guests—camping! After the reception, over 50 of our closest friends and family camped out with us under the stars. At first I was skeptical of the idea that folks would want to "rough it" for a night, but many of our guests decided to forgo the expense of a hotel room and join in the fun. Although not for everyone, camping was a wonderful way to end our wedding weekend. Just be sure to follow the Leave No Trace principles, including minimizing campfire impacts and being considerate of other visitors. (Learn more at http://lnt.org)

Camping in a park on one's wedding night is in sharp contrast to what the high consumption, consumer-driven, $70-billion wedding industry is all about. Vote with your dollars and support your values. Reducing the environmental impact of your wedding shouldn't break your budget. In fact, going green can cost a lot less than the average wedding. It's about tradeoffs. Organic food can be a little more expensive, but Kristi and I saved hundreds of dollars by getting married in clothes we can wear over and over again. The bottom line: reducing, reusing, recycling, and composting not only conserves natural resources but your financial resources as well.

NBC's *Today Show* did a piece on green weddings a couple of years ago. Ann Thompson, the network's chief environmental consultant reminded viewers, "there are many shades of green." You can take the green concept as far as you want. Anything you do to reduce the environmental impact of your wedding will help our planet in the long run. Most importantly, remember that any event can be green, not just your wedding day. So ditch the paper coffee cups and box lunches at your next meeting and go green! Congratulations on your big day!

Starting an Ecotourism Business

by Lisa Kivirist

Wake up to the smells of a full-bodied organic, fair trade–certified Sumatran coffee brewing and a sumptuous vegetarian breakfast prepared with ingredients harvested from less than a hundred feet away. Before leaving your cozy bed, nestled between organic sheets, to take a water-conserving shower with water heated by the sun, you run through the day's upcoming adventures: biking the Badger State Trail that winds through the countryside and a tunnel; grabbing lunch at Baumgartner's located on the Historic Monroe Courthouse Square, savoring a cheese sandwich of locally made cheeses and washing it down with an award-winning Berghoff beer from the brewery right down the street; catching a double feature at the Sky-Vu Drive-In Theatre. A quick glance out the window onto the kitchen gardens and at the wind turbine spinning confirms that the good life doesn't have to come at a cost to the planet.

An ecotourism business cares for the environment and customers who travel for authentic experiences without negatively impacting the areas they visit. It nurtures the land and selects vendors that likewise operate in more sustainable ways. Ecotourism businesses showcase and help preserve the unique natural and cultural heritage of its community. More than a buzzword, *ecotourism* represents travel that helps protect, restore, or enhance the natural and cultural heritage of an area while contributing to the local economy. Because of its elusive definition, however, other terms have also become common when referring to this approach to travel, including *geotourism*, *green travel*, and *sustainable travel*.

Recognizing the double-digit growth of ecotourism, along with a determination to make the world a better place by harnessing the power of business, my husband John and I launched our ecotourism business a little over a decade ago in the form of Inn Serendipity Bed & Breakfast, based on a five-and-a-half acre farmstead located outside Monroe, Wisconsin, also known as the "Swiss Cheese Capital of the U.S.A." Earning accolades for our stewardship of the land, approach to business, and success at powering our operations by the wind and sun, we strive to incorporate various aspects of green design, natural building, renewable energy, and the conservation of limited resources or restoration of the ecological systems on which our business depends.

Nature serves as our model. It guides us in our organic gardens, from which we harvest about 70 percent of the food we serve our guests, and challenges us in our purchase decisions where we mindfully try to operate in a waste-free manner. In nature, there is no waste. My husband and I adopt an ecological "systems approach" to operating the ecotourism business which encompasses food, living, and energy systems as well as a livelihood that supports ecological stewardship and health. We found prosperity possible without destroying the environment or exploiting people.

Place-Based Features of Ecotourism Businesses

There are many creative ways to run an ecotourism business, based on your interests, location, and budget. The International Ecotourism Society offers helpful ecotourism principles for eco-travelers and ecotourism business owners alike: minimize impacts; build environmental and cultural awareness; and provide direct financial benefits for conservation as well as financial benefits that stay in the community.

The small ecotourism hospitality business John and I established roosts in an area known for its cheese, beer, Swiss heritage, and a network of bike trails following old railroad corridors that traverse the patchwork of rolling countryside. Providing milk for the award-winning cheeses made in the county, the cows here still outnumber people. Guests often hit the bike trails, pick up cheeses directly from factories, or join in one of the numerous festivals—including the world-renowned Cheese Days celebration that takes place during even numbered years—in nearby small towns. Bruno Hodel, a Swiss-born cheesemaker, owns the Alp & Dell Cheese Store, which features the area's largest collection of European-style cheeses. His store is part of the Roth Kase Cheese Factory, where visitors can watch cheese being made.

Since we enjoyed hosting people, traveling, and cooking, our decision to run a B & B was a great fit and an important aspect of our diversified livelihood. Interest in the local food movement, the hundred-mile diet and vegetarian cuisine further distinguishes our unique little inn. Recognizing that eating lower on the food chain and more locally are immediate steps that we can take to combat global warming, we prepare seasonal and often fresh-that-morning meals that might include rhubarb muffins, zucchini-feta-cheese pancakes, fresh strawberry smoothies, and oven-roasted new potatoes. Our guests enjoy our seasonal cuisine so much that we've created the *Edible Earth Cookbook*, which contains some of our favorites. An ecotourism operation, however, could have just as easily been a restaurant featuring local organic foods or a bicycle shop powered by renewable energy. An ecotourism business isn't so much what you do, but how you do it.

Conservation and Efficiency First

With a limited bank account, we opened up two rooms in the farmhouse after completing numerous "green renovations," including removing the carpets to expose natural hardwood floors, repainting the B & B with paint free of VOCs (volatile organic compounds), adding guest bathrooms featuring tile made from recycled glass, and installing an EPA-certified woodstove. Conservation measures covered everything from switching incandescent to compact fluorescent light bulbs to line-drying laundry and replacing windows with super efficient double-pane inserts. Just about every major appliance was replaced with Energy Star-certified energy-efficient equivalents, many costing only slightly more upfront than other options, but are more cost-effective due to the amount of energy saved.

By running our small ecotourism operation, we've found that our energy-conserving changes transformed our operations from fossil-fuel based to fossil-fuel free and helped save hundreds of dollars in energy costs. The back-to-basics farm experiences we offer are enthusiastically received by the like-minded guests we often attract. No drones from air conditioners here. Not much traffic either. We're often sharing experiences of canning or root cellaring our bountiful crop of leeks that we eat through March of the next year.

Our investments in renewable energy, green building practices, or sustainable design pays dividends both in cost savings over time and attractiveness as a destination. We make investments incrementally; as funds are saved, they're earmarked for projects. Some projects were possible, in part, because we secured state grants. Knowledgeable neighbors with years of experience in the gardens or with renewable energy systems guided our plans. Partnerships with nonprofit organizations like the Midwest Renewable Energy Association and Wisconsin Focus on Energy also supported us.

About five years after opening the B & B, we added a recreational cabin, Inn Serendipity Woods, located on thirty acres outside Hillsboro. The cabin, which we rent during the summer, features a solar thermal system for domestic hot water, sustainably harvested hardwood floors, a bathroom with tile made from recycled glass, and an EPA-certified wood stove for heat. The cabin accounts for about 20 percent of our gross income, and the proceeds are applied to the sustainable management of twenty acres of forestland and a three-acre conservation-reserve program—an afforestation buffer along a stream (three acres are rented to an Amish farmer for organic cultivation of corn).

Renewable Energy Systems

With energy conservation and efficiency efforts exhausted, our investment in renewable energy generation became more cost effective, especially since we could use the existing electrical grid to "bank" our surplus electricity. We harvest the solar and wind energy to spin our electricity meter backwards most of the year, making our operations a net producer of renewable energy.

While an initial investment needs to be made, our solar thermal systems and 10 kW Bergey wind turbine, as examples, will pay for themselves in five and eighteen years, respectively. In less than a decade, we've managed to sever our dependency on utilities to meet our energy needs. A grid intertied photovoltaic, or PV, system provides electricity from sunlight-generated power during the summer when production from the wind turbine is less consistent. The hybrid wind-solar electric system offsets about $1,200 in electric bills we would have paid each year. Instead of costing $500 to $1,000 a winter to heat

John D. Ivanko, innserendipity.com

The Inn Serendipity Bed & Breakfast has a solar thermal system on the roof and shower water heated by the sun.

our home-based business, it now costs almost nothing at all thanks to the super-efficient wood stove, which burns locally secured, downed, and seasoned hardwood. As an added bonus, the top of the stove is used to simmer sauces and soups.

Sometimes social and environmental costs are more important than economic payback windows when considering the alternative energy source to utility-owned coal-fired electrical power stations. For a grid-connected home and business, our decision to add PV was about more than the economics of energy, since reducing carbon dioxide, nitrous oxide, and mercury emissions and achieving greater energy self-reliance were just as important. It's a matter of operating our business in as responsible a way as possible, within our financial limitations.

Natural Building and Green Design

Many ecotourism businesses exemplify natural or green building practices, employing various strategies to use natural, nontoxic materials, recycled products, energy efficiency, and local or reused materials. From the sustainably harvested hardwood flooring used in our kitchen to homemade natural cleaning supplies like baking soda and vinegar, we explore ways we can reduce our harm on natural systems. Around the farmhouse and property, we've added evergreens for wind breaks; a wildlife pond adjacent to the house; and simple water encatchment systems are used, connected to gutter downspouts.

A strawbale greenhouse, one of our retrofitted farm outbuildings, serves as an example of natural building and green design. Heated with a solar thermal system and biodiesel-fueled furnace, the greenhouse is insulated with straw bales. It features a second floor tropical growing space with south-facing skylights and a first floor growing space for shade-tolerant, cool weather plants. Papayas, lime, and banana are experimental crops grown to possibly offer our B & B guests in the winter. It's used in various other ways to extend our growing season or get a jump on the next one.

To become better land stewards, we've committed ourselves to recycling and reusing, to a large degree turning others' junk into something useful and practical. My husband's old baritone is reused as a lamp in our creativily-themed guest rooms. Thanks to neighbors who've warmly adopted us and who possess far more tinkering talents than we do, we've been able to reuse old furnaces, wood, and salvaged materials in many aspects of the business. For example, we collaboratively transform used fryer oil from area restaurants into emission-reducing biodiesel to burn in our backup greenhouse furnace.

Our favorite tinkering adventure, however, is working with our neighbors, Phil and Judy Welty, who helped restore an all-electric-powered 1974 CitiCar. After spotting it outside a barn near Janesville,

Wisconsin, Phil and John hauled it back to our farm to be restored and largely rewired by Phil. Since about 80 percent of our driving is less than twenty-five miles round trip, the all-electric CitiCar—now powered by an off-grid solar electric photovoltaic system—will keep us moving around locally, completely powered by the sun.

Buying Local, Buying Organic and Fair-Trade

Ecotourism thrives on local interactions, commerce, and community. To every extent possible, we support local family farm operations and small businesses. Our eggs come from a family farm four miles north of us. Whether for printing needs or garden transplants, building a strong local community is crucial. The rapidly expanding farmers' markets and Community Supported Agriculture (CSA) options for buying food, for example, help link visitors to what is grown in the community.

When buying local is not feasible, as with coffee, we select a vendor with a track record of environmental and social responsibility. Inn Serendipity serves organic, fair-trade certified, shade-grown Equal Exchange coffee and we also purchase their cocoa for drinks and cooking. We use a buyer's club, pooling our order with other families or area businesses, to secure organic and healthier food staples in bulk, like sugar and flour.

Carbon Negative

With our heightened awareness of global warming, we endeavor to operate our business carbon negative—sequestering more carbon dioxide than we emit—by both how we operate as well as by purchasing carbon offsets from the Carbonfund.org Foundation. Many similar programs now exist, providing ecotourism businesses with more options to mitigate the impacts of their operations.

Recognizing that most of our guests would arrive to our farm by car, we partner with the nonprofit organization Trees for the Future and purchase "Trees for Travel" certificates. These certificates represent trees planted in communities in developing countries. Besides sequestering carbon dioxide through the natural growth, the trees can stabilize degraded lands and provide community development opportunities.

An aggressive tree-planting program, soil restoration, water conservation, and the use of local or green building materials like Forest Stewardship Certified sustainably harvested wood also reflect our commitment to sustaining the living systems and cutting Inn Serendipity's carbon dioxide emissions. If putting up a wind turbine to meet your electricity needs may not be possible, you could purchase "green energy" through your local utility like we also do, or buy "green tags" and similar programs that place needed investments in renewable energy production, rather than coal or nuclear power generation plants.

Because vehicle emissions are among the largest contributors to global warming, we've switched our long-range car to a Volkswagen Jetta TDI diesel, using biodiesel blends in warm weather months. For local commuting, the 1974 all-electric CitiCar moves us around, recharged using a stand-alone 0.5 kW off-grid photovoltaic system.

Attracting Ecotourism Travelers

According to Paul Ray and Sherry Ruth Anderson in their book, *Cultural Creatives*, there are 50 million people who are deeply concerned about the environment and myriad problems facing the planet. This same group enjoys learning about and experiencing other ways of living and are willing to pay more for products or services that help heal the planet. Ray and Anderson's findings echo the Travel Industry Association of America's Geotourism Study, revealing that nearly 55.1

John D. Ivanko, innserendipity.com

Interior of the straw-bale greenhouse, which provides a variety of produce for guests, including papayas.

million people in the United States express a preference for unique and culturally authentic travel experiences that protect and preserve the ecological and cultural environment.

Marketing to these eco-minded travelers is a matter of walking the talk and engaging them in the experiences you've created, with social and ecological considerations in mind. We've found that our renewable energy systems and focus on organic foods are competitive advantages. Inn Serendipity is one of the few B & Bs in the world powered by renewable energy. Such an emphasis on sustainable operations has resulted in guests who choose us over other lodging options.

Instead of buying advertisements in glitzy magazines, we've found that supporting conservation organizations with fund-raising auction donations or advertisements in their newsletters to be effective communication channels. In nearly every significant renewable energy system addition—wind turbine, PV system, strawbale greenhouse, and solar thermal systems—we found an interested and engaged media eager to share our story about living more sustainably on the land with their audiences.

Our guests tend to watch little TV, instead seeking out news and information through more progressive and positive outlets like renewable energy and sustainable living fairs or expos. Most of our guests arrive at our doors because they, too, share a vision for a more sustainable world and need a place—as we all do—to relax and unwind. They often arrive driving hybrid cars, and once, on bicycle. Complimentary tours of the farm have lasted as long as three hours; conversations around the campfire or breakfast table can linger for hours.

We relish our "business as unusual" approach to operations. By cementing our values with our operations, the business becomes a part of the solution to global warming, pollution and other environmental issues that we care deeply about and want to help solve. Our customers recognize this commitment, supporting it by staying at our B & B. As a result, we consider every aspect of how we communicate with our potential cultural creative customers, starting with our brochure (printed on recycled paper) and Web site (explaining our business philosophy). Communication with guests or participants of ecotourism businesses remains a foundation for our operations. By being green and running our ecotourism operations, we've become more profitable while helping restore the health of the soil and improve water and air quality.

Like other B & Bs, restaurants, and many other small businesses, the most effective form of advertising is by "word-of-mouth" from satisfied guests. We managed our cash flow carefully when starting out, since we realized that it could take upwards of five or six years to become established. Other income-generating enterprises provided the time necessary for the ecotourism business to develop a following.

Ecotourism Certification

While no uniform global certification program exists that is widely adopted by businesses, organizations, or communities, most certification, labeling or similarly conceived programs tend to address the following key aspects:

1) Energy conservation and efficiency through green building, management, sustainable materials, and appliances.

2) Use of renewable energy and biofuels and in other ways reducing or eliminating the impacts of transportation.

3) Waste reduction, reuse, and recycling.

4) Restoring, enhancing, or conserving natural and cultural resources, including water, air, soil, human relationships, and other place-based attributes.

5) Engaging customers through active participation in the area's natural and cultural heritage.

6) Purchase of sustainable and socially responsible products or services from locally owned businesses, including food, energy, supplies, and materials.

7) Local community benefits and charitable giving practices, including an educational aspect that involves customers, employees, and the public.

Certified Green

With the widespread growth in ecotourism, numerous organizations now serve as beacons for further development, some offering certification programs. Co-op America's Green Pages (www.coopamerica.org/pubs/greenpages/) provides an opportunity for ecotourism businesses to be listed after being reviewed based on their practices, as does Eco Hotels of the World (www.ecohotelsoftheworld.com). The

International Ecotourism Society (www.ecotourism.org) provides resources and networks of ecotourism lodges, attractions, and operators spanning the globe. Inn Serendipity is a member of The International Ecotourism Society and Co-op America's Business Network.

To help travelers locate ecotourism operations, new certification programs have been developed, most notably for businesses within Wisconsin by Travel Green Wisconsin (www.travelgreenwisconsin.com) and within Minnesota through Renewing the Countryside's Green Routes program (www.greenroutes.org). Such certification programs provide travelers with more reliable information related to ecotourism practices. Inn Serendipity is certified by Travel Green Wisconsin while also being listed in the growing number of green travel Web site portals such as It's a Green World (http://itsagreengreenworld.com) and the U.S.-based Green Vacation Hub, (http://greenvacationhub.com).

Being Part of the Solution

From using nontoxic cleaners, no-VOC paints, stains, and finishes to selecting organic linens and adopting organic growing strategies in our gardens—and powering it with renewable energy—we offer our guests a more healthy and safe environment to enjoy while making the world a better place. By operating an ecotourism business, we help the very things that first attracted our guests' interest—clean air, pure water, healthy soil, sweeping countryside vistas, and an attractive downtown courthouse square—remain that way.

The Rise of Ethical Fashion: Can We Change The World With Style?

by Elizabeth Laskar

With the news media bombarding us with information about war, poverty, and potentially devastating environmental change, making pretty clothes an issue can sound downright petty. But it shouldn't. The fashion industry is large enough to have a profound impact on these global issues.

Consumers spent well over 1 trillion U.S. dollars on clothing and fashion-related accessories in the year 2000—not a bad haul to ring in the millennium. And since then? Statistics tell us that our spending on clothing continues to rise at an ever-increasing pace. Just a few decades ago, fashion seasons rotated a couple of times a year, but in the new millennium we are seeing many brands introducing new collections every couple of months, creating a real buzz—and we feel the desire to keep up with it.

Not only do we have the desire, today we have the means to keep up. Never before have we had the collective global buying power to

Fashion Facts:
Did You Know?

• At least 8,000 chemicals are used to turn raw materials into clothes, towels, bedding, and other items that we put next to our skin every day.

• Worldwide, the cotton industry is worth more than $32 billion.

• Child labor has been reported worldwide throughout the manufacturing and production chains in fashion, such as the hundreds of thousands of children that the Uzbekistan regime forces to pick cotton.

make this happen. It's the era of "fast fashion" and we can re-brand and re-invent our image on a weekly basis and pretty cheaply at that. It's great . . . isn't it?

Under the Garment Industry

But is it all that wonderful? What is the story behind the design, the garment, the cloth, the crop? What's the real cost of looking good?

Have you ever wondered how many countries your T-shirt has traveled before it hits the retail store? The crop is often grown in one country, spun and woven in another, designed and cut in another, sewn and finished in another. How much carbon dioxide and fossil fuels has the travelogue of your T-shirt cost the planet?

How about the workers involved in the production—have they been fairly treated? Has child labor been used? Where are the laborers from? With these questions in mind, suddenly our T-shirt has unveiled a tremendous story behind it that we have, in most cases unknowingly, fully supported through our purchase.

The Rise of Ethical Fashion

Over the last two years, we have seen the mainstream rise of "ethical fashion," an exciting arena that is tackling the issues causing the statistics mentioned above.

Although there has been activity in the area of ethical fashion for decades, it's all been behind the scenes, and it's largely been media coverage of environmental issues that has helped bring attention to the "real" beauty of fashion—fashion and ethics.

The statistics above are terrifying and it is wise to remember that it is not about pointing fingers at the culprits, but starting to make informed choices and focus on the solutions. How about we help alleviate poverty and environmental damage stylishly?!

So What Is Ethical Fashion?

Simply put, would you knowingly purchase and wear a garment if you knew that it had damaged the environment, employed children, and even killed people? I suspect that the answer for most people is "no." Putting these ideals into action is ethical fashion.

On a broader scale, ethical fashion engages in and promotes a fashion industry that acknowledges environmental and social issues. While determining the criteria for "ethical" practices may be the subject of debate for many years (note the debate over organic food labeling), we have got to start acting now.

The fact is consumers are currently supporting a fashion industry that engages in unethical practices. With our desire to keep up with the latest style, a market for "disposable" clothing has been created. And manufacturers have responded to our needs. Clothes are getting cheaper and cheaper for us to buy and we are buying more and more. Why? Because clothing is so cheap! How many pairs of jeans do we really need? Is $2.99 really a value if it doesn't factor in the costs to the Earth?

www.indexopen.com

Price is only one consideration for conscientious shoppers.

If we care about the environment, humanitarian issues, ourselves, and our future we need to take a closer look at how we spend our dollar. The way we spend has national and international power and we can start to save our environment and the people in it by making a few simple choices in our day-to-day living practices. It may not be easy—but what challenge ever is?

The exciting news about ethical fashion today is that you don't have to look like a hippie or wear unfashionable clothes. Gone are the days of ethical fashion being associated with hard-line activists wearing large rainbow baggy jumpers. The pioneers in the sector are giving us choices that are design-led and stylish—often using some of the most exclusive, innovative materials and techniques in the world. The industry and designers are striving to move toward becoming holistic, though this will take its time. A design label may be using organic materials to manufacture its garments, but it may not be fair trade.

With London, Paris, and New York fashion weeks starting to take notice of ethical fashion and devoting special areas to leading designers and brands within the ethical fashion sector, we know that things are set to get even better.

Five Key Elements of Ethical Fashion

The ethical fashion sector has five key areas—organic, fair trade, vintage, recycled, and innovation. Make a habit of reading clothing labels and looking for certifications in these areas—it's a good start toward becoming a more informed consumer.

Organic

Organic clothing concerns the fabric of a garment. All our clothes are made from different fibers that have been spun to give us a workable yarn and woven fabric. Fashion masters can then work at creating beautifully designed clothes. The textile industry is one of the largest

Fashion Facts:
Did You Know?

- Over 7 million tons of clothes are thrown away and end up in landfills in the United States—only 2 million tons are recycled. In the UK, over 1 million tons of unwanted clothing and fabrics are put into landfills every year. The tonnage is increasing and the landfill space is decreasing—do the math! Besides the amount of clothing, we're also "throwing away" the time and energy used to produce and buy the initial garment.
- Mismanagement of irrigation of Uzbekistan's $1-billon cotton industry has had a massive environmental impact in the drying up of the Aral Sea. Uzbekistan's cotton farming uses over 20 trillion liters of water every year. The Aral Sea has been drained to 15 percent of its former volume.

polluters of the world, so farming organic is an effective way to help save our environment.

Many farmers in the industry use poisonous pesticides that not only harm the farmers and grazing animals, but also devastate the topsoil, absorb deep into the substrate layers, and seep into our rivers. Sadly, the pesticide story does not end there. Residues of the chemicals stay in the harvested crop and are still present in the finished garment. Although the garment may not be immediately harmful to our skin, it certainly is not healthy.

Farmers now have the option of growing materials organically, which helps protect their lives and the environment. It is best for the farmer to seek certification from an established, reputable organization such as the U.K.-based Soil Association, PANUK, and German-based Oeko-Tex. Doing so lets consumers know the farm is following strict regulations. The industry is still fairly young and there are other certification bodies on the scene with standards of varying rigor, which should generate both interest and some skepticism—we need to tread with some faith and plenty of questions.

Much like growing organic food, the worldwide market for organic textile crops is growing, reducing the risk for organic farmers. Many high-street shops and up-market designers are starting to opt for organic textiles.

Fair Trade

Fair trade should not be muddled with free trade. They are most certainly linked, but are absolutely not the same things. Fair trade deals specifically with humanitarian and social issues when it comes to manufacturing a garment. The usual concerns for fair-trade businesses incorporate the following issues:

- **Helping the disadvantaged by creating opportunities:** This may involve investigating and recognizing opportunities to help the disadvantaged, providing business skills, education, and training
- **Transparency and accountability:** Being open about business practices ranging from profit and wages to hours worked by each staff member
- **Capacity building:** Helping businesses grow and find new markets for their products and services
- **Awareness:** Sharing the stories about the people in fair trade and their businesses
- **Trade relations:** With social, economic, and environmental issues at the core of business, they rely on relationships of mutual trust
- **Gender equity:** Learning about the needs of its female workers and making sure their needs are met
- **Working conditions:** Safe and clean working environments

Fashion Facts:
Did You Know?

- Globally, the workforce in clothing and textiles was about 27 million in 2000. Compare that to the auto industry, which directly and indirectly employs 70 million workers.
- According to the Pesticide Action Network (PAN), manufacturing one cotton T-shirt takes one-quarter pound of chemicals; a pair of jeans requires the use of two-thirds of a pound of chemicals.
- Unfair wages have been reported to be as little as 2 pence (4 cents) an hour in places like Bangladesh, which manufacture for much of the West.

• **Child labor:** With respect to the United Nations convention on rights of a child, local laws and social norms are considered

• **The environment:** Encourages better practices that help sustain the environment, like sourcing sustainable materials

There are many fair-trade certification bodies worldwide and again, when you see one on a label, it needs to be questioned. The certification industry is fairly young in the garment sector and sadly, full of "freeloaders" who have seen the opportunity and deliberately try to deceive the consumer. When buying a garment, take a look at the certification mark, which should have a web address. Make a note of it and then go home to do some research. If you are satisfied, then go back and buy. It's not easy, but it is a worthwhile task. One reputable certification body is IFAT (International Fair Trade Association) a global network of fair trade organizations that supports thousands of businesses worldwide. It is important to remember that some businesses may be in the process of applying for certification—best to ring them up and ask.

One of the most wonderful things about fair-trade products are the stories behind the pieces. You'll find that you value your garment just that little bit more and instead of wearing a story of horrors you wear a story worth telling, and guess what? Good news travels fast.

Vintage

This exciting area of ethical fashion is all about finding those hidden fashion treasures, parading them with pomp, and being totally in style all at the same time.

Vintage celebrates the master craft of fashion, including couture, from the past and brings it to play in the present. Pieces are always designed by acclaimed international designers, impeccably sewn together by teams of master craftspeople and made with some of the

www.indexopen.com

We make our fashion decisions and develop habits early in life.

most luxurious fabrics in the world. The excellent construction and selection of high-quality materials often mean that they can continue to look good and stylish for decades.

Our fashion times have called for us to rummage around in our grandparents' or parents' dusty wardrobes and thrift shops for those masterpieces that can be shown off with confidence today. You only have to look at today's top stylists to realize the relevance of vintage fashion and how a piece can make a comeback year after year without ever going out of fashion. The Banana Split dress by Mary Quant would be a great stylish piece to parade on today's fashion scene.

Today's celebrity and fashion icons always have vintage apparel in their wardrobe and we should not be afraid to join the club.

Recycled and Redesigned

On a recent visit to Germany, someone had scribbled this on the old Berlin Wall: "how can you throw things away when there is no away?" That really says it all.

Recycling is all about rescuing a garment from the landfill and finding a better and/or a new use for it. But we still have to be smart and consider all possible consequences. For example, the laudable act of donating your old clothes to a charity shop is not always the best method because shipping clothing to developing countries has had detrimental effects in itself. The idea should be to buy less, buy clothes that suit you, and buy quality.

The growing trend of recycled clothing is now also expanding to re-design—nothing really that new as the war years give us stories of wedding dresses made from silk curtains.

Another great trend in the UK at the moment is chic clothes swapping parties. Themed into dress and suit evenings, the night is spent catching up with friends and walking home with a stylish new outfit. Not a bad way to spend an evening.

Using eBay is also another great way to recycle clothing and make some pocket money at the same time.

Many amazing, talented, young designers are coming up with novel ways of using recycled clothing. Leading designers like Junky Styling (UK) and From Somewhere (UK and Italy) are great examples of how a little imagination teamed with excellence in design and construction can bring a new dimension to ethical fashion. Dresses, skirts, tops, trousers—an entire new wardrobe redesigned from clothes that would

The detailed work of designers can come through on any fabric.

have gone into landfill. Junky Styling has a fabulous bomber style jacket made from a jogging top and a gentleman's suit jacket that retails for about $200. From Somewhere offers a patchwork tailored coat made from cashmere offcuts from top fashion houses in Italy. You would never be able to tell that both garments were once on their way to a landfill. Redesign is certainly one of the most challenging areas and one that is growing in popularity year after year. For a designer to commit to redesign is labor and talent intensive, but also has a huge creative edge to it. The design work is amazing and they guarantee that you will not find a piece like it anywhere in the world. "Be unique" is the motto of the redesign industry.

Innovation

Science is helping create new textiles and fabrics. These new fibers perform well with our bodies and are kind to the environment.

Fashion Facts:
Did You Know?

- The World Health Organization (WHO) states that over 20,000 deaths occur each year from pesticide poisoning in developing countries—many of them cotton farmers—not including the suicide rate among farmers. (Suicides are sometimes related to debt to loan sharks, who farmers are forced to turn to at times to buy pesticides.)
- Cotton is a pesticide-heavy crop that uses about 25 percent of the world's insecticides and 10 percent of the world's pesticides. While a lot of clothes use synthetic fabrics, cotton is still very much a staple and a preferred fiber—60 percent of global consumers said they wore more cotton than any other fiber according to a recent study by the Global Lifestyle Monitor.

The ethical fashion sector has seen leading designers using unconventional textiles like hemp, bamboo, and soya. Bamboo or hemp jeans are a wonderful alternative to regular cotton, and you don't have to worry about them not looking like jeans—they look like regular jeans but the difference is that they don't "cost the Earth."

Hemp is by no means a new fiber for fabric. You only have to take a peek into America's history to find out that the original flag was made out of hemp and the American Declaration of Independence was signed on hemp paper. In the past, hemp was a part of popular farming in the United States. These days the United States doesn't allow the farming of hemp, but Canada still grows and exports hemp. Industrial hemp is not the strain you can smoke to get a "high" on, it's registered safe and is a very strong and ecofriendly fiber.

A great example of new fiber technology is the European Eco Award winning TENCEL®, a material that is a biodegradable fabric made from wood-pulp cellulose. TENCEL boasts antibacterial qualities, the ability to absorb more moisture than cotton, and a soft-touch that's great for sensitive skin. It's important to note that this fabric performs differently when treated with dyes, so natural color may be the best way to go. As always in this field, there is continual testing to produce a better product.

So there we have it, the five main areas of ethical fashion that are taking the fashion sector into a new arena. And because of the emergency of climate change and our responsibility to alleviate poverty in the world, perhaps we can look at our choices when we buy clothes. And guess what? The good news is that we can look good and save the planet at the same time—a win-win formula.

What Can We Do?

One of the best things we can do is become good at asking ourselves and others questions about the clothes, accessories, and footwear that we are buying. Again, it's important to remember that we all support the fashion sector because we all wear clothes—and that's exactly why we can make a difference. Let's focus on solutions that are both ethical and humane while also being amazing and stylish!

10 Practical Tips

1. Support Ethical Fashion. For every two pieces of nonethical clothing that you buy, buy one ethical piece. Mix ethical fashion with mainstream fashion.

2. Learn, Ask Questions, & Raise Awareness. When you go to your favorite shops or designers, ask what they are doing about ethical fashion. What materials are they using? Where are they manufactured?

What labor standards are they employing? Write to your favorite shops and designers and ask them kindly to support ethical fashion—get a local school, your workplace, or community to do the same.

3. Make Ethical Fashion Fun and Innovative. Have a clothes-swapping party every fashion season and theme the parties. For example, have a party frocks evening. We all have an amazing dress or two in our cupboard that could go to a better home. The idea is not to sell the garments, but to exchange and perhaps have a donation bowl for a fashion project nationally or internationally.

4. Celebrate and Have a Party. Celebrate world fair trade by putting on small fashion shows that encourage community participation.

5. Know Your Colors. Book yourself with an image consultant, learn about what colors suit you, and then take your color swatches around with you when you shop. And guess what? This is a great guide for decorating your home too! We have all had the experience of buying something and getting home and realizing that it was not right for us. In the long run, you can save yourself a lot of time and money!

6. Become Your Own Stylist! Not everyone is born with style but it can be learned. Look at magazines, department store window displays, pictures from the past, paintings—figure out what you like and how the look was put together and copy it. Once you get the knack, it is amazing how styling can change the look of an old tired outfit. Don't be afraid to experiment.

Accessories change your look very easily and make you feel and look fresh and in style. The essentials are belts, necklaces, earrings, bags, and the icing on the cakes are brooches. If there is anything that you should be treasuring, it is a small chest full of accessories. Good accessories can help you use and drape an outfit in several ways and make it look different every time.

Elizabeth Laskar

Vintage parachute dress featured amid a room entirely decorated with secondhand furnishings.

www.indexopen.com

The "addition by subtraction" concept can be the best advice for certain outdated wardrobes—hopefully not your own.

7. Shop for Your Body Shape, Not Your Size. There is nothing worse than ill-fitting clothes and standard sizing on labels can have varying fits from shop to shop. Work out your shape and learn to shop for it. Are you a wonderful pear shape, straight, or triangular body? Knowing your body shape will not only make shopping easier (you'll know which cuts flatter your body), but will also give you the confidence in buying something knowing that it will look amazing on you.

Here's a test. Go into your wardrobe and pull out everything you have only worn once or have not worn for over a year. Then estimate the total cost. I suspect the figure will alarm you . . . all that money and time wasted! Male or female, you need to see a reputable image and style consultant or, failing that, buy a book and learn about it yourself.

8. Share. Most of us hate sharing our clothes, but it is time to give it a shot. Sharing means you can always have a fresh, updated look without buying. Perhaps lend selected pieces to your friends or family for six months—when they are returned you will find that you wear it like it was brand-new. If you're nervous about sharing, try introducing a fun "penalty" if the garment comes back damaged—like a trip out to your favorite organic restaurant or a new fair-trade fashion piece.

9. Practice Slow Shopping. Do we really need to go out shopping every weekend to buy something new? We all have our wants but what do we actually *need*? Instead, how about spending the time with your friends or family and visiting some inspiring places? Perhaps you could spend time on a new community project. Also, visit your local thrift shop on a regular basis and only buy when you see something that suits you and fits you.

10. Re-Design. Next time you are weeding your wardrobe, put your clothes to one side and find an innovative local designer who can re-design the pieces. Re-design is all about new ideas and different ways of thinking. One designer in the UK makes dresses out of vintage parachutes and another makes dresses out of shirts and trousers. It's a very unique way to use the clothes you would have put into the landfill or taken to the thrift shop.

The wonderful thing about ethical fashion is that we can be inspired and have fun while we are saving our planet and alleviating poverty. Changing the whole fashion arena will take time, so it's all about taking one step at a time. Remember, it is not about pointing fingers but focusing on the solutions. We can play our part by understanding our responsibility and acting on the solutions. We can look good and do good. What a perfect way to help make the world a better place. Let's fight this battle in style!

(Fashion Facts come courtesy of the Well Dressed Report 2006 and the following organizations: World Health Organization, Soil Association, Fashioning and Labour Behind the Labour, Environmental Justice Foundation, Clean Clothes Campaign, and the Ethical Fashion Forum)

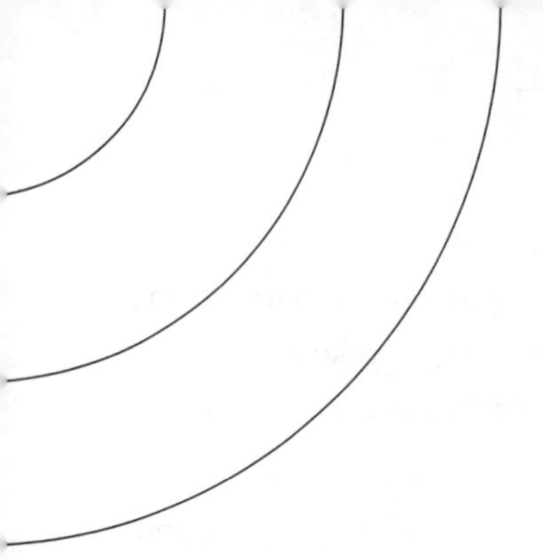

Greening Mealtimes for Children

by Lisa Barnes

Starting the "greening" process with babies and children is a natural way to grow and nurture the next generation of environmentally conscious and healthy adults. When buying organic foods, educating children about food and cooking, making green choices for preparing and storing foods, and bringing families together at mealtimes, we empower parents and children to start a lifetime of healthy eating habits.

Baby Meals

Babies usually triple their weight during their first year, so if "they are what they eat," this is the most important time to give them the best. According to the U.S. Environmental Protection Agency and Department of Health and Human Services, the greatest (and potentially most damaging) exposure to pesticides and chemicals is during a child's first four years. This is why so many advocate providing organic foods for children whenever possible. Sometimes organic is more expensive than conventional foods, because of the higher cost of growing methods, land conversion, and raising practices. However, when you consider the cost of your child's health, development, and well-being—as well as a decision to support the environment by helping preserve water resources and prevent agriculture-related problems—the hike in your grocery bill can be a bargain. In fact, a move away from prepackaged foods can sometimes be more cost effective. Here are some of the benefits of providing your baby with organic food:

Reducing Health Risks

Buying organic reduces health risks that can be attributed to commercial pesticides and herbicides. No matter how well you wash certain fruits and vegetables, traces of potentially harmful chemicals still remain. Babies' bodies are much more vulnerable to pesticides because their brains and immune systems are still developing. There are also, according to the EPA Web site, "critical periods" in human development when exposure to a toxin can permanently alter how an individual's biological system operates. Also, pound for pound, babies eat two to four times more fruits and vegetables than adults, and thus are exposed to a higher percentage of possible contaminants.

Increasing Health Benefits

A study at the University of California at Davis (my alma mater) shows that organically grown strawberries, corn, and blackberries are richer in cancer-fighting antioxidants, sometimes 60 percent more, than the same conventionally grown crops. Other studies have proven the same for organically grown peaches and pears. Researchers theorize that organically grown plants may produce more antioxidants because they have to work harder to fight off the pests and disease that are otherwise killed by pesticides and chemicals.

Reducing Nitrites

Some fruits and vegetables you'll want to introduce to your child have high levels of nitrites—naturally occurring chemicals created when plants break down nitrogen—due to the fertilized soils in which they grow. The nitrite levels also increase when these foods are stored in your refrigerator. Although many of these foods are healthy overall, nitrites are difficult on a baby's system because their stomach acidity is too low to properly break them down. Overexposure can cause anemia or encourage oxygen to be displaced into the bloodstream, resulting in rapid breathing and lethargy. Buying these high-nitrite produce items (beets, turnips, spinach, mustard, carrots, green beans, butternut squash, strawberries, and cantaloupe) grown organically will lessen exposure. If you buy high-nitrite foods grown conventionally and make your own baby food, wait to introduce these foods until your baby is over eight months old, when the stomach can properly break down nitrites. Or buy these food items in jarred options since manufacturers are able to test nitrite levels.

However if you can't always buy organic, you can lower your family's exposure to pesticides by up to 90 percent if you avoid the twelve most contaminated conventionally grown fruit and vegetables. Here's what The Environmental Working Group (www.ewg.org) calls the dirty dozen:

apples	bell peppers
celery	cherries
grapes (imported)	nectarines
peaches	pears
potatoes	red raspberries
spinach	strawberries

Buying Organic

There are now many organic baby-food options both in the jarred and frozen sections of the supermarket. While baby food choices have increased over the last few years there are even more benefits to making your own organic homemade foods for baby. These include:

More Nutrition

Homemade food is more nutritious than commercially prepared baby foods because it retains more of the nutrients, especially vitamins A and B. This is because the food is less processed. The jarring process necessitates the use of very high heat under pressure—much more than you can generate when cooking at home. Unfortunately, many vitamins are destroyed by that heat.

Better Taste

While sometimes convenient, a big drawback of commercially jarred baby food is that it bears little relation to the real food. Fresh, seasonal food just tastes better. You probably can't remember what eating baby food was like, but it did have a role in your development. By eating homemade baby food, your child will appreciate real foods from their first bite. These will be the flavors and food items that they will continue to enjoy as they grow. Jarred or frozen baby food is not available in every fruit and vegetable, nor is it seasonal. You may miss the opportunity to introduce fruit and vegetable options, which you want your baby to eat later with the rest of the family. Some children get used to bland, smooth, jarred foods and have difficulty being reintroduced to the same real foods and textures later. Like with any meal, the freshest and most flavorful ingredients will yield the best-tasting results.

Less Waste

Making food gives you control over quantity, taste, texture, and expense. You will not have to throw away partially eaten jars of food. Instead, you can cook what you know your baby will eat, prolong the life of your homemade food in the freezer, or eat the food yourself.

Lower Cost

The cost for making your own baby food is often less than buying commercially prepared baby foods if you shop smart and cook in larger quantities. For instance, a 4-ounce jar of baby food ranges in price from 60 cents to $1.20 each, and 12 ounces of frozen food can be $3 to $4, depending on brand and place purchased. However, by making your own baby food—and following our tips for creating less waste and buying in-season whole foods—you can actually save money. I purchased enough organic apples for an apple puree for $2 at the farmers' market, and my recipe yielded 16 ounces, thus my cost is only 50 cents per 4-ounce serving.

No Special Shopping

There's no last-minute rush to the store to buy baby food. You can buy the foods you and your family already eats, so you always have ingredients for homemade food at hand. By creating a variety of foods for various ages and stages from a single, whole-food item you shop and cook only once. For example, when making baked sweet potatoes you can puree some (for baby), cut pieces into soft chunks (for toddler), and leave the rest whole (for mom and dad). Because your homemade purees are made with whole foods, the leftovers can be made into soups, side dishes, and sauces for the rest of the family.

Shop Wisely and Save Money When Buying Organic

Some parents say they don't or can't buy organic foods due to cost and availability. Here are a few ways to make organics more affordable and easy to purchase.

1. **Do not always assume organic is more expensive.** Look at the prices of conventional and organic products and compare. You may be surprised, that for some items, there is little or no difference in price, depending on where and when you buy.

2. **Buy in season.** These items will be the lowest priced whether you're shopping at a specialty market or local farmers' market.

3. **Grow your own.** Even a small window-box can yield some organic herbs or tomatoes. Larger areas can accommodate lettuce, strawberries, broccoli, carrots, and more. A garden is also a great classroom and hobby for children and adults alike.

4. **Shop at one of the more than 2,500 farmers' markets in the United States.** The produce here is as fresh as possible because the food is usually picked within 24 hours of your purchase. This is a great place to check prices with little effort. Becoming a regular shopper and getting to know growers personally is a good way to get the best selection and price.

5. **Join a food cooperative.** A food co-op is kind of a buyer's club for affordable, fresh, local, organic, and natural products. It is an actual store where members buy "shares" of the business to provide the capital necessary to run the store efficiently. You as a member directly influence the kind and variety of products and foods available, and also receive a discount in the store. Many co-ops allow you to "buy" shares by volunteering several hours per week or month.

6. **Visit a farm and pick your own produce.** Children love to experience something new, especially when it involves dirt and food.

According to the CUESA (Center for Urban Education and Sustainable Agriculture),"Parents had reported that their children started to eat more vegetables after visiting a farm on a school field trip, having experienced for the first time the process of gardening."

Kids' Meals

It's never too late to purchase organic foods for your children and family. Even if your baby was only offered conventionally grown produce, your child will not know if you switch to buying organic whole foods. A juicy ripe pear grown organically will be safer as well as tastier for your child—but they won't even know it.

Furthermore, starting an organic diet can provide immediate benefits regardless of previous eating habits. A 2005 study supported by the EPA measured pesticide levels in the urine of 23 children in Washington State before and after a switch to an organic diet. After five consecutive days on the diet, researcher found that pesticide levels had decreased to undetectable levels—and remained that way until they went back to their conventional diets.

Of course there are organic processed foods such as peanut butter, breads, and cereal that children may have to get used to a new brand, flavor, or texture. It may be difficult to substitute a familiar favorite with a new organic version. Rather than make a wholesale change, as a parent, you might need to decide where it will make the biggest impact on your child's health to favor organic over nonorganic foods. Just because a processed food product is labeled "organic," this may not mean it is healthier than the nonorganic version. However some companies that manufacture organic foods also avoid additives, coloring, trans-fats, and preservatives. Also, do not assume that because a food product is marketed to children that it is good or appropriate for them. You'll need to read the labels to make wise choices.

Getting Children Involved

Growing

If you have the outdoor space, consider growing some of your own organic fruits and vegetables. Gardening is a great way to teach your toddler about nutrition and get them to eat healthy foods. According to a study at the Saint Louis University Medical Center, young children who regularly eat homegrown fruits and veggies eat more than twice as much of those healthy foods than kids who seldom get fresh-from-the-garden produce at mealtimes. "Garden produce creates what we call a 'positive food environment,'" said study author Debra Haire-Joshu, director of the university's Obesity Prevention Center. She and her colleagues found that garden-fed children were more likely to see their parents eating fresh fruits and vegetables, and that people in homes with gardens had access to a greater variety of produce. "When children are involved with growing and cooking food, it improves their diet," she said. "Students at schools with gardens learn about math and science, and they also eat more fruits and vegetables. Kids eat healthier, and they know more about eating healthy."

Shopping

If you don't have the space to grow your own, you can certainly create a family field trip to visit a local farmers' market, grower, or self-pick farm. Exposing children to farming and growing with a day at a farm can be very valuable and fun. Children love to see dirt and tractors. On the farm, children can experience food with all five senses: the smell of the ripe fruit, the look of the colors and shapes, the taste of the fresh-off-the-vine produce, the touch of the textures, and feel of picking vegetables from the soil. And finally, hearing about the growing process and stories from the farmers themselves will pique interest and questions from children. The whole family will have a new appreciation for food and respect for the land and farmers.

Cooking

Once purchased, children can experience the foods in their own kitchens. They'll take great pride and interest in helping prepare a meal, especially with foods they've carefully chosen. Even the smallest children can get involved by sorting and washing fruit. Older preschoolers can help peel vegetables and toss salads. The greater the participation, the greater the satisfaction and confidence instilled in children—and the more they'll taste, eat, and share.

Eating and Enjoying

Even eating and presenting the food can be a lesson for children. Why not use the good plates and cloth napkins? If our good things are shared with our children, they too appreciate them and feel honored to be part of the celebration. Why do we eat outside? To be connected with the outdoors and environment. Children love picnics, eating outside, and special gatherings. Those traditions and rituals connect family, friends, and community.

"Greener" Food Packaging and Storage

There are many packaged meals marketed as "fun" for children and "convenient" for parents. Unfortunately, these choices are usually the least nutritious and most processed foods around (not to mention the overabundance of packaging material). With a little time and energy you can make lunch healthier for both your child and the environment. These green on-the-go tips work for all ages and venues, whether they're headed to school, daycare, or a family outing.

- **Pack foods in insulated lunch bags to keep perishables cold.** There are many PVC- and lead-free choices. Allow your child to choose his favorite bag so he looks forward to carrying it. Rather than using an ice pack, you can freeze items such as yogurt or water, which will thaw and be ready by mealtime.

• **Pack drinks in reuseable, nonplastic bottles and drink holders.** Thermos containers made from stainless steel and aluminum reduce waste and concern of leaching of toxins such as Bisphenol A, which is linked to birth defects, miscarriage, and prostate cancer. There are many fun and colorful options for kids to choose from. Green baby bottle choices include glass and Bisphenol-free varieties.

• **Wrap sandwiches in foil instead of plastic wrap and baggies.** Unlike wax paper and plastic wrap, aluminum foil is available in 100 percent recycled form, is recyclable in most areas, withstands heat and cold, and works better than plastic and wax paper at keeping moisture in. Aluminum is also oil free and is not made from petroleum, the way that wax and plastic are. You can also reduce landfill waste by eliminating plastic bag use, as they can last up to 1,000 years.

• **Store foods and leftovers in ceramic and glass containers.** They are nonreactive with food, long lasting, and very versatile for cooking and heating (safe for refrigerator, freezer, microwave, and oven). I recommend using ramekin containers to feed babies and children as they are inexpensive, come in a variety of sizes, not easily knocked over, and easily go from refrigerator to table.

• **Freeze individual servings of purees, sauces, and broths in ice trays.** Covered trays are easy to stack and reduce the potential for spills and absorbing other food smells. Frozen cubes can be popped out of trays and put in freezer bags/containers to conveniently defrost individual servings.

• **Pack metal or ceramic utensils that can be used and washed.** Your child must remember to bring them home. Or provide bamboo renewable and biodegradable forks and spoons, rather than plastic.

Talk at the Table — Outside Influences

You've taken precautions for your child to eat healthy foods and impact the environment as little as possible, but will he eat it? And what will the other children at school think?

I thought I'd be asking and answering these questions much later, as my son is only in preschool. However I was very wrong and caught by surprise at how early outside influences come into play regarding food. Media, television, and marketers spend billions of dollars enticing children with foods of dubious nutritional value. And although your child may not watch television or eat supermarket foods plastered with the latest movie character, his friends at school do. Children are often introduced to processed snacks by watching their peers at the lunch table. Once children see the foods being enjoyed by their friends or older siblings, they catch on quickly. They then notice the foods and packaging when taking a trip to the grocery store. Limiting exposure is the best way to curb these desires. Avoid the supermarkets and food emporiums when shopping with children, especially the inside aisles (where food is processed and least healthy). This will cut down on many fights and explanations about food choices if your child is not tempted by all the colors, names, and packaging. If they beg for something at the farmers' market—what's the worst choice they can make?

No child wants to feel different, but healthy food choices can set him apart at the lunch table. Make your child's food look as good and appealing as everyone else's (if not more so). From across the lunch table, preschoolers can't detect the difference between one peanut butter and jelly sandwich and another version made with organic peanut butter and organic berry puree spread, or an organic apple vs. one conventionally grown. Be sure to pack some of your child's favorites, so he is not tempted by the food choices around him.

www.indexopen.com

Mealtimes can be entertaining, interactive, and enjoyable.

Here are a few tips for minimizing the impact of outside influences on your child's diet:

• Give children a good foundation. The healthier they eat from an early age and see your family enjoying healthy meals, the easier it is to ignore the "junk" and processed foods.

• Explain to your child how his healthy, organic food choices will help make him strong, fast, smart, and healthy.

• Let him know his peers may be looking at his food the same way he looks at theirs—with interest and curiosity. They may wish they had fresh, organic pineapple slices too.

• Try not to ban foods. Telling a child they can't eat something they see elsewhere may make them want it more, if only to test or defy you.

• Enlist your child's help. Allow your child to choose which foods to make and pack so he looks forward to his lunch and feels responsible for his decisions.

The Family Table

Changes in diet and eating habits are difficult for children as well as adults. Creating a "greener" mealtime does not need to feel strange or radical. Start by making small changes that work for you and your family's lifestyle. In the beginning, there may be an investment of money and time, such as purchasing glass baking and storage dishes and taking extra shopping minutes to read food labels; however, you'll be saving expenses and resources in the long run. Soon enough you'll be trying new recipes and foods and establishing healthier habits for shopping, cooking, and eating.

The most important factor in "greening" foods for children is to lead by example and share together in the family table. If children see parents and siblings eating healthy, organic whole foods, that becomes part of their habits and routine as well. Mealtime is an opportunity to connect to family, friends and community. Food brings everyone together as it nourishes the body, mind, palate, and soul.

Besides choosing organically grown foods in the high pesticide risk group, these simple steps can help limit the amount of pesticides (on conventionally grown produce) and harmful bacteria (on all fruits and vegetables) your family consumes:

• Peel fruits and vegetables, and remove the outer leaves (on lettuce, cabbage, etc.).

• Wash fruits and vegetables thoroughly under cold running water for at least 20 seconds (sing the alphabet song or "Row Your Boat" two times). Most people do not wash long enough. A produce wash product (made from citrus extracts and plant oils) or mild liquid soap can aid in rinsing.

• Serve a wide variety of produce. This will limit repeated consumption of the same pesticide.

• Choose produce that is free of mold, bruises, and decay, as these are likely to harbor more pesticides.

• Trim the fat off meat and the skin off poultry. The pesticides found in these foods are concentrated in the fatty parts and skin.

Recipes

Here are two recipes with organic apples as an important ingredient. Apples make a great puree for baby (recipe below), a simple snack for children, and a sweetener for baked goods (see muffin recipe below) for all ages. Apples are on the EWG list of fruits to buy organic for limited pesticide exposure. A single conventionally grown apple may be sprayed by pesticides and chemicals up to 16 times before reaching the supermarket for purchase.

Apple Puree

Apples are a great first food because of their sweetness and versatility. Besides baby food, this puree can be used in all kinds of recipes. Use it to sweeten baked goods, as a topping for pancakes, or even to dress up grilled meats.

Golden and Red Delicious, as well as Fuji apples have the least amount of acid, and thus are the most tolerable for babies. You may peel apples before or after cooking. Cooking with skins on allows the apples to retain more nutrients.

All you need are six organic, medium-sized Red Delicious apples, washed, quartered, and cored just before cooking. Makes four, ½-cup servings.

www.indexopen.com

Breakfast is a great time to develop healthy eating habits.

Steamer Method: Place prepared apples in steamer basket set in a pot filled with about 1 to 2 inches of lightly boiling water. Do not let water touch fruit. Cover tightly for best nutrient retention and steam for 10 to 12 minutes or until apples are tender. Apples should pierce easily with a toothpick. Set apples and cooking liquid aside to cool.

Scrape apples to remove skin and puree in a food processor with a steel blade. Add tablespoons of reserved cooking liquid to puree to make smoother and adjust consistency.

TIP: An apple a day . . . When baby is ready for more texture, chunks of steamed apple make a good finger food. If your baby is teething, freeze steamed apple slices for a soothing treat.

Mini Banana-Apple-Bran Muffins

These mini-muffins have all the flavor of a big muffin, but fit nicely into little hands. (Of course, you can also make these in a regular full-size muffin pan, just increase baking time to 15 to 18 minutes and check for doneness.) These are great to pack in lunches and to share at play-dates and school events. Makes 24 mini-muffins or 12 regular muffins.

1 cup organic wheat flour

½ cup organic oat bran

½ teaspoon salt

1 teaspoon baking soda

½ cup (1 stick) unsalted butter

¾ cup homemade organic apple puree (recipe above) or organic applesauce

3 medium organic bananas, 1 mashed (about ½ cup) and 2 sliced

½ cup organic light brown sugar

2 cage-free, organic eggs

Preheat oven to 375 F. Grease 24 mini muffin cups or 12 regular muffin cups. With a fork, combine flour, bran, salt, and baking soda in a small mixing bowl. Melt butter in a small saucepan over low heat or in a microwave for 25 seconds on high. In a large bowl, combine butter, applesauce, mashed banana, sugar, and eggs. Mix together with a rubber spatula. Add flour mixture to applesauce mixture and stir until just blended. Batter will be lumpy and very moist.

Spoon batter into prepared muffin cups, filling two-thirds full. Place banana slice on top of each muffin. Bake for 12 minutes, or until golden brown and set. Cool muffins in pan on a wire rack for 5 minutes before turning out muffins.

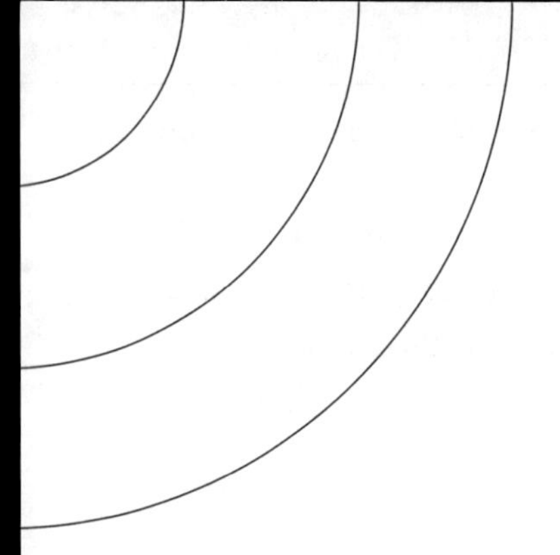

City Chickens

by Kari C. Tauring

It's early on a school morning and before waking up the children, I take my coffee and scone to the garden bench. She hears me coming out the back door. "Bacaaaaw chuck chuck chuck," she greets me and waddle-runs across the lawn for a morning treat. "Rrrrip, chick chick chick," I answer back. Katie was the last of our chickens. She outlived her sisters by a full year, during the course of which she became more like a dog than a chicken. Soon the rest of the city wakes up, neighbors smile and wave, trucks barrel down the alley, air traffic picks up. But I enjoy my quiet cup of coffee offering nibbles of scone to my Old English Bantam.

While we didn't think through every detail in advance, the decision to keep chickens wasn't made on a whim. My mother had grown up with chickens and my mother-in-law used to come down to the cities in the winter and sell chickens on ice door to door. I had even said, "I would like to have a big fat hen running in the garden." My husband picked up a free catalog of chickens and we admired the different breeds at the State Fair. It seemed quite natural that we

www.indexopen.com

Feeding a flock of chickens by hand.

would have a chicken, even though we lived in the city. Then on April 18, 1998 (the day after my youngest son turned one), we received twenty-six pullets (baby chicks) via UPS from the Murray MacMurray Hatchery in Iowa. We have since discovered that you can buy a single chicken at a farm store. I don't recommend buying in bulk!

We built a nesting box and cleared the living room table. We put up a heat lamp and some torn newspapers and straw for them to nestle into. A few of them died en route and a few others died a week later. In the end, we had twenty healthy little chicks of who-knows-what sex or how large they would get. We had ordered Cornish game hens, some were Old English Bantams, and some were a mix of fancy chickens. Soon it was warm enough to move them to the porch and they were big enough to need two boxes. Just because it's cheaper to order a big batch, I would not want more than three to five chickens on a city lot.

Living near the Mississippi River in Minneapolis, Minnesota, our main concerns for the outdoor coop were cats and dogs, raccoons, foxes, and birds of prey such as hawks and eagles. My new 8 × 8-foot garden shed became the barn. We built inside roosting areas and cut a door to the outside. The outside pen was created from strong chicken wire dug a foot deep and an old futon frame served as walls. The pen was enclosed on top to prevent them flying out and cats dropping in. One mistake we made was not building the coop tall enough so I could stand upright inside. That made cleaning more difficult. Of course, in an urban environment, we needed to be sure the pens locked so that kids or other curious folks couldn't get in.

The Cornish game hens grew so big and fat, it was obvious we didn't have enough room. Our neighbor's uncle was a farmer and he took all but three of our chickens. We kept three lovely little Old English Bantams, a very hardy and beautiful heirloom breed, our three girls. Lucy and Lissetta lived with us for seven years and Katie for eight. Our entire community benefited from the presence of these birds. They were some of the first of many chickens that came to live in the Longfellow Community of Minneapolis.

In our city, a simple and inexpensive permit is required to keep poultry. You need the permission of neighbors within 100 feet of the chicken coop. My neighbors all had their own special relationship to the chickens. They loved hearing Katie crow (the job of the lead chicken in lieu of a rooster). We kept them in the pens for the first few years. Once in a while a girl would get loose and go visiting around the neighborhood. We could usually herd her in by clucking and calling and using a long supple stick to startle the ground before them if they should stray from the path. We relaxed quite a bit, as a new parent would, as they grew. I made chicken runs in the little vegetable path and herded them around to different gardens if the slugs tried to escape them.

Permit Required for City Chickens

Permits vary from city to city, so you need to check with your local animal-control agency for the regulations. Many cities allow chickens but not roosters—they crow day and night, are not essential for egg production, and are sometimes used in the grisly and illegal business of cock fighting.

With three chickens, there was no reason to keep a rooster at all. With larger flocks, however, the rooster serves the purpose of herding the chickens, keeping them protected and safe, and interfering with severe pecking order politics among the hens. In the larger flocks (ten or more) the girls can get really vicious with one another, and pecking politics may even cause the death of a runt chicken. The three girls I kept certainly had their order and did some bickering, but serious pecking was never a problem.

The girls would have many visitors besides the surrounding neighbors. Living a block away from the school and park we had contingencies of onlookers with strollers, as well as more formal visits of entire classrooms from the community school. Our yard became an outdoor resource for the teachers who would take walking field trips from the school to our home.

The chickens were a valuable resource for our family on many levels. Chicken droppings are one of the best fertilizers available. We would clean the pens once a month in summer and mix it into the compost. That would cause the compost to cook more quickly and created an amazingly rich soil for the gardens. As I mentioned, they ate the slugs off of lettuce and hosta alike. I also read that deer ticks and mosquito larvae are favorites of Old English Bantams. And of course, we finally got eggs!

They began to lay tiny eggs at first. There were a few here and there that first autumn, but winter was coming and their energy was directed toward growing feathers. These heirloom breeds will molt in the fall and get longer winter feathers and more down. Apparently they did not need artificial heat and light as the hybrid layer-chickens did. Since no electrical wiring had been run to the backyard, we just filled the cracks of the coop with straw. One Web site suggested not cleaning the coop in the winter as the droppings and straw will compost, generating heat for a small area. Still, I was nervous that first winter.

We had to go out twice a day with fresh water. It would freeze so quickly that I started bringing it out warm. Sometimes they would stand in the warm water while they drank. They seemed to love that. We purchased grain at the local Fleet Farm and later, when we only had one to feed, we bought it by the pound at the Southside Farm Store near our neighborhood. They also liked eating greens from the table, apple cores, rinds of melon, and strawberry stems. We would give them the crusts of sandwiches from fussy eaters and whatever crackers went stale. On long winter nights, you would find our three ladies snuggling and roosting together on their inside perch, heads tucked under each other's wings.

The first egg heralded spring for eight years. Chickens ovulate on the sun cycle according to how much light there is in a day. Our heirloom girls quit laying eggs around Fall Equinox and started up again near Groundhog Day. When the first egg appeared, we shared the news of spring's arrival with our neighbors—in a way, it became our groundhog ritual. My children would ceremoniously present the egg and we would cook it up and serve it on toast. Everyone would get a nibble of the first egg. The hens would lose some of their long winter feathers and finding these was also fun—yet another resource they provided my family and my community. Many feathers ended up on

cow on the carton? I thought that was just a logo like, you know, the cereal rabbit."

Astonishing.

That experience taught me a great lesson. You cannot educate children about where their food comes from without putting them in the process. We wouldn't need to bus kids out to the country for a milking field trip if we only had a well-placed cow in a park or school grounds, or perhaps with a neighbor who lived nearby! Alas, no. We stopped at our three chickens, though I did check into having a cow. The ordinance in Minneapolis says that we may keep any animal that isn't naturally wild as long as we meet the minimum square-footage requirements (which vary by animal).

"You mean we could have a goat, or a cow?" I asked the animal control officer, who stopped by to check on our chickens in the early stages. He just laughed at my enthusiasm and said, "Sure!" However, my grandmother warned me about the wily nature of goats and advised against that idea, and cows are way too much work.

As my boys grew up, I did a lot of volunteering and curriculum design around the need for urban green space. We created and participated in many programs to help connect city children with the origins of their food, their very well being. We grew beans and some pumpkins, flowers, and medicinal plants all around the community school and in the park gardens. Kids learned to sew pillows and stuff them with herbs and roses from the school gardens. We composted, led nature walks, and visited the chickens. Though my boys were too young to join, there are great urban 4-H clubs. There is a Youth Farm Market project we are sure to buy our flowers from at the many farmers markets all over the city. There are resources on the web, in libraries, through the university extension programs, and many other places to get help with urban greening and keeping chickens.

I really had no idea how long chickens of this sort live. After year five, I began to wonder. Factory chickens whose lives are spent indoors laying eggs don't live very long. And most of the time, meat chickens are in the stew pot before they are two. My neighbor, who got inspired to raise some chickens himself, used to tease me about why my birds weren't dinner yet. Well, they are such little birds that they wouldn't make a meal and besides, it's a bit too harsh to eat the animals that were named after my son's best friends at school.

One of my neighbors brought her farming family over to see the chickens one summer day. It was fun to chat with them. Their experience with chickens was very different than mine. They found the reality of chickens ovulating on the sun cycle as fascinating as the children did, because they were raising hybrid chickens, not old breeds. And they had been heating and lighting the coop to keep egg production up during the winter.

People with less farming expertise tended to ask trendier questions. In 1999, we were often asked if the hens were part of our plan to prepare for Y2K. More recently the question became, "What about the bird flu?" My standard response was, "They don't get to walk around in my house." The bird flu is passed to humans who are actually living with their birds. Also, most often, the bird flu is a condition that primarily afflicts large flocks. My three girls were very unlikely candidates for the disease as their conditions were clean, organic, free from stress, and just plain happy.

More like pets than livestock, we grew accustomed to their habits and personalities as they meshed their routines like part of the family. This was evident to most everyone.

A few years after we got the chickens, Gilbert the kitten wandered into our lives. He used to tease the hens by chasing them a little, but we kept a good eye on him. Somehow, I think he understood these were family and, well, we don't eat family. He even became protective of them, chasing other cats away and laying in front of the coop with a sphinxlike expression.

In the spring of 2005, Lissetta, the middle girl in the pecking order, laid an egg with a shell too soft. It broke before she could lay it fully. This is what is called "egg bound." A neighbor with whom I had collaborated on many urban greening projects helped me get the egg out of her with mineral oil down the gullet and gentle massage. We got it out but she was protracted—her inside walls were not strong enough to suck back in. She never really recovered.

From this point on, it was interesting to watch how the last girl on the pecking order found herself more dominant. Lucy started strutting and pecking—and her crown actually got more red and full. But, she got too "cocky," as they say. Before egg-bound Lissetta died, Lucy was taking her chances in the next-door neighbor's yard. They have a pointer, a bird dog. He was very well behaved and usually just pointed at the birds—usually. But there was spring in the air. I heard a scream and then my name rang through the alley. Poor Lucy! Just as she was coming into her own, it was time for the bird-dog to fulfill his destiny. I rounded the corner quickly and could see him, proud as ever a dog was, pointing at the lifeless chicken. Here is where my educator, artist, and farmer roots twine. I thought she was a lucky creature who was here to learn and teach and lay eggs and strut around. She had a good life, and what better death than helping another creature realize his destiny?

Lissetta died a week after Lucy, she just couldn't hang on. I began to wonder if Katie would go too, having no sisters to roost with. Fall came and then winter. Katie didn't mind being the lone chicken. In fact, she really enjoyed it. We called her "Katie the chicken lady, circus star" all summer as she would jump up like a puppy to get at a bit of bread or scone. She would follow me around like a dog, and she even started sitting on my lap and shoulder! She was a lot of fun to have around. She made it through the winter with no one to roost with and another full summer. Katie saw her last day on Fall Equinox 2006. From looking at the scene, we deduced that she died feeding a raccoon. So goes the cycle of the life and death of chickens in the city. Everyone they educated, entertained, and befriended along the way knows the story of these city chickens. I miss their feathers. I miss the extra composting ingredient. I miss knowing when spring arrived with the first egg and when winter was here with the last one. I feel somehow less protected against deer ticks and mosquitoes. But I am glad to have my garden shed back!

Selecting a City Chicken

All the Old English Bantam hens are small. We saw a variety of beautiful small birds at the State Fair—silver blues, whites, blue-tailed puffs. But as one Web site points out, Old English breeds are louder and feistier than other breeds, are able to fly, and are more likely to revert to a feral state. So, while my experience was lovely, they may not be the best choice for everyone.

The best thing to do is research the breeds, talk to local farmers—go to a farmers' market and see who is selling fresh eggs, then start a conversation. Think about your winters; cold, hardy breeds are available. There are many online resources. Try searching "city chickens" or "keeping urban chickens." Also, call your local university extension office for advice. Another resource you'll want to check out before getting the birds is a veterinary clinic that deals with fowl. Knowing where to go is important if one of your birds is in trouble.

The Green Dining Market: More Choices in More Places Every Year

by Anne Sala

Choosing to eat local and organic foods is becoming easier every year. Even meals typically considered "fast food" are getting a green makeover in some places, meaning there are more ways for consumers to put their concern for the environment first when making their dining decisions.

Eating locally raised, organic food is a great way to reduce your intake of harmful chemicals and lessen your carbon footprint. Furthermore, animals raised for food in small-scale operations are more likely to have been raised humanely. While growing your own livestock and vegetables is a viable option for some, it is not your only choice. Farmers' markets, organic co-ops, and health-food stores provide other ways to purchase local, organic food.

Sometimes, though, making food for yourself is not an option. In recent years, the number of times the average family dines out has increased dramatically. Subsequently, it's not surprising that the demand for healthful, organic, sustainably grown food has been met in increasing numbers by dining establishments of all shapes and sizes. These entrepreneurs research local food purveyors, make the right purchases, and sell you the organic fruits of their labor. In at least one instance, the call for more restaurants of this nature has brought one small storefront onto the national stage through an unlikely venue: the airport concourse.

Many of these businesses are also expanding their positive impact by building environmentally friendly restaurants and ensuring all their workers make a living wage.

Fertile Territory

Over the past hundred years, there has been a dining shift away from eating locally produced foods. Improvements in transportation has made it easy for the consumer to get whatever they want to eat, whenever they want, and at the cheapest price. Humans love novelty, and in the United States, it almost feels like instant gratification is written into the Bill of Rights.

However, in her book *Animal, Vegetable, Mineral*, author Barbara Kingsolver writes, "In our country, it's a reasonable presumption that unless you have gone out of your way to find good food, you'll be settling for mediocre at best." This presumption is beginning to change as more restaurants are making a commitment to serve local and organic food. It is possible that eating organic will soon be an easy choice for every cosumer to make.

According to the Agricultural Marketing Resource Center, the organic agriculture sector has grown about 20 percent per year since 1999. The All Things Organic 2006 Manufacturer Survey states the overall organic food market had sales of about $14 billion in 2005. A market analysis completed by the Nutrition Business Journal concluded that within the $550 billion United States food industry, organic food sales were about 2.5 percent of all retail sales of food.

This is an exciting time for the green movement, because every organic food purchase a consumer makes has the potential to send waves through market reports, and mainstream companies are taking notice. Hopefully, the environmentally friendly choices that consumers make today will have a positive influence on the choices food companies make tomorrow.

This way of thinking may seem like the green movement is helping the long entrenched enemy, Big Business. Each individual must set their own priorities based on the aspects of their lives that they can control. The environment will not be saved by only those who have the means or wherewithal to grow their own foods or have access to farmers' markets and food co-ops. If each consumer is given the choice of going organic in as many different places as possible, then that is one more person who can have a positive influence on the world.

As the organic market grows, however, consumers must continue to demand that the guidelines for "certified organic" remain tightly regulated, otherwise all efforts to improve the environment will fail due to lowered standards. The United States Department of Agriculture's National Organic Program regulates the standards "for any farm, wild crop harvesting, or handling operation that wants to sell an agricultural product as organically produced." As more businesses file for certification, and the USDA refines its Organic Foods Production Act of 1990 and the "national list" therein—which names the substances that can be used in the production of organic products as well as the prohibited ones—it is crucial that consumers advocate for maintaining strict guidelines, rather than allowing the USDA to expand its standards to include practices that may not truly be "organic."

Sowing the Seeds

Many chefs in expensive restaurants have known for years about the superior taste of organically grown meats and vegetables served at the peak of freshness. In their never-ending quest for the best tasting food around, chefs found that the food with the most flavor always seemed to come straight from a nearby farm rather than from the refrigerated delivery truck from a national wholesale distributor. Upon seeing what the farmers had to offer, the chefs set about doing what they do best: creating dishes that taste good, are filling, and make the customers want to come back.

Recently, chefs have been playing with a new novelty: eating foods in their seasons. That is, eating only what is naturally growing during this part of the year and in this part of the country, just like the world did in "the old days."

Serving only local food is a chancy undertaking because chefs risk disappointing customers who have become accustomed to instant gratification at the dinner table. The average consumer might not be prepared to order off a menu that only offers the limited number of seasonal food choices available during the middle of winter in, say, Wisconsin. What, no tomatoes?

Nevertheless, there are chefs out there that brave the skepticism and choose instead to patiently introduce their patrons to potentially unfamiliar flavors, and to the joys of vibrant, locally grown cuisine.

It is hard to say when, exactly, it became trendy for restaurants to serve local foods. An oft-mentioned touchstone of this phenomenon is the 1971 opening of Chez Panisse by Alice Waters in Berkeley, California. She wanted to showcase local meat and seasonal produce whenever possible in her restaurant. Her set-menu dinners were groundbreaking at the time and became a model for many other restaurants that have followed her local foods formula.

Chez Panisse was considered expensive, but people took notice of how the food there was different from anything else available at the time. The customers began asking questions themselves, eager to know the origins of the foods they ate. As their interest grew, other restaurants began to take notice of local foods' popularity and began to market their own organic and/or locally grown menu items.

Growing the Cause

It seems hard to even turn around nowadays without finding local or organic foods.

At the 2007 Northland Bioneers conference in St. Paul, Minnesota, a panel of local and organic food purveyors were asked about the general public's recent-seeming upswell in interest in their products.

"Consciousness is rising," said Eric Rivkin, Live-Foods Health Chef and founder of Viva La Raw. "Be better to yourself, be better to the environment."

"There really are some epidemics out there," said Lynne Gordon, founder of French Meadow Bakery and Cafe, in Minneapolis, the longest running known organic bakery in the country. "[There's] diabetes, heart disease . . . baby boomers are getting older. And we have an environmental crisis. People are bringing more attention to it."

To satisfy this demand, the food service industry is meeting people where they are: on the go.

In 2005, Gordon expanded her organic business by opening a French Meadow Bakery & Cafe at the Minneapolis/St. Paul airport. Next, she says she is working on opening a branch in the John F. Kennedy International Airport in New York.

"French Meadow is proud to . . . be leaders showing the way for travelers who want a healthy eating alternative," said Chief Operating Officer Steve Shapiro in a press release.

Slowly but surely, organic foods are changing the whole scope of the food industry. Even when people need to grab their food and run, they can stick to their ethics because the movement has found a friend in the fast food chain, Chipotle.

According to area manager Corey Van Scoyk, Chipotle Mexican Grill is the largest purchaser of natural foods.

"We call [our mission] 'food with integrity,' " he said.

The first Chipotle opened in 1993. There are now more than 670 of them across the country. About seven years ago, the company decided to start seeking out local organic food purveyors to supply their restaurants. Now, they have found enough naturally raised local pork that meets Chipotle's standards to supply all of their restaurants. Chipotle is also looking for farms to provide them with naturally raised chicken and beef, as well as organically grown beans and growth hormone–free dairy products. Currently these items are only available in certain restaurants around the country.

Nourishing the Movement

Eating locally grown, organic food is good for the environment, but can we do more? In order to keep the food and the movement sustainable, other commitments to the environment must be made as well. Some restaurants are rethinking the construction of their buildings, trying to make them as environmentally friendly as possible, and a few are even striving to attain Leadership in Energy and Environmental Design (LEED) certification.

This certification was developed by the United States Green Building Council, a nonprofit organization committed to expanding sustainable building practices. They created the LEED Rating System in 2000 as a "practical rating tool for green building design and construction that provides immediate and measurable results for building owners and occupants." Certification takes into account the use of renewable materials in construction; reduction of light pollution; use of materials, such as paint and adhesives, with low volatile organic compound (VOC) emissions; and many other things that reduce waste and excessive energy use.

One of the first buildings in the world to receive LEED certification was The Sundeck restaurant in Aspen, Colorado. The owner, Aspen Skiing Company, decided to rebuild the restaurant from the ground up, installing energy efficient lighting and using wind power for 30 percent of its energy needs. It also recycled as much of the old building as possible to use in the new building.

In Minnesota, the first LEED-certified restaurant opened its doors late 2007. Built within an existing warehouse in Minneapolis, the Red Stag Supper Club is furnished with salvaged excess building materials, like marble and leftover booths from other remodeling projects and used Forest Stewardship Council–certified wood. Since the restaurant is decorated in a rustic Northwoods-style theme, they even salvaged a vintage beer can collection from a relative's own Northwoods bar. This is the third restaurant for Kim and Kari Bartmann, all of which serve organic food.

One of the ads for their Bryant Lake Bowl restaurant boasts their organic eggs are "plucked from under the butts of Larry's chickens for us since 1993."

LEED certification is not just for independent establishments. Last year, McDonald's opened its first LEED-certified restaurant in the LEED-certified Abercorn Common retail development (which is itself the first all-retail center in the United States to become LEED certified) in Savannah, Georgia. It has large windows that allow daylight into the building, reducing the need for artificial lighting; bike racks; preferred parking for hybrid vehicles and employees who carpool; porous pavement to encourage natural drainage of rainwater; and a white roof.

The other element required to maintain the green movement's sustainability is the continued support and education of people, because without them, this upswell in interest will decline like a fad instead of spurring on more environmentally conscious reforms. Customers can research the places they eat and urge restaurants to consider purchasing local and organic ingredients. In turn, restaurants can continue to support local farmers, reassuring them that their effort to grow organically is appreciated and valued.

Consumers must also commit to paying a little bit more for this high quality food. Going green is more expensive for many reasons. For example, the higher price paid for organic food ensures the farmer can pursue environmentally friendly farming practices, USDA Organic certification, and still make a living wage. When consumers understand that, they usually are more inclined to purchase the item.

Keeping It Going

Almost all the panelists at the Northland Bioneers conference said their commitment to local and organic foods was not easy.

"It's very expensive," said Gordon of the French Meadow Bakery. "Profit margins are lower. Those who are here [participating on the panel] are risk takers."

Van Scoyk said Chipotle had to raise the price of their beef options by one dollar when they introduced naturally raised beef.

"It was a leap of faith," he said.

Many restaurants have also chosen to express appreciation to their own employees by striving to pay a living wage.

"We pay a fair wage," said Gordon. "It's important to survive [for] the sustainability of the business, the workers, and the products."

Van Scoyk said Chipotle scrutinizes their food purveyor's practices, confirming the wages they pay their workers and making sure there is adequate housing, if the company uses migrant workers.

"In our restaurants," Van Scoyk said, "we hope to have 100 percent internal promotions to management [positions] in 2008."

Help Along the Way

Becoming an advocate for a movement can sometimes feel a bit directionless, but commitment to the cause is what it's going to take to continue the green movement's momentum. There are organizations out there that can help educate consumers and offer their moral support.

Members of Slow Food International are standard bearers advocating in favor of the local/organic food cause. Founded in Italy in 1986 by Carlo Petrini, the Slow Food Movement is committed to appreciating fresh food and the work that goes into bringing it to the table. Currently there are about 80,000 members.

According to the Slow Food USA Web site, they "seek to catalyze a broad cultural shift away from the destructive effects of an industrial food system and fast life; toward the regenerative cultural, social and economic benefits of a sustainable food system, regional food traditions, the pleasure of the table, and a slower and more harmonious rhythm of life." (Legend has it that Petrini started the organization in reaction to the first McDonald's opening in Rome.)

The FoodRoutes Network is a national nonprofit organization that helps people construct community-based food systems. Their mission statement says, "FRN is dedicated to reintroducing Americans to their food—the seeds it grows from, the farmers who produce it, and the routes that carry it from the fields to their tables." They are strong advocates of the "Buy Local" campaign.

There are even networks for restaurants, such as the Chefs Collaborative. It is a nonprofit organization that helps connect restaurants to local food suppliers. Their mission statement declares the Collaborative "inspires action by translating information about our food into tools for making knowledgeable purchasing decisions."

The strongest way to support the growing organic food market is for consumers to frequent establishments that serve it and to bring your friends. Growing your own tomato plant helps, too.

Resources

Chefs Collaborative: 89 South Street, Lower Level, Boston, MA 02111 www.chefscollaborative.org

FoodRoutes: PO Box 55, 35 Apple Lane, Arnot, PA 16911 www.foodroutes.org

Organic Trade Association: PO Box 547, Greenfield, MA 01302 www.ota.com

Slow Food USA: 20 Jay Street, Suite 313, Brooklyn NY 11201 www.slowfoodusa.org

United States Department of Agriculture:1400 Independence Avenue, S.W., Washington, DC 20250 www.usda.gov

United States Green Building Council: 1800 Massachusetts Avenue, NW Suite 300 Washington, DC 20036, www.usgbc.org

Chipotle Mexican Grill: www.chipotle.com

French Meadow Bakery & Cafe: www.frenchmeadow.com/cafe

Northland Bioneers: www.northlandbioneers.com

Red Stag Supper Club: www.redstagsupperclub.com

Slow Food International: www.slowfood.com

Viva La Raw: www.vivalaraw.com

Sustainable Communities

www.indexopen.com

A Taste of Permaculture

by Dave Boehnlein

After years of trying to make an environmental difference in ways that have always felt like fighting against something, I've finally found something that is solution-oriented: permaculture. Permaculturists aren't fighting against environmental problems; they're just getting their hands dirty and fixing them. Sending letters to politicians about environmental problems and buying toilet tissues made from recycled paper are great things to do, but they just haven't made me feel like I've been very effective in improving the world.

My friend, Ben, seemed a bit skeptical about my latest prospective venture to make a positive difference in the world as we sat in his cozy Minnesota home. He knew I was an environmentalist—I had a degree in environmental studies and had been involved with the Student Conservation Association, YMCA environmental programs, and the Friends of the Great Green Macaw—but he had never seen me so intent before. Like many, Ben was unfamiliar with the topic but let me continue the explanation over a pot of tea.

Permaculture is a design science, like architecture or industrial design, only the medium is the biophysical and social landscape in which people dwell. This design approach is a key distinction among those who care about our planet. As a result of acknowledging the very real damage we have done to the earth, many people in the environmental movement are really down on humans. However, this attitude touches on the root of the problem: the view that humans are separate from the environment rather than a part of it. Permaculture seeks to integrate people back into the natural landscape, where we belong, but without interfering with the natural processes on which we all depend. We can change and modify the Earth for our needs, as the beaver does with dams, but we have to do it with great care because our changes can have repercussions of a greater magnitude.

The idea of permaculture was conceived by a couple of Australian guys, Bill Mollison and David Holmgren, back in the mid-1970s. It is based on three ethics that are so elegant that anyone can agree with them: taking care of the Earth, taking care of people, and sharing our surplus with those around us. That seems like a good start to me.

Needless to say, the conversation continued long after the tea got cold. I had recently gotten a glimpse of permaculture while traveling in Costa Rica and was intrigued. After some further research, I caught the bug and began telling everyone I knew about this approach to sustainability and why I couldn't stop thinking about it.

I wonder how many people around the world were having conversations over a cup of tea at the same time we were. It makes me think about the near universal importance of food and drink in cultures across the planet. So many great ideas and questions are formed while enjoying a meal or drink, and experiences and knowledge are shared and passed on by those with whom you share your meals. In fact, it seems quite fitting to frame my experience of permaculture meal by meal.

Isla Ometepe, Nicaragua

A year after that conversation I found myself on Isla Ometepe, Nicaragua, at a fledgling forty-three-acre educational permaculture site called Finca Bonafide. I had weaseled my way into a two-week permaculture design course as a late sign-up and I was hell-bent on learning everything I could to find out if permaculture was the real deal or not.

Upon arriving at the site, I sat down and shared my first meal with the folks who lived there. We had fish that had been caught by local fishermen from Lake Nicaragua, fried plantains that had been grown on site, and juice made from a passion fruit-like item that was growing wild in the nearby forests. It was all about as local as it gets and grown without chemicals. Sounds like something that might cost an arm and a leg at a natural food store.

At the table were North Americans, Nicaraguans, and Italians with lifestyles and occupations running the gamut from farm workers to wandering translators to recent MBA graduates. The meal had brought us all together. It struck me that if a community in the second poorest country in the Western Hemisphere could provide so much for itself, everyone should be able to do it. With a little forethought and some appropriate technologies, humans and nature could both flourish.

Finca Bonafide was a great place to see permaculture getting off the ground. The owner, Mike, was eager to show me a rare, grafted mango tree he had planted. At first, the prized tree seemed a little out of place to me, so I asked. Mike told me that it was placed along the path from his house to his toilet so he would be sure to check on it several times a day. This exemplifies the permaculture principle of relative location. Where to put things in a landscape is one of the most important considerations you can make. If that mango had been in the back forty, it could have died from lack of care before anyone noticed a problem. However, since it gets checked regularly it has a higher chance of success (and let's face it, during mango season eating baskets of those addictive, fiber-filled mangoes will guarantee you make that trip fairly often).

Another thing that impressed me about Bonafide was their scheme for dealing with degraded landscapes—areas that have already been strongly impacted by poor human management. (Deforestation, erosion, and pollution are all signs of degraded landscapes.) When disturbance occurs in nature, regeneration is usually close on its heels (like when a tree falls and allows light to reach the forest floor). However, some landscapes that have been degraded through human use no longer have the stability and resiliency of a functioning ecosystem, so succession is greatly slowed.

At Bonafide, they sought to accelerate succession as much as possible. Accelerating succession means taking the land through the same stages of development one finds in natural systems (e.g., bare sand to grass to shrubs to pioneer forest to climax forest), but making it happen faster so that the land begins providing the desired functions again sooner. Typical methods of accelerating succession often include enriching soil, mulching for moisture retention, and planting pioneer and late-successional species at the same time.

An example of this was evident one baking-hot day at Bonafide when we tried to beat the heat by working in a shady area where the previous owners had planted conventionally grown plantains. We began chopping out about 50 percent of the tall, lush stalks. Each plantain we chopped had a fruit tree seed crammed into its fleshy stump along with a couple pigeon peas (a legume). The idea was that the remaining plantains would provide shade and moisture for the growing fruit tree while the legume (a pioneer species) would enrich the soil. Today, almost four years later, most of the plantains are being shaded out by the fruit trees, which are beginning to produce heaps of food.

One of the best things about this method of converting chemical plantains into an organic food forest was that the residents were obtaining a yield the entire time. Right after planting the fruit tree seeds the area still produced tons of plantains. After nine months, residents were able to harvest a large crop of pigeon peas. Today, there is a diversity of tree fruits. By making sure there was some sort of yield early on, the folks at Bonafide guaranteed that they wouldn't be hungry while waiting for the fruit trees to grow.

Orcas Island, Washington

While at Bonafide, I found myself wondering how all of this might work back home in more temperate climes. So, eventually I packed my bags and headed out to Orcas Island in Washington State to embark on what I presumed would be a six-month internship at the Bullock's Permaculture Homestead, an operation run by the Bullock family. (I was still there four years later.)

It was March when I found myself looking out the window of the ferry on my way to Orcas, which reminded me of a similar ferry ride several months earlier in Nicaragua, only here the landscape was drastically different. While reading up on permaculture, I noticed that most literature focused on warmer climates (what the Aussies referred to as "temperate" was, by my estimate, bordering on subtropical), so I was intrigued by what I would find here. It was cold and most of the deciduous trees were still without their leaves. What would I eat?

When I arrived at the farm, I was immediately welcomed to dinner by several hardy, bundled-up interns. I was expecting the worst during this lean time of year, but I was surprised by what was served. There were kale, turnips, collards, parsnips, and cauliflower all fresh from the garden. (Orcas is mild enough for year-round gardening with the right techniques.) There were winter squashes, apples, pears, and kiwis from cold storage and a good supply of canned goods that had been stored in the fall. This made for quite a succulent, warming repast while the rain drizzled down outside.

As time passed, I began to get a feel for the magic that was happening at the Bullock's. It differed from Bonafide in that it was a fairly well established, twenty-five-year-old permaculture site. The learning opportunities I found there exceeded my expectations.

One thing that impressed me was the variety of uses for small stock (namely chickens and ducks). Permaculturists seek to identify multiple functions for anything they incorporate into their systems. Chickens, for example, provide eggs and meat, can be used in the gardens to eat pests like slugs and snails, act as efficient weeding machines, and produce rich manure. Who knew chickens were so glorious?

By the same token, any needs in a permaculture system should be able to be met in a multitude of ways. Take the water system at Bullock's. If you tried to draw this system on a piece of paper you would end up with what looks like a plate of spaghetti. Functionally, however, it is quite elegant.

Gardens and nurseries need plenty of water during dry Orcas Island summers. Therefore, there should be at least three different ways to provide it so that, in the case of some sort of water mishap, the plants won't die. The Bullocks have the option to water the gardens using solar-pumped marsh water (from either of two systems), gasoline-pumped marsh water (in a bind), or domestic well water (in a real bind). I saw one of these systems go down during my time at the Bullocks and with the turning of one valve, the gardens (and our veggies for the next nine months) were saved.

Another thing I liked about the permaculture design I saw here was how everything was set up to encourage efficient use of energy. For instance, the compost area was located on a terrace just below the intern kitchen. When you needed to empty the five-gallon compost bucket (which filled quite quickly) you walked downhill and dumped it on the nearest pile. There was space for about six medium-sized piles (four-foot cubes). As the first pile got full, it could be turned over into the second position and new material could continue being put at the kitchen end. Over time, the compost piles navigate their way from one end of the terrace to the other in ascending stages of decomposition. By the time they reach the end they are finished compost and it is just another short downhill jaunt to the garden where it will be used. Wow! I liked the idea of never having to take a heavy load of compost uphill.

One of the most striking features of Bullock's is the nine-acre marsh. When the Bullock brothers arrived, the marsh had been long drained and served as a field capable of yielding prize-winning potatoes. The Bullocks thought hard about what they wanted for this area . . . a perennial water source or really good spuds? They decided to fill in the drainage canal and restore the marsh.

By doing so they did more than guarantee year-round water for the gardens. The landscape of the property now had diversity in spades. By restoring the marsh, the Bullocks created a whole new ecosystem. Where before there were potatoes, there were now redwing blackbirds, fathead minnows, cattails, waterfowl, caddisfly larvae, and much more. This area went from monoculture to incredible diversity in less than a year. In fact, late blight or wireworms (a serious problem for potato growers) could have devastated the entirety of the biological community in this area once—pretty easy since there was only one species, potatoes, to devastate. Now the biodiversity has made this ecosystem much more resilient and productive. It provides clean water, cattail tops for eating, wildlife habitat, basketry materials, etc. And there are still enough potatoes to feed everyone living on the property grown in small plots slightly uphill from the marsh.

Evan Barr

In the Pacific Northwest, slugs can be a huge problem. At Bullock's, muscovy ducks eat slugs like candy, controlling the population and protecting our gardens.

In permaculture circles there is a maxim that gets bantered around: "The edge is where the action is." This implies that where we have edges (where land meets water, forest meets field, river meets ocean) we will have more diversity.

One day in late summer, I found myself standing in the middle of that marsh covered head to toe in muck. I paused as I considered what we were doing.

When the Bullocks restored the marsh they decided to construct peninsulas all along the edge because a linear perimeter would offer a lot less edge than a perimeter with fingers extending from it. By doing so they not only gained the species living in the marsh and the species living on land, but also increased the potential for all the species that live right on the margin.

In the interest of creating edges, there I found myself, up to my waist in chilly water working with a group of forty jovial students to heap marsh glop on top of a pile of sticks that was soon to be an island. Once we built the island up high enough we planted it with pears and berries. Now I can canoe to the island and harvest pears, berries, and a variety of basketry materials where the deer won't get them first!

One fall day I sat in my cabin reflecting over a cup of nettle tea. I learned an incredible amount during my first season at Bullock's. I saw and helped implement a variety of different projects that all gave me a better understanding of the natural world around me and the place of humans in it. I thought back on the cup of tea I had been sipping a couple years earlier with Ben, and it seemed that permaculture was delivering everything I had touted and even a bit more.

Big Island, Hawaii

After my first year on Orcas, Douglas Bullock invited me to the Big Island of Hawaii to help out with a Permaculture Design Course he was teaching there. "Here we go again," I thought to myself as I packed for another stint in the tropics.

I got off the plane in Hilo, Doug picked me up in a borrowed pickup, and we headed out of town toward the Puna District. Eventually, after passing through sugar cane fields and dense forests, we found ourselves traveling through miles of conventional, chemically grown papaya farms planted on bare lava. Ultimately we arrived at the site, a long, narrow piece of property named Surya Nagar, which was purchased a few years before by a friend from the mainland. Stepping out of the truck, we got a reminder of one big difference between the tropics and Orcas Island in Washington State; in the tropics things grow year-round. Since the site had been largely abandoned for about a year, the weeds were over our heads. "Succession seems to be sufficiently accelerated," I said to Doug.

With the help of local volunteers and the other instructors, we had things cleaned up and ready just in time for the course participants to arrive. During the first night of the course we talked a bit about local Hawaiian culture. I found myself learning quite a bit about how the traditional Hawaiian lifestyle had a lot to offer those of us seeking to create permaculture designs (as do many traditional indigenous lifestyles).

Afterwards, we headed out to a local Hawaiian community to "talk story" with a Hawaiian elder named Uncle Robert. We had our first truly Hawaiian meal there. We ate delicious breadfruit from a tree that was growing above Uncle Robert's house. We brought a variety of perennial salad greens that were growing abundantly back at Surya Nagar in spite of the lack of attention for the last year. We finished our meal by sharing kava, a traditional calming beverage important in Hawaiian culture, while we talked.

Uncle Robert spoke to us about the Hawaiian sovereignty movement and his efforts to preserve the traditions of his native culture. He told us that the places of bounty that we sought to create using permaculture were exactly what the Hawaiians had always created.

During the brisk ride back to Surya Nagar in the bed of the pickup, I had ample time to contemplate our conversation. It seemed to me that the values of diversity extended far beyond the world of plants and right into the realm of cultural knowledge. A little contact with folks who had never lost their connection with nature gave me a lot to ponder.

At Surya Nagar I was impressed with the way biological resources were used. Instead of importing expensive chemical fertilizers from offsite, most of the fertility needs were met on-site in the form of aquatic plants growing in the ponds and tanks. By mulching trees with these aquatic "green manure" plants during the course, we gave

Dave Boehnlein

In Surya Nagar, an orderly profusion of hundreds of species now productively share the space once occupied by a conventionally grown, monoculture payaya farm.

all the trees a fertility boost and helped lock moisture into the soil around their root zones.

Biological solutions to obstacles are often the best because they are inherently regenerative; nonbiological solutions typically are not. For instance, you never get as much energy out of chemical fertilizers as you have to put in to create, package, and ship them. However, by utilizing a biological fertility source right at home, we were able to meet fertility needs while expending a minimum of finite resources, such as petroleum. And the best part is that this fertility source will grow back without any effort from us!

One afternoon, we braved the mosquitoes in the dense, strawberry guava-covered hinterland of the property. We headed back and divided into teams. Some worked on binding welded wire mesh into a large cylindrical form about four feet tall and ten feet across. Others set up a tarp structure with gutters. Yet others cut pond liner (a type of polyethylene or rubber sheeting typically used to line ponds in areas where the ground will not hold water) to the shape and size of the cylinder. By the end of the afternoon we had created a quick-and-easy water storage tank. This allowed us to catch rain from the tarp, which could then be used to help establish fruit, nut, and timber trees and native Hawaiian plants.

The idea here was to take advantage of an energy source that was moving through the property (in this case, water moving from the sky to the ground water). We recognized this energy flow and tapped into it to meet water needs during the establishment of a diverse forest. Most of the water will still end up in the ground water where it was headed anyway. We were just slowing it down a bit to suit the needs of the site.

That evening as I sipped a glass of fresh star-fruit juice and scratched my mosquito bites, I thought about how elegantly permaculture seemed to approach dilemmas. Whenever there was a problem to be solved, the answer often accompanied it. As I considered this, my eye began to wander around the gardens near the main house. Here again I found a permaculture principle sneaking up on me.

What I was seeing was the intensity of the plant systems that were growing there. To many, it probably would have looked like a helplessly messy bunch of weeds. But what I was noticing was the squash poking out through the sweet potato vines that were crawling over the Okinawan spinach, which, in turn, was climbing up a papaya tree. In order to produce this much food in a conventional, monocultural system one would have to use five times the amount of space and a ton of fertilizer. Yet here it was in front of me, enough food for several meals growing in about ten square feet of space. It struck me that if we grew all our food like this, we could leave a lot more land alone, never bringing it under the plow at all.

Looking Back

As I sit here now, once again with my cup of tea close at hand, I can't help but think that the true beauty of these permaculture principles is their universality. They can be applied on the tundra, in the desert, inside your suburban home, or in your urban neighborhood. Why not plant snack fruits along the path leading from your house to your garage—you know, the path you walk twice a day on your way to work and on the way home? Why not put a window-box with herbs right outside your kitchen so you don't have to drive to the store and drop a small fortune on those little plastic containers of basil—they're pretty outrageous, aren't they? Why not make sure you have three different ways to make light in your apartment in case there is a blackout.

I'd like to leave you with my quick list of five things you can do to learn more about permaculture:

- **Read *Introduction to Permaculture* by Bill Mollison.** It's quick and easy and gives a good understanding of permaculture principles.
- **Cultivate your eye for reading landscapes.** This can be as simple as spending more time outside just observing what is going on, asking the question, "Why?" and finding out the answers. For example, if you pay close attention you may notice that the wind always comes from a certain direction right before a big storm. Finding out why (through research in books, the Internet, and asking locals) will help you to better understand what is going on around you.
- **Analyze your home, school, workplace, or community in terms of how things function and relate to one another.** Figure out what works, what doesn't, and how it could be better. In the kitchen, for example, the hot pads should be within reach of the

oven. If they aren't, you've probably already recognized that this isn't ideal, so figure out what it takes to fix it (perhaps a little hook where you can hang them). You can look for creative solutions to problems like this at any scale. Is your community pedestrian-friendly? If not, how could you make it more so? Could you also increase wildlife habitat and food for people at the same time? By practicing analyzing the systems in place around you and looking for creative ways to improve them, you will be starting to make the shift to seeing the world through the lens of permaculture.

• **Plant a garden.** There is no better way to gain insight into natural processes than to interact with them at home, in a community garden, or in the median strip outside your apartment.

• **Take a permaculture design course.** This will provide you with an opportunity to ask questions, network, and find other opportunities in the permaculture community.

My tea is cold again. I seem to have this problem a lot when I start talking about permaculture. Don't worry, though. "Thou shall drink cold tea" is not one of the principles. The tea I'm drinking today is plain old peppermint. It's delicious. I grew it outside my cabin with the water that flows out of my sink drain. I feel pretty good about that. I certainly couldn't say anything like that several years ago when I was having that conversation with my friend Ben. Learning about permaculture has given me a new lens through which I see, and interact with, the world. Through this lens, I'm no longer seeing just problems, but also solutions. And abundance. And happy people. Speaking of Ben, it's been too long since I've visited him. I think next time I see him I'll make him a cup of piping hot peppermint tea.

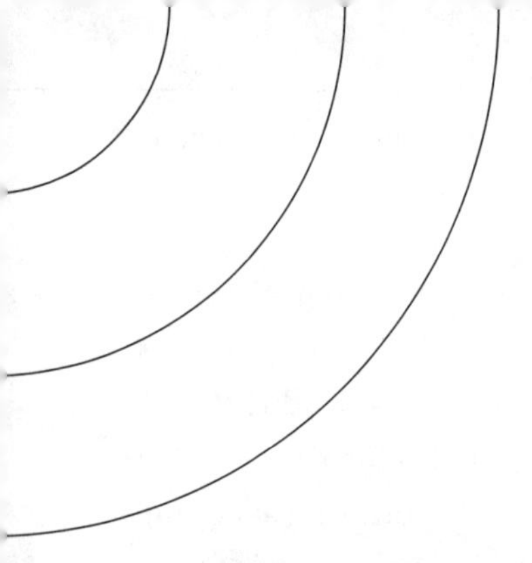

Ecopreneuring: Small, Local, and Restorative

by John Ivanko

Our job title doesn't fit on a two-by-three-inch business card. In fact, my wife and I operate a diversified business that could be its own zip code: an award-winning bed & breakfast; a creative services consulting company; an electricity utility, harvesting power from the wind and sun; an organic farm producing vegetables, fruit, and herbs; a microbiofuels processing facility, transforming waste fryer oil into biodiesel to use in the backup heating system in the greenhouse. We also write books and freelance for national magazines. Some enterprises generate revenue and others save on expenses, all with a mindset of wanting to make this world a better place.

We're the sole CEOs—Chief Environmental Officers—of our business, responsible for the success of our operations and its environmental and social impacts. Mostly, we eat what we grow, use energy we generate or produce ourselves, and create the meaningful work we desire. In other words, success is relative to our worldview and based on what we find meaning in and value. Rather than make

Earth Mission

An Earth Mission is the overarching springboard from which your business, livelihood, and life launches forward that respects nature and fosters socially just relationships with all life. Wealth without purpose is poverty. Ecopreneurs create enterprises that are ecologically restorative, socially responsive, and just—and measure their success in how they build community wealth in a living economy.

money from working at a job, we put our limited funds to work for us through our business to serve what we call our Earth Mission. We define our business qualitatively, not quantitatively.

Ecopreneuring promotes the idea of using small business as a powerful, positive tool for social and ecological change. By transforming our lives from relying on others for paychecks to crafting our own livelihood and legacy by doing our part to better this world, empowerment erupts and change occurs. Think of "ecopreneur" as a subset of "entrepreneur," a business with a mission-driven mindset using creative tactics under the green umbrella to protect the planet. Ecopreneuring is not about making lots of money, though some ecopreneurs will achieve significant financial returns (some already have) because their ideas and businesses can find a ripe market today. Ecopreneuring helps you craft a livelihood to support your values, quality of life, and your pursuit of happiness. And ecopreneurial businesses are the types of enterprises that will emerge as the culturally defining institutions in the twenty-first century: small, human-scaled, ecologically and socially responsible, and local.

In many ways, entrepreneurs and ecopreneurs are similar. Both are idea-driven, innovative, creative, risk-tolerant, flexible, adaptable, freedom-minded, independent, and not afraid to fail. However,

Entrepreneur	Ecopreneur
Values Money	Values Life
I want to be rich	Passion, purpose, meaning, fulfillment through work
Return on Investment (ROI) • capitalist model, based on scarcity • depleting natural resources	Return on Environment (ROE) • nature's model, based on abundance • enhancing or restoring natural resources
Free trade • extractive, exploitative	Fair trade • cooperative, socially responsible, just
Externalize environmental and social costs	Internalize and imbed costs in business
Following regulations • meet governmental regulations	Setting (voluntary) standards beyond regulations • recognize responsibility, take action, innovation, opportunities
Stakeholders = stockholders • financial results driven	Stakeholders = everyone and everything • considers nature, community, future generations
Technology will triumph • technology will save the day	Technology is a tool • appropriate, individualized, one of many options
Super-size me • bigger is better • ride the Titanic	Human-scale, Micro-size, small-mart • small is beautiful, less complex, adaptable • paddle a kayak

ecopreneurs go beyond organic certification standards, beyond compliance to laws and regulations, beyond consumerism, beyond minimum wages, and beyond the free-market economy to conduct business. However, instead of working for money, successful ecopreneurs find ways to let money work for their aspirations, dreams, and hopes for what we want to see the world become—our Earth Mission.

Free Market Dementia & the Four Horsemen of Ecopreneur Opportunity

We've suffered too long from Free Market Economy Dementia: a state of suspended belief in the free market despite the existence of the alternative reality of ecological destruction, concentration of financial wealth in fewer hands and diminished happiness, community life, and family cohesiveness. How can the free-market capitalist system that allows 5 percent of the planet's citizens (living in the United States) to use 25 percent of the planet's resources and produce 40 percent of the planet's waste and pollution be considered a successful economic model? The free market cannot grow infinitely because we can't find substitutions for everything when there's nothing left. It's not the economy, but the ecology that matters. No economy can be sustainable in the long term without a balanced, prosperous, ecological system and at least some sense of social equity.

Our human impacts on ecosystems, climate, and cultures around the world have led to what my wife and I call the Four Horsemen of Ecopreneur Opportunity—climate change, ecological collapse, peak oil, and our indebted nation. They represent problem solving opportunities for businesses, not signs of the Apocalypse. A swelling movement of inspiring and multifaceted innovators—seeking meaning over money, satisfaction over status, and preserving the planet over growing profits—have emerged because of an increasing awareness that if we don't start solving our planetary problems soon, we will face what Keynesian economic theory calls diminishing economic returns—with declines in our quality of life, condition of our natural environment, and, perhaps, human civilization itself.

Small Business Is Booming

While hanging out a shingle and becoming a small business owner is nothing new, mindfully serving the planet through what and how our business operates is. Today's ecopreneurs recognize that profit, while a necessity in our world of mortgages and motors, is not enough. We keep a holistic outlook on the big green picture: How can we do well, make a difference, and make a living? How can I take advantage of existing small business structures and incentives to benefit both our business and the planet?

Running a small business provides freedom to independently control inputs and outputs, from the projects and clients we may work for to the 100 percent post-consumer waste recycled paper we put in our printer. The traditional bottom line of increased profits and stock prices is overrated. Our limited funds passing through our small enterprise generate passive and portfolio income; we invest in income-producing assets rather than splurge on stuff we really don't need. We try to be conservers, not consumers.

About 33 million people in the United States are small-business owners and entrepreneurs, making up 25 percent of our workforce. The vast majority of "free agents" (a term coined by Dan Pink, author of *Free Agent Nation*), run very small businesses. These "job-hopping, tech-savvy, fulfillment seeking, self-reliant, independent" workers represent about 16.5 million soloists, 3.5 million temporary workers (temps), and 13 million microbusinesses that include everything from construction contractors, real estate agents, nannies, direct sales ventures (i.e., Amway), services subcontractors, and accountants. Operating as a microbusiness, or what Pink refers to as a "nanocorp" with three employees or less, is both a personal preference and competitive advantage. The downshift in size enhances the owners' ability for incredible adaptability, innovation, and creativity. Our subchapter S corporation is a nanocorp committed to ecological restoration and social change while turning a modest profit.

Like us, you might be among the 15 million full-time or part-time small office/home office entrepreneurs, or SOHOs. Maybe you're among the 75 percent of all U.S. businesses with only one person at the helm, self-employed. Of the nearly 26 million business firms in the United States, about 97 percent have fewer than 20 employees according to the U.S. Small Business Administration. These small businesses account for about half of the nonfarm Gross Domestic Product, or GDP, generating 60 to 80 percent of the net new jobs over the past decade. While big businesses fired, laid off, downsized, and outsourced jobs, in part, to squeeze more profits for shareholders, small business added economic vitality and employment.

Ecopreneurial businesses grow better, not bigger. Of course, some business models unavoidably demand largesse to accommodate the complexity or scope of the task at hand, like assembling diesel locomotives or manufacturing steel. But fewer Americans are working in these industries as technology plays an expanding role. Recognized as a competitive advantage, many small businesses strive to remain small. Sometimes called personal or lifestyle entrepreneurs, these owners carefully manage their enterprises to achieve optimal efficiencies in whatever niche market they serve—in much the same way as various plants and animals have evolved in nature to fill ecological niches.

Building Value Based on Values

Perhaps you yearn for something more than a paycheck. You want your work to be more about leaving a legacy than making someone else rich by working for their dream instead of yours. Bored, you

John D. Ivanko, innserendipity.com

Lake cabin at Inn Serendipity surrounded by 20 acres of sustainably managed forest.

want do something you feel passionate about that also gives back to our world. You want more time with your family. Maybe you've grown tired of living with the nagging threat of your job being outsourced or company being acquired.

Or perhaps you want to do more than commute to the office in a hybrid car or donate time or money to a charity. Welcome to the emerging social sector, or "citizen sector," of our economy. This sector is characterized by the not-for-profit organization that devotes resources to solve and serve the social, ecological, and community issues instead of rewarding shareholders with dividends—the model championed by big business (and big government) that neglects and sometimes creates many of our social ills.

Today, our family thrives on what one of us made fifteen years ago at the ad agency. Our quality of life has grown exponentially, despite the fact that our earned income on paper declined. At our small-scale Inn Serendipity bed and breakfast—a foursquare farmhouse on five and a half acres—our guests can relax, savor a local breakfast with most of the organic ingredients harvested from a hundred feet from our back door, and drive away knowing that their carbon dioxide emissions were carbon offset through our participation in the nonprofit Trees for the Future Trees for Travel program. The revenues we generate from our business enterprises, besides meeting any financial obligations, are devoted to the good work of improving soil quality, producing more renewable energy than we use, and assisting others who wish to launch their own enterprise or live in a more sustainable way.

Creativity blooms as we freely hopscotch between an intentionally diverse buffet of projects, from running the B & B, writing and photographing for a magazine article for *Mother Earth News*, authoring books, consulting on marketing projects for various nonprofit organizations as subcontractors, tending our organic growing fields, speaking at conferences, and homeschooling our young son, Liam. Both our lifestyle and livelihood blend and reflect our values, like eliminating our contribution to global warming, eating healthy and local, forming community, and renewing the Earth. Our guests, clients, and customers connect with us through the values we share.

Entrepreneurs are problem solvers, possessing an ability to see what was there all along, and then bringing it to market. These entrepreneurs become ecopreneurs when their spirit, boldness, courage, and determination coalescence into a movement to transform global problems into opportunities. Ecopreneurs emblazon the re-greening of Earth, restoring degraded land, cleaning the air, building healthy and safe homes, devising clean and renewable energy sources, offering prevention-oriented alternatives to treatment-focused health care, and helping preserve or restore the ecological and cultural wonders of the planet by changing the way we experience travel.

An Ecopreneurial Business

Ecopreneurs operate sustainable businesses that possess the following key qualities.

The Triple Bottom Line (People, Planet, and Profit)

First coined by John Elkington and articulated in his book, *Cannibals with Forks: The Triple Bottom Line of the 21st Century*, the triple bottom line doesn't drop the idea that businesses should earn a profit. It adds that businesses should do so in ways that take into account environmental and social performance in addition to financial performance. Sustainable businesses can, and should, aspire not merely to mitigate or minimize their impacts on the environment, but in the very way they operate their business, they should make the planet healthier, community more prosperous, air clearer, and bring about greater economic and social justice. It's the fundamental role of an ecopreneur's business to restore, heal, enhance, or nurture the living systems on which we depend.

We measure our success by how we impact the health of our community and others as well by how we help restore or improve the health of the environment. Our focus is on quality of life—not financial surplus or accumulation of goods. A key aspect of this approach results in a focus on stakeholders: customers, employees (if you have them), vendors and suppliers, and investors.

Regional Roots

A sustainable business roosts locally and is inexorably linked to its community for customers and for goods or services needed for the business. This means priorities for both generating and spending

> **Serving Conserving Customers, Not Consumers**
>
> With awareness building about our far-reaching and global impacts on nature and society, ecopreneurs are changing how we live, work, and play—becoming conservers, not consumers. Instead of borrowing from the future or burning through resources, reducing the possibilities for future generations, ecopreneurs are seeking to thrive in a restorative economy that's life giving. It's a change in consciousness, not merely a change in shopping habits. Ecopreneurial businesses, by how they operate and what products or services they offer, foster this conservation-minded behavior.

income stem from our regional area or bioregion. Our place of business defines what we are, how we are connected to other community businesses, and who our customers might be.

Whole Pie Purpose

Whole Pie Purpose differentiates between "principles" and "practices." It's not about what you say—a noble mission statement on paper—but what you do, how you do it, and why it matters. Customers drawn to ecopreneur businesses demand transparency, accountability and tangible practice. The end results matter. How much carbon dioxide has your business sequestered or avoided sending into the atmosphere? How has your business managed to generate more renewable energy than it consumes in its operations?

What Makes a Green Business Green?

Ecopreneurs aspire to continuously push the envelope to do better, with less negative impact on Earth while fostering more positive, restorative changes. Sustainable businesses don't turn nature and labor into private wealth for a select few. They're catalysts for ecological change that use the power of commerce to transform how we live on Earth.

Sustainable, or green, businesses can prosper in all industry sectors, but not all businesses can be sustainable. The Lifestyles of Health and Sustainability, or LOHAS, marketplace consists of five main segments where ecopreneurs would most likely prosper. According to the Natural Marketing Institute, approximately 16 percent of the adults in the United States, or 35 million people, make up this segment of the marketplace most likely targeted by ecopreneurs. The general segments are as follows:

1. **Sustainable economy** (green building, renewable energy, resource efficient products, environmental management, socially responsible investing)

2. **Healthy lifestyles** (organic foods, nutritional supplements, personal care)

3. **Ecological lifestyles** (organic and recycled fiber products, ecotourism, ecological home products)

4. **Alternative health care** (health and wellness care, naturopathy and homeopathy, complementary medicine)

5. **Personal development** (mind, body, and spirit products; yoga; spiritual products)

Multiple Economies of Ecopreneurship

ECOnomics involves operating in more than the free-market economy, the one we commonly think about when buying or selling goods or services. Depending on their scale, many ecopreneurs with smaller operations thrive in other economies as well:

1. **Barter Economy:** Why pay cash (or charge on credit) for something you don't need to buy? Exchanging goods or services or time satisfies needs without draining the bank account. Fruits and vegetables freely flow from our farm; in return, we've received our wooden B & B sign and clothes for our son, Liam. The barter economy often erupts serendipitously, like when a friend who received some of our vegetables presented Liam with a three-string guitar he made himself.

2. **Household Economy:** Self-reliance is underrated, thanks in part to companies that advertise solutions to all our problems—for a price. While most Americans could grow at least some food in a container or small plot to offset their food expenses, few do. Rather than outsourcing our daycare for our son, we created a work-at-home situation where we could care for him, which also optimized our satisfaction as parents.

3. **Collecting and Reuse Economy:** America is surely the land of opportunity—to transform our waste into new materials. From forests filled with wildlife and lakes teaming with fish to piles of discarded tile, bricks, and other building materials, re-using, salvaging and in myriad other ways transforming someone's trash into treasure provides a cost-effective vector for ecopreneurs to outcompete larger companies while saving money and boosting their bottom line. Using www.freecycle.org, www.isharestuff.org, and www.craigslist.org, we pick up things we need and clear out unwanted items, all for free.

4. Volunteer Economy: From donating time at a homeless shelter to contributing food to a food bank, without the volunteer economy, many nonprofits would be out of business. While many equate time with money, people who freely exchange time or services support the activities and services that enhance communities—in some cases adding to desirable communities that are already vibrant with civic life. Ecopreneurs can be on the giving and receiving end of mentorships and informal guidance from social and business contacts.

5. Cooperative Economy: We're members of five cooperatively owned businesses, including the nation's largest retail food cooperative, Willy Street Cooperative in Madison, Wisconsin; a regional sustainable forestry cooperative, Kickapoo Woods Cooperative; and a community land trust, the Mississippi Valley Conservancy. Common ownership in these mission-driven organizations offers opportunities for us to better steward resources and work together to accomplish collective goals.

6. Harvest Economy: Every day, enough sunlight falls on the planet to meet all our energy needs, with some to spare. Instead, most Americans burn fossil fuels that end up polluting and destroying the planet. Ecopreneurs search out opportunities in a harvest economy that are often tax free, climate neutral, and better for the environment. Our businesses harvest so much wind and solar energy that we receive net annual payments from our utility company. Our electronic "storefront" on the Internet—harvesting page views and with the potential to reach millions of people—costs about as much as a taxicab ride in downtown Chicago. It uses a "free network," the Internet, to grow a business in a way that's almost impossible to do with the corporate-controlled TV or radio airwaves.

By operating in these other economies, ecopreneurs short-circuit expenses and boost their bottom lines. The savings flowing from our business are harnessed to work for our Earth Mission.

Getting a GBA: Green Business Administration

There are tricks to the trade that many millionaires—and most of our millionaire politicians—use that allow us to make a life without having to become wage slaves. We agree, it's almost impossible for the working or middle class to get ahead earning a wage income. We've discovered a different way to bend the ends that never seem to meet, instead forming a circle, where assets generate passive and portfolio income and liabilities, like loan interest payments, are minimized or avoided altogether.

The main requirement for a for-profit business is to make profits at least once every three years, according to the U.S. Internal Revenue Service. No requirement specifies how much profit must be made, just some. That's the big difference between a hobby, where generating revenue is not the primary goal, and a business. The nonprofit business, formed as a special type of corporation depending on its purpose, uses revenues collected to fund its mission, whether it's saving open space or planting trees around the world to help mitigate the effects of global warming, provide nature-enhancing livelihoods, and prevent soil erosion.

My family and I approach our passions—writing, photography, hosting people, and desire to restore the planet—not as hobbies, but as business enterprises. You can blog on the Internet about growing your garden or you can write articles about growing food organically for *Hobby Farm Home* magazine. One's a hobby; one's a viable business and provides income from writing about something you love.

There are numerous advantages of operating a business for yourself, in terms of tax savings, control over how natural or human resources are used (or misused) and the freedom to pursue your passions without your boss looking over your shoulder. If you grow weary of climbing the ladder, own it. If you don't like the kind of companies that are offering you a job, then make your own in your vision of what it means to tread lightly on the planet. Our book, *ECOpreneuring: Putting Purpose and the Planet before Profits* dives into practical aspects of how to make your green dreams a reality.

The New Bottom Line: Making Things Better

Small businesses, and increasingly green businesses, are already providing right livelihood to many families in America. You'll find these ecopreneurs working at farmers' markets, launching nonprofit organizations, and tinkering with their green technology businesses at a community incubator,. You can also find them consulting for nonprofit organizations out of a spare bedroom "home office" in their suburban home, and operating a bed & breakfast featuring breakfasts prepared with organic ingredients harvested a hundred feet from their back door, like we do.

Resetting the scales of commerce, ecopreneurs replace the global consumption craze with new, personal, and localized models of business that restore the planet while nourishing our quality of life. My wife and I envision a nation of ecopreneurs, much like Thomas Jefferson may have believed in a prosperous nation of yeoman farmers, harnessing the freedom of the free market and pioneering spirit. We can change the world, one business at a time.

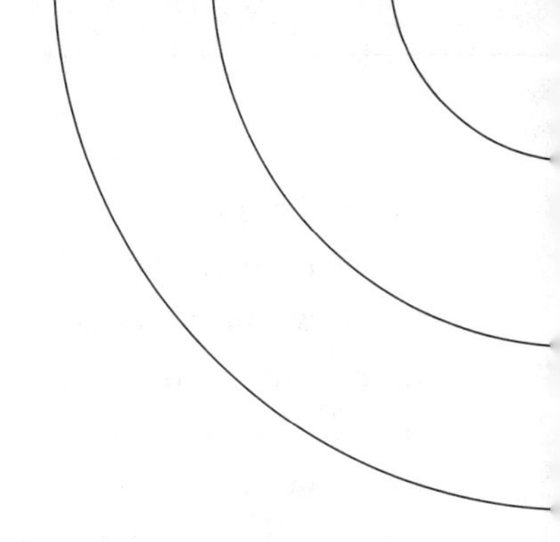

A Family Farm's "Well Beeing"

by Mark Bruland

We live in southwest Wisconsin, where I am proud to report that our state insect is the Honeybee. However, our family's journey in beekeeping really began one hot, summer afternoon in southern California. We were still three years and 2,500 miles from where we would tend our first colony, but it seemed fitting that our oldest daughter, Chloe (only 9 years old at the time), piped up from her back seat as we crawled through bumper-to-bumper traffic on the San Diego Freeway. The question we had pondered as a family was "What would be a good name for our farm, if we ever have one?" With the wisdom and creativity of a child that had been seriously ill much of her life, Chloe proposed "Appley Ever After" as our farm's name. It became a destination, and to this day, a mantra to live our lives by—in harmony with the land, the weather, and even the bugs that share our forty-six acres outside Viroqua, Wisconsin.

Flash forward to the present. Chloe is now in her mid-teens, healthy, and looking forward to getting her driver's license. She enjoys putting on her bee suit, veil, and gloves, and working with me. She has watched me do many stupid things along the way as I learned experientially. Back in southern California, one of Chloe's then-first grade friends, Leanna Gage, once told us, "Everyone has a little 'dumb' in them . . ." Sometimes that little "dumb" has taught us exactly what we needed, just when we needed it most, and helped us become even more successful than some "experienced" beekeepers. Sure, we get stung once in a while, but less often if we don't do something incredibly dumb.

Here are some of the things we have learned about bees and beekeeping. (But in reality, you stand to learn infinitely more by caring for and observing the seasonality of a colony or two on your own place.) We do it for our "well beeing." It is therapeutic on many levels. Furthermore, because honeybees are disappearing at an incredibly alarming rate, each of us can make a difference, one hive at a time.

Why Beekeeping?

At Appley Ever After Farm, we decided early on that we wanted "organic apples and cider" to be our family farm's core business. This meant growing as many quality apples as possible from our trees, which are expensive to plant. Like many other small family farms, we needed to optimize the return per acre on our little farm to keep it going . . . to maintain its "well beeing."

Farming definitely isn't a get-rich-quick scheme. Someone who had many years of experience farming organic apples once asked me "How many acres do you farm?" When I told him about 45 acres, his immediate comeback was, "Good! The fewer acres you farm, the less money you will lose every year." To be sure, farming is full of risk, but raising bees is one way to keep it in check. Honeybees increase the yield in just about any crop. That is the first and best reason to tend bees on a small farm. By seeking out nectar and pollen (bee food), honeybees pollinate fruits, vegetables, flowers, and trees.

www.indexopen.com

Safety practices around the hive include the proper equipment and no sudden movements, which is also good for the bees.

Bees give us a bigger harvest on almost everything that blooms. Even though we have built up to tending 15 bee colonies, the return from increased yields far outweighs any honey profit you will get. For us, this is improved production on our 200 apple trees, 400 blueberry bushes, 3,000 crowns of asparagus, and 450 raspberry plants. (We also have raised 3 litters of pigs, 75 broiler chickens, and 8 turkeys while continuing to collect eggs every day from about 100 hens and keeping 2 milking goats.)

Most of the time, farming involves heavy lifting. Beekeeping is a rare type of "farming" that keeps most of the lifting under 50 pounds. You can learn to be a beekeeper in one or two years, and become relatively proficient if you are patient. Besides helping your other crops, the bees can provide you with a nice "second" income, either from renting your hives for pollination or collecting the honey and selling it directly from your farm.

Hive Rental Pros and Cons

1. Up to 800 colonies of bees will ship on a single semi.

2. Pollination charges currently are anywhere from $25 to $200 per colony depending on how far the beekeeper needs to transport the bees and the agricultural application which they will be used for. (For example, it may only cost $25/colony for local apple orchards, but cost up to $200/colony to move bees from WI to CA for the almond blossom season. The East Coast rates are currently $65/colony minimum.)

3. Moving bees is very stressful on the colonies and can weaken them over time (heat building due to poor air circulation inside the colonies during transport). Loaded flatbed trailers utilize netting over the colonies/boxes to keep the bees from escaping (and causing a potential health risk/insurance nightmare).

4. In many cases, the fees a beekeeper can collect from renting out colonies is greater than the amount of income he/she will see from processing and selling the honey that the bees will produce.

5. One of the only agricultural crops that farmers do NOT hire a beekeeper for pollination services (although they do need to use them) is orange trees. Orange-blossom honey is so highly sought after that the beekeeper will set his/her hives in the orange groves solely for the honey they will collect at the end of that season.

6. Many beekeepers and researchers feel that the added stress of renting out/transporting bees contributes to weaker hives and can lead to colony-collapse disorder.

A Buzz About Town

It takes a special kind of person to willingly stick their head in a box of bees. Beekeeping is definitely full of colorful personalities, and can be the origin of local legend and tall tales. (You can save plenty of money when you turn off the cable TV service and attend a local bee club meeting or two each month.) One time, while teaching a beekeeping workshop out in a local bee yard, a student asked me, "Do you think that your bees recognize you?" I asked the rest of the class what they thought before I offered my opinion. Some were quite certain that their bees knew them. One even practiced reiki with her bees, calming them first with her energy each time she worked with them (check it out at www.reiki.org).

Most days I think that the colonies we have tended on our farm from one year to the next do know our smells and sounds. We can stand pretty much directly in front of their entrances and the bees politely buzz past our heads on their return flight approaches. Occasionally—maybe it's a young bee on a training flight—one will crash into my head, bounce off, and then continue flying home. At first, those occurrences are a bit unnerving. My daughter and I now get a good chuckle when that happens to us. We have never been stung in the process, even when one gets tangled in my daughter's hair. While they buzz up a storm, and my daughter tends to talk faster and at a higher pitch while it is happening, the bees seem to appreciate the patience with which we "guide" them back out of their temporary "jungle" and they take off without stinging.

There was one cool summer evening, however, when my honeybees certainly did not recognize me as a "friendly." I call the tale "The Night Of Nine Stings Ending Not Soon Enough" (a.k.a. "N.O.N.S.E.N.S.E."). One of the best things you can do when you are just getting started in beekeeping is to find yourself a mentor—preferably someone who has tended bees for a number of years and will want to assist you in learning and working through your first few seasons. (Always ask your mentor about the specific nature of his/her "hazing" rituals after you get to know them pretty well.) My mentor was aware that during our first summer we did not have an extractor to remove the honey from our hives. He invited us to bring the boxes of honey over to his place and use his equipment while he showed us how to "spin out honey." Worked great! We spun out a few boxes of honey and came back to our farm at dusk, packing a sixty-five-pound bucket of honey and a number of empty honey boxes. My mentor told me that it would be better to get those "dripping, wet boxes" back on the bee colonies as soon as possible, "they'll love it!"

Here's where being a little dumb taught me a lifelong lesson. Since it was almost dark, I drove my car right up to the hives and turned my headlights on them so I could better see what I was doing. The night air was cool. The bees were usually very calm and pleasant. At the last minute, having never actually done this before, I made a conscious decision to put a protective veil on. I was wearing a white T-shirt, shorts, and sandals because it had been bloody hot earlier in the day. Honey extracts wonderfully when the temperature is above 80 degrees F though. As soon as I removed the top of the first hive to put the boxes back on, I heard a different kind of buzzing sound. Looking back on it, I would say they sounded "agitated." They must have been steamed, because someone that they had previously known as a caretaker had last been in their hive as a robber.

I really do love hearing the bees buzz. To me, it is "The zen of the bees." There is nothing that distracts you (in a good way) more from the day-to-day stress of your life like having your head down inside a colony of about 80,000 buzzing honeybees. It must have looked like the old cartoons though that night—the swarm of bees rising up out of their nest and heading straight toward the dumb guy messing with their hive. They probably thought I was a bear or something.

Anyway, I had bees in places on me and in my clothing that made me more than just a little nervous while I was trying to reposition those boxes on the colonies. I moved quickly back to the car and jumped in. It hadn't occurred to me, as I leaned back in the seat, that there would be a large number of the angry girls crawling around on my back (yes, only the girl bees will sting you).

I learned four new things about bees that evening. First, they don't like waking up in the middle of the night. Second, they don't like bright lights shining in their faces. Third, bees see in ultraviolet, so my warmer-than-the-air invading body was an easy target to locate and sting. Fourth, and I consider it the pearl of the entire adventure, was this: pinch a bee, get a sting. My body leaning back on the seat pinned nine frightened and angry honeybees and they each offered me a sting to learn by. Later that same night in the house, I discovered the main ingredient in many after-sting topical medicines is ammonia. Since then,

Collecting Honey 101

While lightly smoking the boxes, pry open the compartments in a colony that contains just honey (not brood). Lift out one frame at a time, "brushing" off the bees that are on it softly with a feather duster or soft-bristled brush. Put the frame (sans bees) into an empty box, preferably in a closed container or car trunk so that the bees won't find it and latch onto it, taking these frames back to your "honey house." With a hot knife, cut off the top layer of wax from both sides of the frame. You can either use gravity (letting it drain out one side at a time) or put each frame into a centrifugal force "extractor" that will "spin out" the honey, collecting it in the bottom of the extractor.

Getting Started: Basic Tools

1. One hive-opening tool and soft brush
2. A veil/hat
3. A pair of gloves
4. A smoker
5. One or two deep boxes for raising the brood
6. One or two shallow boxes for bees to store excess honey
7. One hive bottom
8. One hive-top (inside cover and outer cover)
9. Optional: a queen excluder that sits between the two deep boxes and the honey boxes, which prevents the queen from laying eggs up in the honey-storage area, but allows the worker bees to slip through.
10. A good basic beekeeping book to read and a mentor close by to call on when you have questions

we keep a bottle of Windex handy. It works just the same as the name brand anti-sting topicals and of course, our windows shine!

How Does One "Get Into" Beekeeping?

People often ask me, when they learn that I tend bees, "What does it cost to get into bees?" The price of honeybee colonies for a start-up operation has gone up rapidly over the years, largely due to the economics of supply and demand. Colony collapse disorder has seriously disrupted the supply. The price of just one box of bees can be over $100. Add to that your equipment, hive boxes, and honey storage, and you are into $200 per colony pretty quickly.

There are many local beekeeping clubs and organizations that you can find fairly easily, no matter where you live. You can check with your local agricultural extension agent, ask your neighbors and friends if they know of anyone that is tending bees, or search for a local connection with the Internet. Finding local beekeepers is easier than you think. Most beekeepers readily welcome "apprentices." This really means they love getting someone else to lift honey boxes, carry their equipment out to the field, and buy their old, used equipment. That might sound like a scam at first, but when you are starting out, ALWAYS know where any used equipment you are buying comes from. There are many unused hive boxes on the market—some are sitting out there because diseases wiped out the former colonies of honeybees. Your mentor will NOT try to sell you such equipment. There is a code of honor among beekeepers. Real beekeepers will help out anyone who they get to know, and who they think are truly interested in learning and perpetuating the art of beekeeping.

OK, so you have purchased a couple of colonies from your mentor, you have the necessary equipment to begin, you are reading up on beekeeping in general, and you are looking forward to staying on top of your colonies and checking on them regularly. Beekeeping has given us a perspective about life and farming at Appley Ever After that we did not appreciate at first. We practice a "Let it bee" philosophy now. And in practicality, it really means, "If you don't know for sure how to make something better, leave it alone—watch and learn from it." It works with everything from farrowing pigs to keeping competitive weeds out of the asparagus field. The same goes for bees. "Newbee" beekeepers do more harm than good by trying to do too much for their bees. Bees are bees. They are not creatures that we need to dominate. They appreciate being left alone whenever possible. They don't appreciate their hives broken into, opened up, exposed to sunlight, breathing in a lot of smoke or chemical "treatments," and they should not be looked at as some kind of nature experiment. The less we have opened up their brood chambers or "wombs" where the young bees are hatching and growing, the stronger our colonies have seemed. We stopped treating them with any chemicals for mites or diseases over three years ago. To this day, we rarely lose a colony and when we do, it is likely due to starvation. What that really means is the beekeeper did not leave enough honey to get through the winter and well into spring when the new nectar and pollen supplies would kick in.

When Should You Start Working with a Colony?

Your mentor will tell you that the best time to start a new colony is in the spring. Once the dandelions come out, the bees are anxious to begin collecting the pollen. We tend an organic farm. When we first started out, we figured that a well-trimmed lawn and orchard looked (and felt) like we were on top of things and "in control." Since adopting our "Let it bee" philosophy, we have learned that our colonies are healthier when we provide pollen and nectar sources as early in the spring as possible, and as close to their bee yard as it can be. When the days warm up in March and April, the colony of bees that has been holed up in their warm hive all winter is anxious to build back up the colony numbers. Some of you may know—perhaps others may not—bees do NOT hibernate. They cluster in a ball inside the hive with the single queen in the center. The wing muscles from the beating of their wings produce heat. A hive will stay above 80 degrees F inside even when the weather is below zero outside. Keeping warm takes energy. The bees get their energy from the stored honey and pollen you will leave them going into the winter. Many of the bees will die during the winter though . . . mostly those on the outside of the cluster. It is a bit weird to see thousands of dead bees (having been carried out of the hive in the middle of winter by their respectful "sisters") laying on the snow in front of the hive. Your heart sinks and you will plead with your mentor asking them what you did wrong. Fear not.

Swarm, Swarm, Swarm!

How big does a colony get before they split up and swarm? It depends on how much room you give them. I would say the average colony that has two deep boxes on it for brood would grow to about 40,000 to 50,000 bees before they would want to split. If you only gave them one deep box and never added anything on (built them an addition) they would need to split at about 20,000 bees.

What happens if you do not collect the swarm? The swarm will look for a hollow in a tree or log where they can begin building their comb and raising their little sisters and brothers. Nowadays, wild colonies are extremely rare. Most "splits" that you will see have come from some beekeeper's bee yard.

It's all good. But in the spring, the queen's instinct once she knows there is a "nectar flow" happening is to quickly lay as many eggs as she can to hatch out more worker bees. Springtime is when experienced beekeepers will "split" their colonies as their bees begin to build up numbers and strength. We have found that when we split an existing colony and let the split raise their own queen naturally (instead of buying one in the mail and "installing" her in a box full of some other queen's progeny), the colonies are extremely strong, healthy, and productive. We have done it both ways. In some cases, when we wanted to build up our number of colonies quickly, we purchased new colonies. They arrive in a wire cage with about 3,000 workers—and one queen in a smaller "cage" inside the larger one. The workers free her in about three days by eating through a candy plug on one end of the queen's cage. By that time, the pheromone from this new queen is the one that the worker bees key in on and they instinctively want to care

Three Common NewBee No-nos

1. Opening up their hives too often during the year or too early in the spring.

2. Not leaving the colony enough honey/food for them to get through the winter.

3. Setting the hives up in an unfavorable location (morning sun and afternoon shade are best in the Midwest, and they should be protected from cold north winds in the winter).

for her from then on. Our recommendation is to "bee patient" and let the bees develop naturally. True, you may not get honey as quickly, but you will be rewarded with honey sooner or later.

Springtime is when colonies that build up quickly become congested and nature decides to make a split of the colony on its own. These are called swarms and at first we would almost cry when one would be seen leaving one of our boxes. Remember, "Let it bee?" Now, we watch as they fly off, grateful for the fact that the colony is so strong. That's the ONLY reason they will ever swarm, because they are big and strong. We have learned that this is NO reason to be saddened. Of course, catching swarms is one of the things that beekeepers love to do the most. Picture someone in shorts and sandals, maybe a T-shirt, maybe not. They step up to a cluster of bees hanging from a branch, and without a veil, gloves, or a smoker, simply tap the branch and catch the ball of falling bees in a simple cardboard box. Then close it gently and take it back to their bee yard, transferring it into an empty box. We in the industry like to call them "free-bees." The colony in a swarm is not protecting any territory—they are on a mission to find a new spot to make their nest in. (In a way, you're their real estate agent showing a nice place. If you don't collect the swarm, they continue to search for a hollow tree or log to call home.)

You will not even need a veil or gloves to catch the swarm. It drives the neighbors nuts when they see you bare-handing a ball of bees. If you don't pinch them, they won't sting you. We usually discover swarms in trees around Memorial Day each year. Two years ago, we captured our first swarm thanks to the keen eyes of one of the neighborhood children out riding her bike. Important point here: kids can be your best swarm scouts. Let the neighborhood kids know that you are a beekeeper and that swarms will NOT hurt them. Treat them to free honey whenever they are over—I like to call them honey shooters. I tell the child to hold out their cleanest finger, and I squirt about a half teaspoon on their finger and let them lick it off. Addict them young, and they will probably be lifelong scouts for you. A lifetime supply of "free-bees!"

I hope what we have shared with you about beekeeping on Appley Ever After Farm convinces you that tending bees on your own place is something that you can learn and do easily. I know that it will promote your own "well beeing." Live in peace and bee well.

www.indexopen.com

Bees, as the saying goes, tend to keep busy.

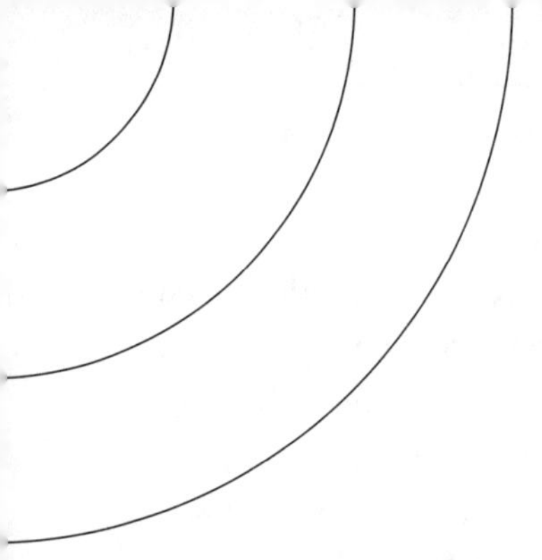

Finding Myself in the Dark

by Laura Gardiner

It's 15 degrees Fahrenheit outside; I come in bringing the cold with me. There is nothing like coming home to good friends and warm food. The five of us currently living in this snug apartment sit around a candlelit table with a refreshing silence that stands in stark contrast to the city that surrounds us. A yellow glow pours in the windows. How did I ever become so lucky to have time to sit nearly every night with some of my best friends for a long dinner filled with idle chatter, philosophizing, laughter, and everything in between?

Living simply was a concept that was introduced to me in high school, but it took meeting the people of what is now the Allium Collective, a group united by convictions to make this world a little simpler and a little happier for all those who inhabit it, to truly realize it. Out of a common desire to organize to raise awareness about the overconsumption of resources that plagues our nation, as our first major project we decided to fast from electricity for thirty days in the dead of winter. Our aim was to demonstrate the discrepancies in this world and the necessity for change in a way that might be heard. The success of our first experience turned the fast into an annual event.

The idea came about not from a desire to make an environmental statement, but a political one. Our first fast was a part of a campaign against the war in Iraq. A Chicago organization, Voices for Creative Nonviolence, organized a monthlong campaign called "The Winter of Our Discontent" in which they encouraged people to take a nonviolent stand against the war by lobbying, standing vigil, and fasting from food for thirty days in the U.S. capitol. Because a food fast did not fit with any of our schedules (it's rather hard to teach a class of twenty-five students all day when you haven't eaten in several weeks), we came up with the idea of a different sort of fast. At the time, the effects of the war and inefficient reconstruction efforts left most Iraqis with, at most, four hours of electricity per day. The idea of an electricity fast to specifically highlight the power situation in Iraq, with the added environmental connection, sat well with all of us. Our second fast however, had a predominantly environmental message, although our initial concerns about the political consequences of overconsumption were still present.

The first time we fasted from electricity, I'll be honest, I was scared. What if it didn't work? What if, after telling everyone I knew that I'd be doing this, we couldn't actually make it work? Looking back, it's difficult to understand what I was so nervous about. Perhaps it was simply a fear of the unknown, or a fear of failure. Although the first week I might have lost my keys, poured toothpaste in the sink instead of on my toothbrush, and cooked some absolutely dreadful dinners only to find I couldn't see well enough to wash the dishes, I discovered that these failures were a part of the success of the experiment and, as it turned out, an enormous factor in my growth as a person.

The winter of 2006, I sat, unsure of what thirty-three days without electricity would mean. I rationalized that it must be possible because over 1.5 billion people around the world live without electricity every day[1]. What makes me so different that I cannot live without electricity? Well, nothing really. And I was right—not only was it possible but it was also enjoyable. Our lives in the United States can be quite sterile, prepackaged, almost mass-produced. But while fasting I realized to a greater degree than ever before that this prepackaged lifestyle leaves much to be desired. With all the gadgets, television shows, new movies, entertainment centers, video games, and frozen dinners out there, few of us spend much time just being with the people around us. Without electricity, there is no other choice. When the house is dark, you've eaten dinner, and there are no TV, movies, computer, lights to read by, or music to listen to there truly is nothing to do but sit around and talk. If you ask me what I enjoy most about going without electricity, I will without hesitation answer: it's the time that I can just be.

The second year that we decided, as a community, to fast from electricity for a month, the fear was replaced by anticipation: mental planning, worry, and preparation. The first few days feel strange, working a little harder than before to keep things just so, but soon enough everything falls into place. Make no mistake, like so many Americans I enjoy surfing the Internet, having a cell phone, and oh goodness, the music. A month without music is a strain on the soul. But there is a certain spirituality to going without.

The second time around we also had a much better idea of what to expect and what was possible. Where we had originally bought fresh produce daily to enable us to go without refrigeration, we now realized that it is about freezer-temperature outdoors and refrigerator-temperature on our enclosed porch. So began our outdoor refrigerator (think: plastic storage tub full of food). Additionally, we quickly learned which candle types were most efficient for which activities and made sure we had the proper candles already set up where we'd want them. The previous year we were always hunting for a lighter, hunting for a candle. And the most exciting addition—which almost felt like cheating—the hand-crank flashlight / radio! Granted, you have to crank it every ten minutes or so to get the radio going, but it is contact with the outside world.

You're probably thinking, "I still don't get it. What good does that do?" Or maybe you're more like my mother and are thinking, "Well, that's just crazy!" Maybe it is a little crazy and maybe there is no shift in the universe that follows five people going without lights, computers, telephones or a refrigerator. But just maybe it makes a small difference. After our first fast in the winter of 2006, there were a lot of folks curious about the experience, but not so many ready to join in.

"But what do you do?" Well, we talk. We play games. We cook vegan meals and try to convince our friends and neighbors to come over for a candlelit dinner. Really, what we do is finally have time away from the hectic schedules of our modern world to be with one another and with ourselves.

"That's great, but I couldn't do it. I have to work, I have responsibilities." Well, me too. I wish I had found some magical secret to living without money, but I haven't. We all go to work or school and in general carry on with our lives as normal during daylight hours. An electricity fast, to me, is a statement, a way of raising awareness, of tweaking one's perspective on life. Were the lights on in my classroom? Yes. Did I e-mail my students' parents when necessary? Absolutely. Did I call my mother? Well, no, I didn't, but she understood.

OK, let's be honest. It's not really all fun and games, and certainly not as easy as usual. But change is good, right? I now know quite well why the invention of the washing machine has been so popular. Doing the laundry by hand in the bathtub is not exactly fun. And I'll admit, at the end of the first year's fast I had a large pile of laundry that I was waiting to wash until the fast was over. But the next year I made it a point to wash clothes every couple of days so it was never quite the chore that a "full load" would be. It's all about planning.

There are several layers to electricity fasting. The outermost layer, that which is most visible to the public, is the statement. I will reduce my consumption to raise awareness of the inequities in our world and the destruction that is caused to both people and the planet so that we may have these resources. But a bit deeper there is the experiment of what my life could have been like had I been born to another circumstance; to have a greater sense of what it means to not have access to a resource I generally consider to be a necessity. And, for me, the innermost layer is truly that of community. The community that gets lost in the every day hustle and bustle of modern urban life. In our home we are five people, five schedules, and all too often very little meaningful connection.

When you stop and think of the number of people across the globe who, on any given day, do not have their basic needs met, who do not have access to clean water or reliable food, who do not have adequate shelter or the security of knowing they will be safe for the night, it seems like quite a luxury to be able to hear my mother's voice from nearly two thousand miles away at my whim. To be sure, I miss checking in with her, but that loss is nothing compared to the hardship that so many face living every day without reliable clean water, hospitals, or simply not knowing if your loved ones are safe.

The electricity fast has become an annual event, each year with more people joining in. This year there were seventeen people total reducing our consumption; ten full fasters and seven partial fasters cutting back for either a shorter time or in a specific area. Even though, to me, an electricity fast means no lights, TV, refrigerator, microwave, cell phone, computer, etc., the extended community that participated with us the second time around added a new level and helped me revise my own ideas of what is possible. When two friends of ours decided to join in a way that was meaningful to them, I learned that a statement is meaningful so long as it means something to the person making it. For them turning off everything was too much, but they still joined in by turning off their television for a portion of the fast. I believe they experienced the same layers as those of us turning everything off in a way that was just as meaningful to them. And perhaps next year they'll be ready for something a little more.

Part of making a statement is making people hear it. My friend, housemate, and fellow faster Neil Brideau arranged for our environmental outreach to be interactive, leading to greater awareness and community participation. The Chicago Department of the Environment donated compact fluorescent light bulbs (CFLs) to any person who agreed to sign a pledge with us saying they were willing to reduce their energy consumption. Easy as pie. Sign the pledge, get a free light bulb. Install your light bulb and you've fulfilled the pledge. Presto! When all was said and done we handed out approximately 400 light bulbs, which, if they were all installed has greatly reduced Chicago's energy consumption as each CFL uses 65 percent less energy than a standard incandescent bulb[2].

According to the U.S. Environmental Protection Agency (EPA), "the energy used in the average home can be responsible for more than twice the greenhouse gas emissions of the average car. When you use less energy at home, you reduce greenhouse gas emissions from power plants and help protect our environment from the risks of global climate change." Within our household, we calculated that we saved approximately 320 pounds of CO_2 from being released into the atmosphere by not using electricity for thirty days[3]. After each fast we seem to find new ways to cut our energy usage and reduce the waste from our home without fully fasting. Some of the things that we've found in the past include [4]:

- Not using the dryer for laundry. If it's hot and windy, hang your clothes outside. Savings: 215–600 pounds of CO_2 per year.
- The refrigerator is the largest energy user in most homes. But we never use it between midnight and 5 am, so why leave it on? A cold refrigerator stays cold if no one opens the door. Savings: 1,500 pounds of CO_2 per year.
- Make sure the refrigerator is full when in use. Fill it with containers of water (to be used later) if you don't have enough food to refrigerate and/or freeze. This decreases the amount of energy required to keep your food at the designated temperature.
- If you're feeling really motivated, store your food outside during the winter.
- Use a wind-up clock instead of an electronic one. Savings: 100 pounds of CO_2 per year.
- Turn off your computer and monitor when not in use.
- Get rid of your television.

The United States uses approximately 25 percent of the world's natural resources, but has only 5 percent of the world's population. I never needed to be convinced to take steps to reduce my energy consumption. It just made sense. Every day you can read in the news about people suffering the world over for lack of simple things such as clean water, a stable food supply, basic shelter, and security. It is astounding how interconnected all of these things are. However, when we surveyed Chicagoans on the street during this year's fast, very few had any idea where their power comes from. If you don't even know how the electricity is created before it's delivered to your house, I can

Estimated Home Appliance Carbon Dioxide Release

Appliance	Estimated Usage	lbs CO_2 released per year*
Clothes Dryer	2 hours/week	217 – 603
Clock Radio	24 hours/day	101.6
Refrigerator	24 hours/day	7,367
36-inch Color Television	3 hours/day	168.9
Computer CPU awake/asleep Monitor awake/asleep Laptop	5 hours/day	245 / 63.5 317.55 / 63.51 105.85
Dishwasher	4 hours/week	289.5 – 579.07
Microwave Oven	5 minutes/day	26.46 – 38.81
Radio/ Stereo	1 hour/day	29.63 – 169.36

*Energy usage range varies based on model and setting used.

only imagine how difficult it would be to fully internalize the importance of cutting back.

As my co-faster and friend, Leah Patriarco, put it "we rely on our lawmakers and business leaders to put policies in place that will reduce our negative political and environmental impact on the planet, leading to little or no actual change. Meanwhile, we engage in activities that help fuel these negative effects. We are aware that cheap clothing and other products come from factories in countries where labor laws are lax, yet we still buy these cheap products from chain stores. We know that driving our cars results in higher demand for oil and more pollution, yet we still drive our cars to work every day. It is only through changing the way we as individuals live that we can hope to see changes at the global level." It is the belief of the members of the Allium Collective that we need to show, as people living in the United States, that we are willing to let go of our excesses and live in the world more equitably. We need to refuse consent to the taking of resources from others both in our country and abroad. If we personally reduce our demand for resources and invite others to do the same, we will alter the general demand and our country's negative impact on the planet.

With each day I fast I learn something new about myself, something I can easily change to help make the world just a tiny bit safer and cleaner for those I share it with, and something about the people in my life. All in all, I can't recommend any other activity more. I hope you'll join us.

Endnotes

[1] Source: IEA world energy outlook 2004

[2] Source: www.EnergyStar.gov

[3] Approximately (avg. monthly kWh)×(1.16 lbs/kWh)], Source: Energy Information Administration, Updated State- and Regional-level Greenhouse Gas Emission Factors for Electricity (March 2002), http:/www.eia.doe.gov/oiaf/1605/e-factor.html

4 Calculations for CO_2 emissions: [(wattage × hours used/day × days per year) /1000] × 1.16 = lbs CO_2 per year

Blowing in the Wind: Residential Turbine Power

by Lisa Kivirist

You could say my husband and I have a windy site at our home and bed & breakfast business, Inn Serendipity. Located in southwestern Wisconsin, there are times when we come inside after working in the gardens with red faces, not from sunburn, but from windburn. Sitting high on the ridge where we can see for many unobstructed miles in any direction, our place is well-situated for generating electricity with a residential-scale wind turbine. It helps that we also operate a small farm in the country and have enough space for one.

Not to be confused with the old abandoned windmills—designed to mechanically pump water from wells or grind grains—a wind turbine generates electricity by using the wind, a renewable energy source. Unlike coal-fired power plants or nuclear reactors, wind turbines generate electricity without creating any water or air pollution—or leaving behind toxic waste for thousands of years.

The large commercial-sized turbines seem to get all the press these days, huge towering sentinels with slowly sweeping blades longer than a wing on a Boeing 747. Many towering over 180 feet in the air, they generate vast amounts of energy—measured in the megawatts—and have a price tag to match, costing more than $1 million to put up. These systems are typically set up as wind farms, grouped together in high wind areas along windy overpasses or coastal areas. These wind farms often generate electricity for tens of thousands of homes.

But our wind turbine is a residential-sized system, grid-connected, and rated for electricity generation at 10 kilowatts (kW). Residential systems range from small 0.5 kW turbines on modest poles to a larger 20 kW residential system placed atop a steel-lattice tower. Not all turbines operate the same way. We selected the Bergey 10 kW wind turbine for its reputed reliability and minimal maintenance. The more moving parts, the greater the possibility for wear and tear, plus regular maintenance. Besides the wind turbine system, we operate a 780-watt photovoltaic (PV) system, two solar thermal systems for our domestic hot water and to heat our greenhouse, have extensive energy conservation practices and green building technologies, and grow enough food to meet about 70 percent of our needs.

Being grid-tied, or connected to the utility grid, our wind system avoids the bank of batteries needed for energy storage. Instead, we use the electricity grid as storage for excess electricity produced. After all, the grid was, in part, paid for by American taxpayers' money; why pay more for a battery bank when we can use what already exists—assuming that it's reliable enough. When we overproduce in any given year—which we regularly do now—our net metering contract with the public utility entitles us to a credit check. Going completely "off grid" with a wind or solar electric system can be an expensive investment in batteries for electricity storage and increased maintenance costs—in our case likely would have added about $10,000. Off-grid systems are most common where no grid interconnection

Residential-Scale Wind Turbines: Five Main Parts

1. **Turbine (generator):** The electricity generator, which is attached to the top of the tower.

2. **Rotor:** The set of rotating aerodynamic blades that turn when air masses move through. The load on the airfoil-shaped blades is captured by the generator. The amount of so-called swept area is determined by the rotor diameter; generally, the greater the diameter, the better the generation. Two or three blade rotors are most common. Three blade rotors, while less efficient, spin more smoothly, extending the life of the equipment and allowing the turbine to start up at lower wind speeds.

3. **Tail:** The component that tracks the wind's direction.

4. **Governor:** The mechanism that limits the amount of electricity produced, protects the equipment from overproducing and burning up in high winds, and limits the centrifugal forces that might endanger the system.

5. **Tower:** The post upon which the turbine is mounted. It's made from various high-strength materials with three common styles: free-standing, guyed lattice, and tilt-up. The tower helps the generator avoid ground wind drag (friction between the ground and moving air masses) and turbulence caused by obstacles on the ground surface.

has been established, like new-home construction where utilities will charge thousands of dollars to run an electrical line to your home.

Dollar for dollar, investing in ways to conserve energy can work efficiently in tandem with generating your own power. The former owners of our farm property were using about 16,000 kilowatt hours (kWhs) of electricity annually. With extensive steps of energy conservation (using less energy, for example by line-drying laundry) and purchasing more energy efficient Energy Star certified appliances, we were able to whittle down our energy needs to about 8,500 kWhs a year on average for an all-electric home and farmstead.

We replaced the biggest energy hogs first: refrigerator, air conditioning (opting to strategically open and close our windows), and the freezer. Four years into electricity generation with our 10kW Bergey wind turbine, we found that it was offsetting about $1,200 worth of electricity we would have been purchasing from our local utility company a year. In kWhs, we're being paid for the surplus electricity generated amounting to about 1,800 kWhs a year. Barring a major problem with the system, our investment in the wind energy system should pay for itself through energy savings after about eighteen years.

In Wisconsin, and in many other states, residential net metering arrangements whereby homeowners or small businesses can connect to and sell surplus electricity back to the grid are limited to a maximum of 20 kW of combined generating capacity (including wind, PV, and hydroelectric). The buy-back rates vary considerably, depending on your utility. We have a parallel meter in which the meter spins either frontward or backward depending on how much electricity we're using versus how much we're producing. We receive about eight cents per surplus kilowatt hour (kWh), the full retail rate that we're charged for electricity. However, many public utilities will only pay the wholesale cost per kilowatt hour, as low as only two or three cents per kilowatt hour. And many rural electric cooperatives may not even accept grid interconnections, or may refuse to buy back surplus generation.

In recent years, prices for residential-sized wind turbine systems have been dropping. This is matched by rapidly expanding state and federal cost-sharing or cash incentives or tax credits. For our 10 kW wind turbine from Bergey Wind Systems out of Norman, Oklahoma, we secured over $15,000 in state funding support, plus qualified during certain years for a renewable energy generation federal tax credit.

Still, given the initial investment, energy conservation and efficiency options should be exhausted in your home before any investment in a wind turbine is made.

Windy Enough?

There are several keys to successful wind energy production. First, the site must have consistent wind speed averaging at least 8 to 12 miles per hour. A site assessment should be completed using national wind speed data collected by the U.S. Department of Energy or other reliable sources. After a partially state-funded (Focus on Energy) site assessment completed by Mick Sagrillo, a state-certified renewable energy site assessor, it was estimated that a 10 kW Bergey XL-S system, with an annual wind speed of 13 mph at the tower height of 120 feet, would generate about 13,560 kWh/year. Additionally, students from a Penn State engineering capstone class under the oversight of environmental engineering professor Dr. Jack Matson visited our site before we selected our present system. The students evaluated our energy-use patterns (electricity load) and presented several renewable energy options.

In general, any site for a residential wind turbine should have enough space to allow a turbine to be placed on a tower with its rotor at least 30 feet higher than anything within 500 feet of the tower. Typically, a half acre of land would suffice for the actual tower and equipment. In the United States, the U.S. Federal Aviation Administration (FAA) allows towers to be erected no higher than 200 feet without significant and expensive additional requirements. Zoning regulations or proximity to airports can present additional requirements. In our case, our 5.5-acre farm provided ample space about 300 feet from the house to erect the tower in such a way that the "fall zone" of the tower remained on our property.

John D. Ivanko, innserendipity.com

The 10 kW Bergey wind turbine helps Inn Serendipity generate a net excess of electricity. Wind power is part of a comprehensive approach for the business, which includes making use of solar power, locally produced organic foods, working with local businesses, and biodiesel vehicles.

Besides the wind itself, several variables determine how much energy can be generated, with each system having a tradeoff in the cost and complexity (and maintenance). In general, the larger the rotor diameter, the greater the wind-swept area and the greater the energy generated. Additionally, the higher the tower, the faster and more regularly flowing the wind, and the more energy generated. It's usually cheaper to install a higher tower than install a larger wind generator.

Each wind turbine has different features that provide advantages and drawbacks. The key variable for our system, however, was reliability and ease of on-the-ground system monitoring (i.e., where monitoring the system does not mean climbing a 120-foot tower). Our surplus generation sold to the utility company helps offset any services needed from our wind turbine dealer, Lake Michigan Wind & Sun. Neither my husband nor I wanted to be dangling from the top of a tower to do repairs or maintenance.

In Phases

Our most significant investment in renewable energy generation was completed in May 2003 when erecting our 10 kW Bergey wind turbine. The project was completed in phases. About a month before we planned to put up the tower, we contracted with a local excavation and tower construction company familiar with putting in footings and anchors for cell towers. With assistance from our neighbors Phil and Judy Welty—themselves experienced with renewable energy with a small 0.4 kW Solardyne Southwest Wind Power-made wind turbine spinning above their log cabin home—we laid out the guy anchors and tower pad in our grassy field. The Welty's 0.4 kW system supplies the power for their solar thermal pumps and cost them about $500 when they erected it in the early 1990s. Our concrete footings and pad needed to cure for about a month in advance of the 120-foot tower and 1,000-pound turbine being placed on top of it.

Wind Turbine System at Inn Serendipity

Turbine System: Bergey Excel-S, 10 kW grid-connected system without battery bank

Tower: 120-foot guyed lattice tower

Inverter: GridTek 10 Power Processor

Rotor Diameter: 24 feet

Installed cost (labor and in-kind efforts): $39,465

Actual net out-of-pocket financial cost (after $15,595 state grant and in-kind support): $15,480

Annual average generation: 9,500 kWhs

The actual tower and turbine construction phase took place over seven days as an educational workshop for the Midwest Renewable Energy Association (MREA), helping offset about $4,000 in what would have been contracted labor. About ten students, many of whom were electricians, builders, and developers, took classes in the morning under the tutelage of one of the most experienced residential wind turbine installers in the country, Mick Sagrillo, then completed hands-on work in the afternoon.

Each day the MREA workshop students completed different aspects of the project: assembling the tower, preparing the guy wires, attaching the turbine to the tower, running the wire to the house, and wiring the inverter. For grid-tied residential systems, the inverter converts "wild alternating current (wild AC)" from the wind turbine to alternating current (AC), which is synchronized with the electrical grid. The new inverters, in general, provide an important step in the conversion of energy to a usable form for home use; utilities, likewise, have recognized the new, more reliable inverters for grid-connected systems with such safety features that result in the systems operating only when electricity is coming from the grid. Neighbors stopped by to check on our progress or offer the use of their tractor to help move the turbine. A friend in town, who had the proper machine and expertise, was able to help trench the wire run to the house.

Our Bergey wind turbine was rebuilt by our equipment dealer, Lake Michigan Wind & Sun, which replaced the parts most likely to wear out with new ones. The new 11.5-foot redesigned blades were added to reduce the sound of the turbine when spinning and the latest generation inverter, GridTek 10 Power Processor, was added in the basement to complete the conversion of "wild AC" to AC. Since the GridTek 10 inverter has a fan that often runs during the peak generation periods to prevent the inverter from overheating, its careful placement helps avoid possibly disruptive fan noise.

With respect to our grid-tied energy systems with our public utility, Alliant Energy, a simple contract, certificate of liability insurance in excess of $300,000, equipment specification sheets, and a lockable external AC disconnect (to allow our utility to isolate our system when needed) were necessary for the project—similar to how most larger utilities approach grid-connected systems. Our local Alliant Energy representative was fantastic to work with throughout the entire process. Farmer neighbors, many retirees, were contacted in advance of the project, but expressed no objections at the required public hearing. We had to pay various construction permits and zoning fees to our county, but this is variable based on your local regulations.

Being Your Own Power Producer

There are some general steps we've discovered to guide your efforts to generate electricity from a residential wind turbine system.

1. Exhaust Energy Conservation & Efficiency Options. According to the Midwest Renewable Energy Association, every $1 spent on conservation or efficiency is equivalent to about $3 spent (or saved) on renewable energy generation systems. Implementing energy conservation and efficiency makes adding renewable energy systems more easily adopted and less costly.

2. Investigate Renewable Energy System Options & Funding. Renewable energy fairs, workshops, books, and Web sites provide the tools and know-how. See Wind Resources section.

3. Site Assessment. This is usually conducted by experienced professionals (whose opinions count if you are seeking grants and rebates) to help determine your renewable energy resources.

4. Apply for Funding Support. Secure funding if available.

5. Connect with Community. Talking with neighbors about the familiar windmills once used to pump water breaks the ice; the phrase "little or no electric bill" tends to hold the interest.

6. Zoning Permits and Public Hearing (if applicable). Usually required for larger systems or towers higher than 100 feet, the county and city / township requirements vary widely. Knowledge of other systems in your area and state statutes (if available) related to solar and wind energy helps.

7. Order Equipment. Allow as much time as possible and sort out alternatives to shipping costs.

8. Sign Grid Interconnect Contract with Utility (as needed). Avoid costly surprises by making sure the utility is involved.

9. Pour Foundations (as needed). Given all the cell towers going up, choose contractors with related experience.

10. Installation of System. If possible, hire those who have the know-how to troubleshoot problems. Welcome helping hands or host educational workshops.

11. Take Advantage of Tax Breaks at Tax Time. If you're running a business, don't miss out on the possible federal tax credits or accelerated depreciation. Cash in on the federal renewable energy tax credit for kilowatt hours generated by wind, if available.

Besides the tax credit, it's possible to accelerate the amortization for the generator with the Federal Modified Accelerated Cost Recovery System (MACRS; Section 169 of the Internal Revenue Code), by which businesses can recover investments in solar, wind, and geothermal property through depreciation deductions. Grants may also be exempt from federal taxation, since they were mainly used for conserving or producing electricity. Consult your tax adviser for more details.

12. Monitor System. Routine maintenance and "visual" monitoring is needed, much like your vehicle. Many issues can often be resolved by simply pushing a "reset" button on inverters—something we do about five times a year due to irregularities in power supply.

After the first year of data collection, both of wind speed and production data, we detected a shortfall in generation of our Bergey turbine with their quieter blades. But with the excellent dealer relationship and responsive manufacturer, a replacement set of Bergey's next-generation blades were sent to us that are four-inches wider and about one foot longer, designed to boost production but not blade noise. Better yet, their replacement was completed at 120 feet in the air by a service technician with Lake Michigan Wind & Sun, allowing us to become regular net producers of electricity on an annual basis.

Cheering Local Energy: Democratic and Renewable

It's hard to imagine a community coming together to cheer a coal-fired power plant opening up in their backyard. When it came time to throw the switch and start harvesting our own wind energy on site, however, we had attracted a crowd sitting in lawn chairs and a regional TV crew that filmed the whole event, capturing the applause when the blades starting spinning.

As of 2006, our 10 kW wind turbine, in combination with our small photovoltaic solar electric system, has allowed us to become net producers of electricity, sharing about 1,800 kWhs of surplus renewable energy with our neighbors without polluting the environment. Like the booming local food movement, there's power in producing our own local renewable energy.

Wind Resources

Database of State Incentives for Renewable Energy (DSIRE). Locate what incentives or renewable energy rebates might be available in your state. www.dsireusa.org

Windustry. From large-scale to small residential wind turbine systems, this nonprofit program offers extensive wind turbine information. www.windustry.org

Midwest Renewable Energy Association (MREA). Hosting the world's largest renewable energy and sustainable living fair, the MREA also features the ReNew the Earth Institute headquarters, which demonstrates how energy independence is viable today with a hybrid system incorporating solar electric, solar thermal, wind, and woodstove heat to meet energy needs. www.the-mrea.org

National Tour of Solar Buildings. Coordinated by the American Solar Energy Society, this annual national tour held in early October offers the opportunity to visit and tour homes and businesses that incorporate myriad renewable energy, energy conservation products, and green design elements. www.ases.org

U.S. Department of Energy Efficiency and Renewable Energy. Download the Small Wind Electric Systems Consumer Guides for your state or region. The guides,which are produced by the National Renewable Energy Laboratory can also be found at www.eere.energy.gov/windandhydro/windpoweringamerica/small_wind.asp

Transit & Travel

www.indexopen.com

The Right Mix Could Fix Our Chaotic Car Culture

by Graham Hill

Everybody seems to think they have the right ideas to cure the ills of modern-day urban mobility. Given the horrific conditions in many large cities, troubling trends in medium-sized cities, and even the obnoxious inconveniences in smaller places, there are new thoughts and re-energized older ideas making comebacks.

Can we bank on clean(er) cars, trains, increased housing density, bikes, microsized electric personal mobility, and pedestrian-friendly environments to sort out our painful embrace of the gas car? It depends on who you ask. The future of healthy, safe, and efficient urban areas rests on how well they manage the car, deploy land use and zoning (which can match people more to their environment than to their cars), and offer incentives and planning assistance for people who need to be shown how to be a "citizen of consciousness" for the twenty-first century.

We must learn to recognize how harmful stepping into our cars is to the environment over the long haul—especially how "overuse" or "always in use" makes a big impact on the next generation. After

Trolleys can play an important role in a comprehensive transportation system.

all, our children look up to us, watch us model, and then determine how life will be for them by just watching us. Certainly, engaging young people about transportation choices will take some effort. But we are the "demonstrators" for the next generation who will bear the consequences or reap the rewards depending on how we do or do not preserve our natural resources. This includes air and water quality, and by extension, the quality of life.

While many Third World countries are plagued with pre-2000 air pollution problems, they are not the only ones. Here in apple pie land, we seem to turn our heads from horrific conditions that are beyond any reasonable expectation. In Port Arthur, Texas, one gets a strange feeling that something just isn't the way the world should work. The fact that it is a longtime petrochemical base (and once the hub for the largest oil-refinery network in the world) is one thing, but for people to live near it is another. Nobody should be exposed to the toxins that are launched into the air. People are suffering greatly. On a recent visit, I recall it being very grim, with everybody just moving place to place with their cars. I made a couple of U-turns around the area just to gain an understanding of how 65 percent of the tax base is paid for by the refineries.

While the taxes reflect the economic dominance, in light of their environmental and social costs, the petrochemical industries should pay for 100 percent and the money should go to moving everybody out of the danger zone and providing housing. The place should be abandoned and residents should not be exposed to excessive levels of benzene and dangerous ozone levels. Think about this: Any disruptions to these plants can cause major concerns and prompt officials to warn residents to stay inside when excessive amounts are spewed into the air. Children are highly susceptible to these types of conditions. Local activist Hilton Kelly worries about all the people who suffer from asthma, respiratory ailments, skin irritations, and cancer. He needs an army to take up this cause.

The Car Culture

We have come to idealize eras of good times. For our country, that was the post-WWII boom. In fulfilling the dream of owning a big suburban house, a big quality U.S.-made auto, and an open-road life to chain stores, new problems arose, including, in some cases, the loss of a sense of community. However, the old dream continues today despite the mounting evidence of its effects. Unless you desire something more in life—community spaces, less need for cars for all trips, and local stores and businesses that may be owned by somebody you know—we will follow the lead of fast food! This can be summarized as short-term desirability with long-term anguish. The big suburban house is great until you realize you have to get in your car for almost every need. Then, after a couple of years, there is traffic associated with all these trips and you are going to national chains exclusively—because they are only a couple of miles away! So by merely choosing a smaller, more community-oriented place to live, you have resolved the biggest issue facing the ugly world of daily car culture.

That said, it is not feasible nor practical for many people to overhaul what they do daily to reach all their destinations. We must understand this and begin to deploy realistic strategies to overcome the blight of the car bombardment. In most cases I have observed, many strong and workable methods of reducing car use can be combined with other good ideas. These are ideas that could be very symbiotic, but need refinement and leadership to be implemented. The foundation for a lively urban core must include dynamic public transportation, which provides a viable option for all citizens and visitors. Usually trains, streetcars, and trams provide the best chance to get all levels of the economic scale to use them, but good bus introductions work well with frequent headway and a vast, dependable system. By reaching main employment areas, unique and cherished city treasures, neighborhoods, and shopping areas, dynamic public transportation answers the first priority to a city invested in bucking a car-dominated feel.

The next layer of transportation needed to create a functional urban flow is an elaborate bicycle and pedestrian network. This is the obvious connection or overlay to dynamic public transportation. Trains and buses rarely will take you to that final destination, but combined with a short, safe walk or bike ride, many of us will suddenly start to see how easy and convenient it is to get where we need to go. People will go out of their way to avoid car culture (heavy traffic) if there are safe alternatives to get places. We can create these options with the nuts and bolts to a sustainable transportation network.

The tricky part of getting people to identify with dynamic public transportation and a bike and pedestrian path network is resistance to change an established routine. Having already invested in an expensive car, the prospect of stepping out of their comfort zone (their car), is daunting. Other reasons people don't try public transportation is that they don't understand the ramifications of urban travel choices, can't use these methods because of where they live or chose to live, or have jobs that require a car most of the time.

With that in mind, we can't expect these folks to embrace this same plan. These are people who need to be encouraged to drive less and purchase or drive vehicles that operate on alternative fuels. If everybody displays some effort that at least works in the same direction, it will achieve some very impressive results. However, by giving cars priority over the inner-city space that humans need to thrive, we will remain foolish until we halt the 24/7 hypermobility attitudes and learn to add a bike or transit connection to the inner city.

The Second-Car Quandry

With the overview provided for a human-based transportation system as opposed to a car-based transportation system, we must now recognize the "gapers." These are evolved methods that may not be as "pure" of a method to travel locally, but nonetheless represent "street softeners" that can be incorporated to entice many to follow this movement. If at all possible, when we discuss smaller vehicles, we should try to pursue the development of electric-drive technologies. These are technologies driven by the idea that fuel comes from power outlets that can be produced on a renewable-fuels platform (wind, solar, etc.). The list is growing rapidly for these urban mobility nuances, but it presently includes electric bikes, neighborhood electric vehicles, electric scooters, electric cycles, Segways, and now some three-wheel versions. All these methods of urban travel demonstrate a softening of our local streets. When combined with a train or bus trip, they can often replace a second car.

Now the household that works to drive and drives to work also could have a keen interest in new methods that could assist them. One of the new and exciting trends becoming more and more available is car-sharing. In fact, it is bigger than this; it is really on-demand mobility. It is an intelligent way to live locally. You no longer have a second car, but in fact you skip the car for the right to drive several different cars that are appropriate for the purpose of each individual trip. In Boulder Carshare, we can drive a Honda Insight or a CNG truck, and share the same choice with others. Look for these type of Carshare clubs and join others that may have a focus on smaller modes. In fact, a "Modes to Match your Miles," model could also include bikes, Segways, scooters, and even submarines.

Carshare works like a club, where you gain access to vehicles and modes by merely using a phone or PIN. This on-demand method has a tremendous upside. It can meet the individual needs of urban condo dwellers, large families, one-car families, business travelers, and tourists. By reaching out to a community and adding important partners, such as city transportation departments and businesses, a city can embark on community-based transportation options. By creating the public/private partnerships, a clear message can be sent that a city is ready for more change.

An effort behind on-demand mobility will provide a rebirth to a choked city. It is a solution whose time has come. Even though there are no examples of this philosophy playing a large role anywhere (yet), there certainly are micro—if not influential—examples of this platform. Paris has recently "planted" bikes with on-demand technologies all over the city in hopes the locals would use them for their town trips. Carshare itself has spread from Europe; it was first introduced to the United States in the late 1980s. It presently is a thriving option in most metropolitan coastal cities and in some key locations in the middle of the country. In some locations, car sharing has given some local residents even more housing options—the opportunity to live in a more desirable location (dense, but expensive) without the need to find parking and pay the extraordinary costs of car ownership.

Many places in Europe have proven that a single car shared by many can result in huge benefits to individuals and a community. In some cases, fifteen to twenty people in Western Europe are living with the use of a single car. These are people who are not defined or identified by their car, but probably their bike—or even their friendly smile. These folks are not spending 20 to 30 percent of their income on transportation, but rather a fraction of that. They wake daily with a bike or transit commute and feel richer for it.

Introducing a comprehensive system that includes a community-mobility pass that offers access to a dynamic public transportation, bikes, and an array of small electric vehicles might enable us to see past the next bumper! With strong success found in individual mode offerings, imagine what a deliberately planned, comprehensive system might yield. For a large city, a 10 to 15 percent reduction in vehicle trips within one year is a reasonable expectation. By pricing these systems to be affordable for everyone, over time we could see reductions that could cut individual auto use by 50 percent or more. Marketing methods, such as public mandates, neighborhood access, huge tax incentives, and the coupling of location-efficiency mortgages with mobility-demand memberships would give a highly desirable course of action to those who never thought they could part with their extra cars.

Considering All "Alternatives"

We must recognize and remember that people are used to, and demand to be in, a highly mobile society. However, we can only achieve change by realizing that our methods must continue to evolve and hold us all responsible so we are not the victims of our own shortsighted policies. By building superfreeways to meet the demand of new drivers, we obviously are missing the point. Yes, there is a highway lobby in the United States that represents those who make a living by building these expanded roadways, but they will never satisfy all the four-wheel contraptions. Building extra lanes to relieve traffic congestion makes it easy to ignore other modes of transport—until those lanes attract enough new drivers to cause another daily traffic jam, prompting a call for additional lanes once again. Failed policies and continued operation of cars and their infrastructure will spell doom for all species—including us. For the better part of fifty years, the United States has delivered more and more roads and a very unbalanced means of local travel. Nationally, roads receive about $40 billion in annual subsidies; transit, bikeways, sidewalks, and other "alternative infrastructures," only receive a fraction of that amount.

Calling viable transportation options "alternative" is not the right message. Alternative transportation seems like the most repulsive way to describe how folks travel locally. For the many of us who ride a bike, take a train, drive a cleaner vehicle, or simply walk most of the time, the term stinks. If you asked people who drive forty-five minutes in gnarly traffic to and from work every day if they would rather catch a local bus or bike a half mile to work, most would answer, yes. To me, it is not efficient to spend the first hour of every day in your car with thousands of others doing the same thing—so doesn't that seem to be crazy, or "alternative?" Doing something simple seems to be what normal people do. To me, that is living in such a way that you don't have to depend on a car. Those who have multiple-transportation options would not trade it; if you got used to it and had to trade for a car commute, life could become alternatively miserable!

The world got a good look at Beijing, China, for the 2008 Summer Olympics. Very likely, the looming air pollution that typically sits over this site during the Olympics was considered a very big event itself.

Abandoned fuel pumps: a sign of improved transportation choices?

During preparation for the Games, air-quality worries centered on the endurance sports (the marathon). For the 3 million cars that clog up the city streets every day, one suggested approach was to eliminate one-third of these by only allowing driving based on license plates (banning odd and even numbered plates on alternating days). Sure, many other methods were deployed while the world watched and the athletes hoped to withstand the compromised air, but we can take an important message from these Olympics regarding how to address some of these major issues facing the planet. Can you imagine if we campaigned to limit car use based on license plates as a mandate? I can, and I hope we can do it soon!

We must recognize that depending on where you live, some of these examples and solutions exist today or may in the future, and some may never materialize. It is important to know that people usually get accustomed to where they live whether they like it or not. However, I would encourage anybody who desires these options or solutions to visit places like Portland, Oregon; Davis, California; and Boulder, Colorado, which provide some of the better examples of people harmoniously getting along quite well without cars. Try it—you might like it!

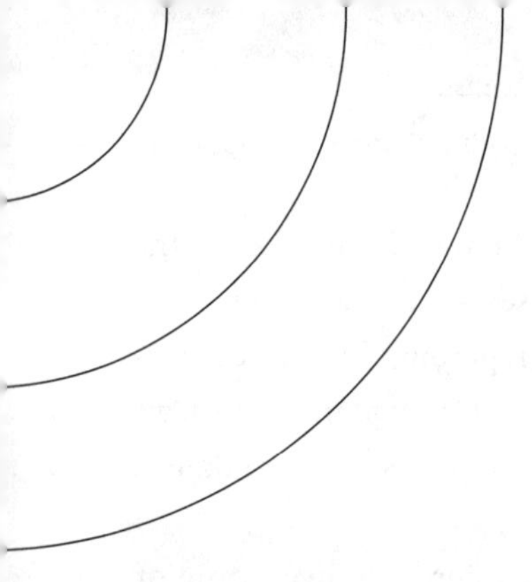

Bicycle Commuting and the No-Car Life

by Laura E. Kreger

When I moved from the rural Midwest to Portland, Oregon, I entered a metro area of 2 million people with more breweries than anywhere in the country and more strip clubs per capita than Las Vegas. My Minnesotan family collectively raised their eyebrows but had faith I wouldn't do anything drastic.

Between its pints and dancers, the City of Roses sways heavily toward environmentalism. This sentiment weaves through a culture of fleece-covered yuppies, dreadlocked beat poets, hipster rock stars, and the homeless man who picks up trash in the neighborhood park. When a co-worker said he didn't recycle, battle cries flew up from a four-cube radius. Somehow, all these groups merge to create a city recognized as one of the most environmentally friendly, and as a result, most bike-friendly, cities in the country.

After just two years in the Pacific Northwest, I found myself making New Year's Resolution 2007: Sell car, buy bicycle.

When I made the announcement, my parents worried that Portland hippies were ruining their daughter but still didn't believe I would take the plunge. Even my roommate, who supported the idea, figured this would go the way of my "Do a handstand" resolution, which ended with me sprawled on my new yoga mat, laughing at myself. I wasn't coming into this adventure an urban biking expert. In fact, I hadn't even sat on a bike in two years. When the car-free plan didn't die in four days like most of my resolutions, the questions started flying:

"Why on earth would you want to be without a car?"

"What would you do in the winter?"

"What if you get sick?"

"How will you carry groceries?"

"How will you bring us to the ocean if we visit in five years?"

All valid questions.

Why On Earth?

Like many things genuinely good for both people and the environment, living car-free isn't mainstream. In fact, it's almost unheard of. According to the Department of Transportation, about 90 percent of people in the United States drive to work. Subtract those who work from home or live in major metro areas like New York City—where driving and parking are logistical nightmares—and you're left with very few people who don't get in a car every day.

I recycle, compost, and don't own a television, but I'm no hippie hero. The tastiest veggie burger I've ever eaten had bacon on it. I've yet to go to a protest for, well . . . anything. And yet, once this car-less thing came to mind, I couldn't get it out. The more I thought about it, the more it made sense. Gasoline will never be sustainable. Pedal power doesn't influence wars. I'm no financial wizard, but paying nearly $2,000 a year on something that decreases in value the longer I own it doesn't seem particularly prudent.

It's also a way to stay healthy. For me, exercising in a concrete gym to offset the stress of spending all day between a car and cube isn't worth the years of life it promises. I confess, I'm not going car-less purely to save the Earth or whales or children seven generations from now. I'm doing this because I want to live simply, and I can't reconcile owning a car with the life I want to lead.

Cavalier Plans in a Cycling Community

Part of my plan involved easing into things, and the rest was pure self-trickery. I'd start exploring mass transit in April and buy a bike in May, while still driving if I was sick or late or lazy. I'd enjoy this new method through bright sun and balmy breezes. Then while biking still seemed like a glorious idea, I'd sell the car so by the time winter hit I'd be stuck.

After posting my '98 Chevy Cavalier on Craigslist one Saturday morning in August, I made plans to run some longer-distance errands. Then an e-mail came, and then a couple phone calls. An hour later I was left with a handful of cash and an empty parking space, watching my car drive away to the suburbs. After a whoop and a short tribal dance around the living room, reality hit with the thought, "So . . . now what?"

A few months before selling the car, I spent $400 on an overhauled Trek hybrid (cross between a mountain bike and road bike) with everything the fatherly shop owner said I needed. I got lights for night riding, fenders for puddle protection, a decent rack, a sturdy U-lock, and a shiny helmet. Although endearing, my bike is conveniently ugly. When your primary mode of transportation could be carried away by anyone with a good bolt cutter and a crowbar, any method of theft deterrence is a good thing.

Portland earns its bike-friendly status largely through a passionate, if not eccentric, bike culture. The city is home to approximately 36 bike shops, community bike events featuring things like bike polo tournaments and pedal-powered cotton candy machines, and the largest Naked Bike Ride in North America. During "bike moves," extremists shun moving trucks and instead rally the troops to help them move all their earthly belongings via bicycle. City planners and transportation officials have come on board to require bike racks on all city buses and continually increase miles of bike lanes. Local business owners have started to team up with the city to take out parking spaces and replace them with on-street "bike corrals." Every summer the city closes portions of all ten city bridges to car traffic, including the interstate, for the third-largest organized ride in the world—the event attracted 20,000 participants in 2007.

Laura Kreger

Not the most attractive bicycle, but it gets the job done.

Despite the city's reputation, not everyone is so supportive. Carless Week No. 1 brought a pickup truck barreling past so quickly that I almost missed its "One Less Bike" bumper sticker. Two blocks later, the door of a red sports car flew open, giving me just enough time to squeak out of the bike lane into the car lane. If it hadn't been empty, I would have had to choose which car to hit. Despite infrequent heart-pounding incidents like these, often I feel safer riding a bike than driving a car. Slower and smaller give more options—I can quickly swerve onto the sidewalk or change directions onto a side street. If I caused an accident, the only one likely to get hurt is myself.

At the same time, I can't take it lightly. When it's car vs. bike, car always wins. Two Portland cyclists have been killed in the last two weeks (fall 2007)—one by a garbage truck and the other a cement truck—both while riding in the bike lane. While bike-commuting in Milwaukee, my friend Wendy was recently hit by an unyielding driver making a left turn. Luckily, all she has is a permanent bump on her shin to prove it.

Winter brings fewer hours of daylight, which also affects safety. Reflective clothes become more important as visibility decreases, and as the days get shorter, I need my blinky bike lights not only to be a law-abiding citizen, but to actually see and be seen.

Raindrops Keep Falling on My Head

Portland winters are nothing compared to the Minnesota winters of my childhood, but they're definitely not rainbows and sunshine. In fact, they're pretty much just rain and no sunshine at all. During my first winter, it rained thirty-one days straight. This melancholic consistency challenges even the most creative meteorologist: "Light rain likely in the morning, turning into rain in the afternoon. Evening will bring showers, with a chance of rain after midnight." On the upside, there are very few days that dip below freezing. Biking at a moderate speed, intensified by long downhills or cold rain, creates a wind chill that makes normally bearable temperatures bite. I've seen cyclists decked out in enough sleek, reflective rain gear to live comfortably at the bottom of a swimming pool. Their less enthusiastic counterparts wear plastic ponchos with grocery bags on their feet. I opt for something in the middle, with a breathable raincoat and rain pants (bought used), and old shoes, which I change at work. Once it gets really cold, I'll add a balaclava and waterproof gloves.

Friends in the Midwest have differing perspectives on winter biking. While some say it's completely unrealistic, Nick made do without a car in northern Wisconsin, even in 3 degrees F and heavy snow. He rode a mountain bike, wore sunglasses (snow glare is fierce), and depended on wicking base layers that kept him warm and dry. One morning, it was below freezing and he got a flat tire halfway to work. When he tried stretching the extra tube around his rim, it snapped in the cold. His advice holds valid for any climate, weather, or transportation mode: "Sometimes it's just better to call someone to pick you up."

Backup Plans

Of course it's not realistic to bike everywhere in all circumstances. Any mode of transportation should have a Plan B, and biking is no different. There are situations like job interviews and doctor's appointments that can't be left to chance. I'm not going to use my bike to pick up my sister from the airport, haul a garage-sale loveseat, or take a ninety-mile trip to the mountains. As invincible as I'd like to be, at some point I'll get too sick or hurt to pedal. With Portland's public transportation system, being car-less would be feasible without a bike, just more limiting. The hardest part about public transit is relying on schedules and routes. If I take the bus, it's suddenly impossible for me to get to work exactly on time: my options are either twelve minutes early or six minutes late. Some destinations take an hour by bus, which I can beat by twenty minutes on bike. However, the bus is a relief if I'm going farther, later, or through sketchy neighborhoods. Carpools come in handy if not abused (paying for gas earns friends). Renting a car for weekend trips or hosting out-of-town visitors is affordable when I consider the $900 a year I'm saving just on insurance. Car-sharing companies like Flexcar and Zipcar are gaining steam, which allow members to use cars parked around the city and pay by the hour. Most mid-sized towns at least have taxis, and family and friends are always the best bet in an emergency.

While some trips obviously take a lot longer by bike, rush-hour traffic can tip the scales. My friend Claudia "bikepools" on a tandem with her husband, and co-workers from the same neighborhood complain that the tandem beats them home.

Claudia's bikepool got me thinking about future options if my family situation changes. I don't have kids now, but biking with them someday doesn't seem out of the question. Older kids can ride their own bikes and babies can be bundled into covered trailers. There are also options for those in between. Every morning I pass a four-year-old in a red rain jacket dancing on the sidewalk, waiting for her mom to prepare their Tag-Along. These half-bikes attach behind the parent's bike and have their own pedals and handlebars. Though the children are not responsible for steering, balance, or keeping up with the pedaling pace (like a tandem bicycle), they can exercise their legs a bit as they have fun and develop a healthy habit.

A Bucket for a Back Seat

Without a trunk or back seat, every trip to the store is an experiment. I have to think twice before impulsively buying things like six-packs of chocolate stout or crystal punch bowl sets. While there are expensive panniers (bags that attach to a bike rack) and trailers, I currently make do with a four-gallon kitty-litter bucket that hooks on my rack. It's waterproof and too ugly to steal. Even when unbalanced, the weight rides low enough to make heavy things like a gallon of milk very manageable. For larger items, I've zip-tied a milk crate to the top of my rack, with mixed results. It holds a lot more, but heavy items make me precariously tippy. I also can't trust a crate to protect contents from the rain or passersby. While riding with a backpack makes my back sweat, it carries a lot without requiring a rack and absorbs enough impact to safely transport eggs. Rumor has it that the water bottle holder doubles nicely for carrying a bottle of wine. The only thing I haven't been able to manage hauling is passengers—despite romantic notions of motorcycle sidecars, my bucket does not fit a boy.

Estimated Monthly Savings On Car-Related Expenses

Insurance:	$75
Gas:	$50
Maintenance:	$85
Parking:	$5
Total:	$215

The Biker's Dress Code

Riding to work (or anywhere you want to arrive presentable) poses two basic options: ride in your work clothes or change when you get there. I work in a large, corporate office with a begrudgingly boring dress code that I almost follow. When biking entered the picture, my wardrobe became even more limited. The standard skirts, while very modest for normal activities, became insta-scandals on a bike. Thankfully the first day I wore shorts underneath, because the skirt hiked to my waist. On day two, thinking I'd chosen more wisely, I ditched the shorts, much to the awakening of construction workers

Jaclyn Ademek

For those who choose to commute by bicycle, the side streets in Portland offer a reasonably safe route and a chance to absorb the feel of the neighborhoods. In addition, some studies indicate that the air is much cleaner as little as one block off the busier arterial roads.

when they saw more than a sunrise. On the way home, I ignored everyone and rode like lightning.

Despite mixed results early on, I now bike in skirts regularly. Full range of motion is key, with fabric heavy enough not to take flight. A little spunk doesn't hurt either. As for pants, the gangster look of rolling up one leg is essential. After getting black chain-grease lines on khaki corduroys, I now roll both legs. After getting some curious looks, I now also remember to roll them down again.

Much to my dismay, biking makes me sweat, even on the short two-mile ride to work on cold days. I wear the lightest shirt possible because even if I'm freezing at first, the exercise soon warms me up. Once I get to work, I head straight to the restroom to cool off my face and arms with a quick paper-towel bath. Deodorant has earned a permanent place in my bag.

Some bike commuters look very cool. They glide by confidently with their hair blowing in the breeze. They do not sweat. They breathe about as hard if they were lying on a beach blanket. I envied this coolness until I realized most of these miracle-bikers don't wear helmets. Then I decided I'd rather look ridiculous than be dead. After riding in 103-degree sun and 35-degree pouring rain, I'm resigned to any uncoolness with the goals of Don't Melt, Don't Freeze, and Don't Die.

A Natural Connection

Don't get me wrong, I enjoyed the independence and anonymity of driving. Being sealed in a little steel bubble at the perfect temperature while listening to clever reporters on public radio was quite nice most days. When I get on a bike, I still feel independent, but I also feel . . . real. Raw. Connected. I notice the crack in the street and how there are more chestnuts to swerve around than yesterday. I mourn the untimely deaths of gray squirrels and bloated cats. My heart beats in time with my rotating feet, and with the wind blowing freedom in my face, I can handle swallowing the occasional bug. My friend Trib, who bikes in Colorado Springs, captured it perfectly: "In a vehicle you're alienated from the natural world around you. On a bike you are a part of it."

There's something about the vulnerability of being on a bike that breaks down barriers with other people as well. Fellow bikers nod in passing as if saying, "Hey, we're in this together." While I've rarely been approached by a stranger in a parking lot just to chat, this happens almost every time I'm at a bike rack. Because I usually choose smaller streets, I see neighborhoods instead of highways. I make eye contact with dog walkers, morning joggers, teenagers skateboarding to school, and construction workers on strike. (Granted, not all acknowledgment is welcome—I could live without the catcalls.)

Resolution Complete; Adventure Begun

Going car-less is big. This isn't a change you can make for a weekend, like deciding to compost your coffee grounds. Without a car, I'm forced off autopilot. I've gained a changed sense of place. I have to be more intentional about simple things like getting dressed in the morning and buying groceries. I arrive at work awake and rosy-cheeked. By the time I get home, I've already burned off the frustration of sitting at a computer all day. I'm getting at least a half hour of exercise a day without even trying. And I'm saving a heck of a lot of money.

Most days I don't even mind riding in the rain—swimming down the street with cold kisses dripping off my nose feels ridiculous and makes me grin. Something I felt guilty about has turned into something gratifying. Car-less became car-free, and I have no regrets . . . except not trying it sooner.

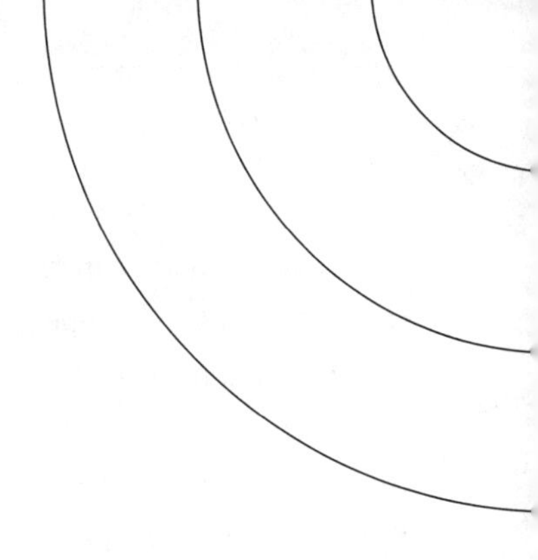

The Patience of the Wild: Learning the Lessons of the Land

by Paige Doughty

The first thing I learned about living in the desert is that even though you can smell the rain in the breeze, even though you can see it in the lower reaches of the clouds, it doesn't mean you're going to feel it—not even a drop.

Somehow, I knew the Great Basin Desert of the Escalante National Monument before I arrived. Located in southeastern Utah on a geologic anomaly called the Colorado Plateau, Escalante called to me like home. For days, I was puzzled by the familiarity of a place I had never seen before. Then one morning when I sat next to a tiny stream that cut through long, flat, red rocks of hundred-million-year-old sandstone and the familiarity dawned on me. It was the sound of the water that did it.

These long, flat slickrocks, cut through by a trickle of stream, looked just like the stratified clay and marl that make up the banks of Lake Ontario in Western New York. That place of seemingly abundant water and this place of almost none met in my mind as a flash of memory: myself as a child playing on the banks of the lake, my fingers covered in the sandy clay along the edge of water. The rocks are strikingly similar in appearance, and although they are not the same, they have been shaped by the same phenomena: water and time.

It is not a "logical" thing to fall in love with the land. It isn't something one normally learns in school or mentions in passing to friends. But love is what I found in Escalante National Monument. There, I embarked on a journey with seventeen other graduate students in environmental education that would fundamentally change my understanding of wilderness and what it means to love and care for a place.

The start of our backpacking trip, early under a brilliant spring sky, saw us scrambling to zip up the last of our bags, lending hands to fit gear into tiny places, rolling stiff tent fabric into tight bundles, and filling water bottles with enough liquid to reach the first stream. One of my favorite moments of wilderness camping is watching people help one another pack. There is a distinct energy in the air during these last moments, an edge of anticipation for what the days ahead will bring and a barely stifled excitement for the beauty that lies only footsteps ahead. Making the choice to leave "civilization" to live from what you can mount on your back, and to go only as far as your own two feet will carry you, seems a revolutionary act in this time of speed and constant connection. Our hike through the wilderness took us thirty-five miles over nine days.

On the second day of our trip, after winding our way into Coyote Gulch, a beautiful canyon-filled area lined by cottonwood trees with a small stream that runs down its middle, we climbed eight hundred feet up onto an unmarked trail to reach Scorpion Plateau. Though we had felt no wind while sheltered in the gulch, the wind outside the protective canyon walls was so fierce that my hair, pulled tight against my skull, was ripped loose from its binder. When we reached the top of the plateau breathless and shaken, I stopped to

Paige Doughty

A view of Stephen's Arch as we approached from lower ground.

rest, crouching behind a boulder like a child in a womb, and looked out at the landscape.

We are walking on the skin of the Earth, I thought as I looked into the divots and cracks of the slickrock. It's the openness that gets to you in this place—the rocks so raw and exposed it seems impossible to imagine anything more beautiful or terrifying. This land has memories millions of years old. Each layer of stone that forms the bedrock of the Colorado Plateau was deposited by a different moment in time; a sequence of seas, deserts, streams, and oceans have come and gone over some 270 million years to form what I experienced on Scorpion Plateau as solid ground.

At that moment, facing three days in this shelterless place, some animal instinct rose in my throat and wanted more than anything to return to the safety of Coyote Gulch below us, where protection from the ceaseless wind felt safer than anything this ocean of rock could offer. Instead, I swallowed my fear and felt the landscape reshaping around me with each gust of sandy wind on my face.

Danger feels real in the wilderness—and it is—but it's manageable, too. It is not danger like the sound bites on television news that make you want to lock your doors and wait for the end of the world. This was danger of survival, of slipping and falling, of sleeping out under the stars, of finding enough water for three days on the plateau.

About 100 million years ago, this land was at the bottom of a massive inland sea that connected the Arctic Ocean to the Gulf of Mexico. Now, 160 days into a drought, the only water we would find was in small slickrock puddles. If these oval crevices in the Navajo Sandstone were empty we would have to press into nightfall to drink from the Escalante River several hundred feet below. Happily we did find (somewhat stale) water, surprising pools, despite the drought.

What water could exist on this raw naked land? I asked myself. It seemed impossible that there was any. Three days on Scorpion Plateau exposed me to the realities of water scarcity like no classroom could teach. It forced me to ask difficult questions: When is it OK to take water in the wild? Is there enough for six thirsty people to drink and eat for two days, while still leaving plenty for wildlife? Is there enough for the coyotes whose scat we found as we hiked? Is there enough for us to take and not feel guilty for our thirst?

Each morning as I pumped stagnant liquid through a filter into my solid-steel bottle, I couldn't help but wonder if I should suffer thirst rather than consume a rattlesnake's water. In the end, I did drink from the pools, but between each sip that passed my lips came a tiny whispered thank you.

At the end of three days, we made our way down into the vein of the Escalante River. Here we found what seemed like plenty of water. The Escalante runs south and west into the Colorado River. It then winds its way into the shrinking Lake Powell reservoir, which is held in place by Glen Canyon Dam. Though we welcomed the sight of this seemingly abundant liquid, even here we witnessed the drought: along the riverbanks, we saw white "bathtub ring" marking canyon walls, a constant reminder that the river was shrinking.

We had to cross the water in pairs, hooking arms for safety. It was thrilling and terrifying to wade into the rush of liquid. We unstrapped the waist belts of our backpacks each time so that the weight of them would not drown us if we fell. We laughed as cool muddy water filled our boots so that each footstep on dry ground was a quick sand sound. With each day in this wilderness we were all falling in love.

Like the energy spike at the beginning of a backpacking trip, there is another height reached in the middle; it's when you've spent enough time in a place without seeing anybody but your hiking party. It's when your group becomes so cohesive that when you come around the bend to find the next most beautiful arch you have ever seen suspended impossibly above you, like someone took a knife and cut a rainbow of rock into a sandstone wall, there is no need to do anything but point, settle back onto your heels, and sigh. It was on the fifth day that we found ourselves so immersed in the canyons of Escalante that we began to forget the rest of the world. It was just us, alone, in the most beautiful place on Earth. And on the next day, suddenly, we were leaving too soon.

On the sixth day, we returned to Coyote Gulch. We entered this time from the southern end that connects with the Escalante River. As we turned the corner of the canyon from the river to the gulch, we met people. Hordes of them. There were children with toys, girls in bikinis, men carrying coolers. Suddenly we realized—it was Saturday. We checked our maps to find there was another trail head nearby. The people we were seeing hadn't hiked for six days to get to there; their cars were parked a few miles away. We looked at them like aliens from another planet. They looked at us the same way.

A group of young boys scrambled along the canyon walls like spiders. Their feet landed in places I knew they shouldn't. There is, in this part of the desert, a complex ground cover called cryptobiotic soil. In the sparsely vegetated desert, it is the "crypto" that holds the soil together to prevent erosion, retains water after a rainfall, and fixes nitrogen for plants to grow. These are all critical jobs that larger shrubs and plants would do in another climate, but that only the crypto can accomplish in this part of the desert. This ground cover is a fragile structure that looks like miniature sandcastles, hardly noticeable if you don't know what it is, the largest formations (about half an inch in size) take upwards of half a century to form. One wrong footstep can do damage that could take 250 years to repair. We watched with mouths wide as children and adults walked all over it.

www.indexopen.com

Lake Powell in southeastern Utah.

The less magical part of wilderness camping is the leaving. When you return to "civilization" you start to notice things you never have before: the ringing of telephones like sirens in your ears, water rushing into the kitchen sink like a hole leaking precious liquid from your finite source, fountains in the middle of a city spouting water out of concrete like it's the most normal thing in the world. In Escalante, we hadn't returned to civilization, civilization had come to us and we weren't ready.

That evening we were silent beneath the canyon walls. Our sleeping bags were spread out under the naked starlit sky in one of the only truly dark places left on Earth. We slept early and listened to our neighbors a few hundred feet away yelling into the gulch to hear their voices echo back to them. They banged pots, shone lights, and shouted well into the middle of the night.

In the morning, all had shifted. We were no longer a cohesive group of people walking on the land, drinking from pools of sacred water, river walkers fording streams. We were just human beings from the same place as everyone else, the one we call "civilization," where people don't talk about loving the land. We had no more right to this place than people who used pots as drums, crushed hundred-year-old soil unknowingly under their feet, or left plastic bottles perched between million-year-old rocks.

We held passionate discussions about wilderness areas. We talked about cutting wilderness off from human beings.

"We have enough of this planet to ourselves." Some of us proclaimed, "Something has to be untouched, left alone for other creatures!"

"But isn't that just creating the illusion that human beings are separate from nature? Isn't that creating the problem we already have?"

"That's why we have to teach people . . ."

"But did you see them? Did you seem them?" One of us finally said what none had wanted to admit aloud. We were judging other people. For all our efforts toward compassion and nonjudgment, we had spent the day before watching people do things we knew were harmful to this place. And though some of us had silently picked up small pieces of trash to carry out, and one had even dared to say quietly to some small children, "You should really try not to step there," we were daunted by the number of people in the gulch, and what felt like our inability to educate or even make a difference.

We didn't want to admit it, but we would have been happier if those "other" people had not been let into this place. And so we talked about education, about what the Bureau of Land Management could do to help visitors understand the delicate and unique circumstances of this ecosystem, about putting up signs, about how most people don't visit visitor centers, about the tragedy of the commons, about how none of us really believed that any person visiting Escalante had bad intentions, and about how "we" were "they" and "they" were "us." We asked all the questions lingering over our heads under a clear blue desert sky and approached the most difficult of all: was drinking rattlesnake's water not just as destructive to this place as scrambling through cryptobiotic soil? Was our presence here just as harmful as anyone else's?

Finally, we sat, still and defeated. Our campground was on the bank of a stream that cut through the middle of a bowl of ancient red rock. There we waited in silence for something to make us feel better as we contemplated what felt like the glaring fact that there are just too many people in the world and not enough wilderness or space for humans and animals alike. Then, suddenly from this darkness came light. It was the rocks and the water and the time that did it.

I was staring into the stream as I had been on one of my first mornings in the desert. I was in love with the sound of the water, with its slow meandering pace, with the way it had carved through time a path into what looked like solid rock. Many of these canyons had started this way—as a trickle. Even the Grand Canyon began as the joining of two small rivers and over millions of years became one of the most spectacular places on Earth. It was this small thought that helped me see: Yes, it was too late to change everything about the world. Yes, more cryptobiotic soil would be lost, more trees cut down, more rubbish left. But there was also the possibility that for that tiny moment in Coyote Gulch, where we sat impassioned and in love with the desert, there were innumerable other moments and places where other people were also falling in love, or could be. They, like us, only had to find the right place.

The last thing I learned from living in the desert was patience. If those rocks and the surprising amount of life they support can wait for rain, I can wait for change and work toward it. And although this didn't feel like enough—every one of us (if asked at that moment) would have abandoned whatever plans we had waiting at home to stay there to protect, and educate, and share that place with other people—we left the next day.

The most important lesson Escalante had to teach me was this: find a place and love it. Explore its beauty and secrets, delights and mysteries, and share them with other people. It is only in experiencing the wild that people have the chance to fall in love. If we do this well, the places we have loved will live on for generations. Like the slow trickle of the stream that over time becomes a canyon, the thoughts and sensations of every visitor to Coyote Gulch are trickling through our heads, and for every person we saw that day, there were thousands of moments when they had the chance to fall in love.

The next summer when I went to Lake Ontario—which does not boast spectacular views or red sandstone walls that tower above you like laughter thrown into the sky—where water seems abundant and cornfields stretch out as far as the eye can see, I started my own garden. In that place, which I have known since I was a child, I watched the sun set every evening with my ninety-two-year-old grandmother. On still nights, we listened to the jet skis break the silence on the water. And with every breath of air, each moment of my bare feet on the Earth, and every sip of water, a tiny thank you left my lips and was stolen by the wind.

Ruth Doughty

Paige Doughty on the banks of Lake Ontario.

The Nuts and Bolts of Self-Contained Bicycle Travel

by Megan Holm

My first bike tour was not something I built up to. I did not take a weekend to try a bike camping trip, or even practice riding with my bike fully loaded with gear. Instead, my first trip was my biggest one, across the United States from Virginia to Oregon. It was my first trip to see both the Appalachians and the Rockies, and my first trip across the continent. I think it was this series of firsts that made it seem so ideal to really see and experience the landscape, not from inside a car or train, but in some way to feel more connected to the people and places along the way. I wanted to explore the country and feel more involved, less like somebody passing through and more like somebody interacting with a place. And such was my introduction to bicycle touring, which is the act of pedaling your bicycle some (usually long) distance while carrying what you need right there with you, on your bike.

There are several different styles of touring, ones that accommodate a variety of expenditures, abilities, and comforts. The main types of touring are: the "sag tour," where a sag vehicle carries your gear and the rider pedals unencumbered by the weight of food, clothes, etc; the "hotel/motel tour," where riders carry clothes, some snacks, and minimal bedding and generally stay and eat at formal accommodations to relieve the need for carrying camping and cooking gear; and "the self-contained tour," where the rider carries everything from a camp stove to toilet paper. And of course there are multiple variations in between, any of which can be great, wonderfully invigorating, depending on what you want to accomplish. My experience has always been self-contained tours, partly due to my desire to take longer trips and the subsequent need to be more budget conscious, but more so because there is something really incredible in knowing that with my loaded bike, I can go absolutely anywhere and have what I need. There is a freedom in being so self-sufficient and simple, no matter what length of time.

When I set out to do that first trip, I talked my sister into joining me, got some maps, some gear, and set out for the East Coast. It was more the trial and error sort of tour, where every couple of weeks I would lighten my load and revel in the lost pounds as another item was sent home from a different post office. It was a trip that began when we rode out of that first parking lot feeling like four bowling balls were strapped to our bikes. This was nothing like the light, unencumbered bike I knew. On that bike I could coast on flat ground! This one I could barely lift. But as we kept going, day after day, I stopped noticing that I pedaled a little more and coasted less. What I noticed was how amazing it was to spend the day outside, going somewhere new—and the only thing to do was ride my bike. The scenery felt even more stunning because I was working for it. Not only that, but by pedaling I was not relying on fuel that depleted resources or created pollution that would harm the very views I was there to see.

Planning a first bike trip can be a bit daunting. There is the bike and gear to acquire, not to mention the trip planning and preparation. I will walk through some of the basics to offer a starting point, and I encourage more research or questioning from there.

First things first. Obviously, some kind of bike will be necessary for the journey. While most bikes can work for touring, there are some designed specifically for the purpose of carrying gear and going longer distances. Touring-specific bikes tend to have a large gear range, braze-ons for front and rear racks, are positioned more comfortably and upright than road-specific bikes, and often have stronger wheels. Touring bikes are built to be sturdy and durable. They can also be expensive, so it is worthwhile considering adapting your already operational bike to be more tourable.

Get the Bike You Need

These are a few things I look for in a touring bike, or that I recommend changing to retrofit an existing bike:

- Wheels with 36 spokes (this signifies a stronger wheel, and since the wheels are what hold the weight of you and your gear, the stronger the wheel the better).
- Handlebars that allow for multiple hand positions—either drop road bars, or consider adding bar-ends to flat bars to allow an alternate hand position.
- A good fit! Make sure that the bike is your size: go to a shop and get advice if you are unsure. An ill-fitted bike may be fine for rides around town, but several days of riding are a different story.
- An ample range of gears: rear gear clusters, or cassettes, come in a range of sizes. Look for options with the most range. Also, in my experience, the more gears the better—24 to 27 gears are ideal.
- If you will use panniers (see next paragraph), you will need eyelets, or braze-ons, so that you can bolt racks to the rear, and possibly

Jim Holm

Megan and Andrea Holm take a break along Skyline Drive in Virginia.

the front of your bike. These braze-ons, now standard issue on all new bikes, are welded on screw receivers where your wheels attach to your bike.

While you don't necessarily need a special touring bike, you do need some specific gear to carry all of your things. The most common option is panniers: bags that attach to racks on your front and rear wheels. Panniers come in a variety of styles—some with lots of pockets, waterproof materials, even recycled plastic buckets. Panniers are easy to take on and off, and are generally centered on your bike, but they do add extra weight and wind drag. Trailers hitched behind the bike where you are actually pulling your gear are another popular option. This method takes the weight off of your bicycle, but puts it behind you, creating heavier pull. Either method works, so go with whichever suits your style, budget, and bike. Talk with your local bike shop for help.

As you acquire the gear you need and work on setting up your bike, the next step is choosing where to go, when, how, and with whom. These factors will largely depend on the time you have available (my transcontinental Virginia to Oregon trek took ten weeks), where you want to go, and what season is best for riding. While technically you can ride just about anywhere you can drive, some roads are preferable to others. Look for roads with good shoulders and less traffic, and as much as possible, prepare your route in advance. Many states offer free cycling maps, there are route books for certain regions, and there is the Adventure Cycling Association (ACA). The ACA is the primary touring resource in the United States. It maps several routes throughout the country that feature many details and frequent updates. The maps give you regional information like weather and rainfall, elevation levels, area bike shops, and places to sleep (campgrounds, motels, hostels, city parks, etc.). I recommend using one of their routes for your first tour, not just for the great maps, but for the likelihood of meeting other cyclists en route.

Selecting Riding Partners

When my sister and I rode the transcontinental route, we ended up keeping a similar pace to a few other small groups heading in our direction for a few weeks. Somebody invested in sidewalk chalk to split among us, and we all left chalk messages along the route saying "Camp spot this way!" or "Good morning!" It was nice to have a bigger group to check in with until eventually our paces changed or schedules made it so some groups had to go farther than the others. Any commonly ridden route is nice for that reason: cyclists abound, biker campsites are common, and small businesses are used to the bikers coming through. Often you can hear about places to stop for the best pancakes, biscuits, or pie, and townspeople keep you posted about other bikers ahead of you.

When choosing your riding partner(s), it is helpful not only to think about who you want to spend time with, but also what differing goals you might have for a trip. Is it a goal to travel great distances for an athletic feat, or are you more interested in seeing sights along the way and riding less mileage? Are you more interested in spending time alone and riding without worrying about other people? Do you prefer to ride with a group that includes bike mechanics for safety or musicians to pass the time? Do you feel comfortable riding alone for some distance or do you prefer to always stick by a riding partner?

I did a long trip down the East Coast (five weeks through Maine, Massachusetts, New Hampshire, Pennsylvania, Maryland, Virginia, and North Carolina) with a group of six, all of us seasoned bike commuters, but with really different paces and styles of riding. There were several breakdowns throughout that month: one person hated the rain and would rather wait it out, another wanted to keep a certain mileage; one of us liked riding in the morning, somebody else preferred the afternoon. Put all of these preferences together, and then add in a permeable route that changed from week to week with no set camp spots, physical exertion, and rain, and you get some hard times. Communication—especially in advance—with any ride partners can help manage the dynamics and needs of a group.

There are many positive qualities to traveling with others: shared cooking and carrying capacity for tents and supplies, the ability to draft off of one another in the wind, a support person/people, and a variety of personalities to encourage you on the trip. The challenges include managing differing expectations, riding styles, and personalities. Likewise, the advantages of riding alone include: complete autonomy to ride exactly as you want, quiet, calm, and solitude, and the ability to plan a trip without relying on anyone else. The challenges of a solo trip on the other hand, are loneliness, lack of camaraderie, and the lack of support people if something were to go wrong.

I did my first solo trip in 2006 in upstate New York on into Canada—five days of biking over ten days. I planned the route to start and end in places where I knew people, and was able to ride on trails most of the way. My favorite part was when I got to Niagara Falls on the U. S. side in the middle of a drizzly day. I really wanted a hot beverage, but didn't feel like heading into the tourist frenzy that seemed to be the entire town. So instead, I pulled up to a bench in the national park just off of the Rainbow Bridge, pulled out my camp stove, and made some coffee right there while watching the falls. I had my own spontaneous picnic on the water before pedaling my way across the bridge into Canada. It was a moment where I felt so fulfilled with that one cup of coffee, and also so proud of myself for being there.

Starting Away from Home

A final detail to keep in mind while planning your trip if you don't always want to start from your home: transporting your bike to your start/end destination. Some common options include:

Train (Amtrak): Amtrak supplies extra large bike boxes at most larger depots (for a $10 fee) that will be considered an oversize piece of luggage with an added charge of $5 to $15. The boxes are much larger than a standard bike-store box, and you only need to remove the pedals and handlebars to fit inside.

Air: Different airlines handle bike boxes differently, so talk to the airline before booking a flight. Typically, bikes on flights in the United States, Canada and Mexico are charged $70 to $100 as additional oversized luggage. Bikes must be boxed. International flights increase the bike box charge to $150, though some airlines allow one oversized bicycle box for free.

Bus: Greyhound offers both a shipping service if you want to send your bike box, and they also charge a variable fee of $20 to $50 for the oversized luggage if you are traveling as a passenger. Bikes need to be boxed, and often the bike will not transfer on the same bus as you. (Do not count on simultaneously arriving with your bike at your end destination.)

Shipping: UPS and FedEx can be good options for transporting your bike. The cost is usually $45 to $75, depending on where the bike is being shipped. Bikes need to be boxed and addressed to a specific address.

Vehicle: If you are able to leave directly from home to begin your trip, or are touring somewhere nearby, using a vehicle and bike rack may be the easiest and only method for transportation, so long as you can secure a driver!

As you maneuver through trip planning, the remaining part of the process involves personal trip preparation and expectations. When my sister and I set out on our 4,000-mile trek across the country, I wasn't sure what to expect. I wasn't sure what it would be like to ride my bike every day, and I was definitely not sure what it would be like to ride up mountains. I had envisioned the mountains as sequential giant hills, where you started at the bottom, took a break halfway up, and ultimately got to the top, looking down at the road where you started some hours before. Once I started climbing up the switchbacks, I laughed at the idea of how steep a direct road up a mountain would be. Sometimes I would look down at my speedometer those first few weeks in Virginia, in disbelief that my bike could stand up at only four miles an hour.

Riding days for me can take on a rhythm, and there can be as much flexibility to them as you want. I like to ride somewhere between 25 to 70 miles per day and generally ride less in the more scenic areas. When I biked throughout Ireland, I rode only 30 miles a day because towns were so close together and the country was much smaller. Plan a mileage that sounds achievable and enjoyable, and think about how

A Day on the Road

Now after many tours, I am familiar with a kind of riding routine. Every person will ride differently, but an average day (depending on stops and towns) for me on the saddle looks like this:

7 am: Wake up, cook oatmeal for breakfast, pack up the tent and gear

9 am: Ride 20 to 25 miles with snack/break in the middle

11 am: Stop for a second "diner" breakfast or lunch

12:30 pm: Ride another 10 to 15 miles, stopping if there is a scenic area

2 pm: Stop in town for dinner groceries, the library, post office, etc.

3 pm: Ride the last 5 to 10 miles to campsite

4 pm: Set up tent, wash out bike clothes, bathe, cook dinner, relax

8 pm: Write or read until I fall asleep!

much you do or do not want to push yourself. Look at the region and map, and make sure there are places to stop or that you are prepared to carry extra food and water with you.

If you do not ride much on a weekly basis, it will probably be helpful to put in some miles to better physically prepare for your tour. A good general rule for me is to be able to ride in a week at home what I expect to ride on an average day of my tour. That ratio seems to minimize the chance of overworking certain muscles or joints, and also allows for a gradual increase of mileage. It also helps to make sure that you are used to your bike seat since increased hours on your saddle will inevitably create some new pains.

Aside from physical preparation, general bike maintenance knowledge is a final task to get some basic know-how before setting out on your tour. Be familiar with any tools you might bring along, including tire levers and a pump for fixing a flat, and a basic multi-tool to adjust breaks and gears. If you are interested, taking a basic bike maintenance class can give you a good idea about the mechanics of your bike. Wheel truing can be especially useful since spoke tension tends to be affected by heavily loaded bikes. But, that said, knowing how your bike works is not necessary to touring, just like knowing how to fix your car is not necessary to a car trip. There will be people to help you if something goes wrong, and being on a bike is much easier than being stranded in a vehicle!

Megan Holm

Time out for a self-portrait along a waterway near Ithaca, New York.

Though the details of touring are fun and important to consider, the nuts and bolts of a bicycle tour are not what keep me riding year after year. In this time where society tends to cultivate a sense of fear to leave what is familiar, it is easy to miss a lot. It is easy to roll up the windows to shut out the weather and the strangers walking by. It is easy to lose curiosity in the fast-paced world we live in because so much around us becomes a routine. But on a bike, I can't help but watch the night storm off in the evening distance over the Kansas wheat fields. I learn to watch the weather and really pay attention to it because it affects my day and how I ride. I get curious about where I am and who might tell me about it. I rely on other people to help me find the right road or the best food in town, and I depend on them if a big storm comes or if I get lost. It is a risk to be in unfamiliar territory, to challenge myself to meet and see someplace new, and to venture away from the comfort of my home. Every time I tour, I meet new people who invite me into their house, share their backyard for camping, or ask me to join them for dinner. People approach me and want to know where I am going. Touring ultimately makes me feel closer and more connected to people and places beyond my own neighborhood. That kind of connection is well worth riding against the wind in a downpour while dragging a wet tent, and with only a bowl of spaghetti for my evening's entertainment.

Annie's Big Bike Adventures

by Annie O'Grady

I am pedaling and pedaling hard up a 7 percent grade. The more I pedal, the more rhythmic my breathing becomes and the more I am aware of my heart pumping, my nostrils flexing, and my thigh muscles burning. I am enjoying the sights, but also suddenly aware of the hint of carbon monoxide I am inhaling which is lingering in the air. It's subtle, but I realize I am breathing in pollution and wondering what it's doing to the nature surrounding me.

Physically fatigued and my mind drifting off on yet another massive brain teaser, I couldn't be happier. This is what I've always wanted to do, even if I didn't always know it.

At the tender age of six, I spent many school days aimlessly staring out the window across the playground into the woods beyond and wondering if the rest of the world looked the same. By the age of 40, curiosity was killing me! A transplanted American now living in London, England, and staring down death, destruction, and a dead-end job, I decided to make my passion come alive. With less than a month before my adventure, I crafted a clever note to say that

Lois Evans

Annie takes a break on a roadside in Europe.

this cherubic middle-aged workaholic was going to cycle across 3,870 miles across America and they could check up on me through my blog. It was hard to imagine, as I did not even own a bicycle. Before I knew it, my bags were packed and I was off on an incredible daring journey to cycle America "the beautiful."

Sending that fateful note transformed my life. Not only did I cycle across America in 2006 but in 2007, I covered 2,870 miles across Europe from London to Istanbul. I'd always enjoyed traveling, and the face-to-face communication and sharing of experiences that I believe helps build a more peaceful global community—but this was even better! I stumbled upon two great adventures and a wonderful sport that is good for the soul, body, mind and the environment! With a growing awareness of the environment I have now shifted my sightseeing adventures to a bicycle.

The Adventures by the Numbers

North America

3,870 miles across 11 states and 2 countries in 50 days and 5 rest days.

Average miles per day: 82

Climbing: 110,000 Feet (Mount Hood, Ochocho Pass, Keyes Pass, Dixie Mountain, Tifton Mountain and Snall Summit, Summit Pass, Togwotee Pass, Black Hills, Adirondacks, Appalachian Mountains, Green Mountains, and Hogback Mountain)

Countries: USA and Canada. States: Oregon, Idaho, Wyoming, Minnesota, Wisconsin, Michigan, New York, Vermont and New Hampshire

European Tour

2,850 miles across 9 countries in 57 days with 15 rest days.

Average miles per day: 68

Countries: England, France, Germany, Austria, Hungary, Slovakia, Romania, Bulgaria, and Turkey)

Pre-trip Planning

Other trips I've taken have always required some grit to handle new places, faces, and foods—that's part of the fun—but never before had a trip tested my fitness level. I am no Lance Armstrong—just a gal with a crazy dream when I set off to cross America by bicycle. For what little sense I had, I made the wise move to make both trips with professional bike companies for the camaraderie and relative safety in numbers. However, I had more than a bit of trepidation once I realized I was in the company of a few world class athletes.

A month before taking off, I purchased my bicycle: a Trek 520, which was a good starter bike for long tours; not the fastest but quite reliable. My first challenge was that I landed (from the UK) in Boston and I needed to get to Oregon. With the risk of cutting my training regime (or what little there was) short, I added one more of my life's dreams to this trip: Taking a train across America! I hopped on the Empire Builder from Chicago to Seattle, traveling along the northern states of the USA, capturing the beauty of Wisconsin, Minnmesota, North Dakota, Montana, Idaho, and Washington including the wonderful sites of Libby, Whitefish, Glacier National Park, Cut Bank, Shelby, Havre, Malta, Glasgow, and Wolf Point. Boarding the train filled me with nostalgic thoughts and I was immediately daydreaming of all the Old Western movies I have ever watched. Each stop had breathtaking views and cool fresh air. It was a wonderful alternative to a direct flight. Of course, heading to Istanbul was quite a bit easier, leaving London was simply stepping out my door and hopping onto my Trek 520!

There is nothing like a two-month bike trip to make one aware of how few material possessions one really needs in life. On each of my trips, I was limited to two bags no bigger than a breadbox. So like many of the old women I saw in Romania washing clothes in the river, I became accustomed to washing my clothes in the sink and then hanging them to dry and in the process becoming more eco-friendly than I realized! In fact, a Cambridge University study found that washing and drying accounts for 60 percent of the energy associated with clothing—over its life, a single T-shirt can send up to nine pounds of carbon dioxide into the air. All across Europe and America on sunny afternoons, we were taken in by the beauty and tranquility of clothes blowing softly in the wind. And for me, apart from cycling 80 miles per day, there is nothing that puts me to sleep faster than air-dried sheets. Since the trip, I have purchased a clothesline and become a fresh-air convert.

The Contrasting Adventures

You might miss it from the inside of a tour bus, but from the street-level vantage point of a bike, it was apparent that Europe promotes cycling as a means of practical everyday transport. In Paris, an incredible abundance of cycle paths provided easy navigation around the chaotic city traffic in a nonintrusive, manner making it safe for the cyclist and stress-free for the autos. With convenient cycle paths and a prolific number of bicycles in the German university towns; it seemed to naturally lend itself to eco-friendly communities. With more than 900 miles of bicycle paths, many Germans take their holiday on the Danube and I was in disbelief seeing a boy no more than ten with at least forty pounds of gear attempting to climb a steep 10 percent grade hill (a 10-foot vertical rise over 100 feet of road surface). Many retirees were pedaling leisurely as they enjoyed their healthy vacation. Moving toward the former Eastern Bloc countries, the bicycle was a utilitarian necessity, not a choice. Most astounding was the senior-citizen population making use of the two-wheel contraption to head to the market. One lady in her 60s speaking Romanian provided us many hand gestures to demonstrate that her bicycle could turn a motor on after a pedal start. Likewise, I was in awe and trepidation as I saw a man carrying gas canisters balanced on the bike handlebars. The bike was not a hobby here but a part of life.

While the European conurbations of largely self-contained but interdependent contiguous villages creates small eco-friendly communities, traveling long distances by bicycle in Europe felt a bit more hazardous and very arduous. Most frightening was England, where we had to negotiate the abrupt end of a lovely bike path to navigate a major road with no shoulder and cars whizzing by at 70 mph. Across

Lois Evans

The Parliament of Hungary sits on the shore of the Danube River in Budapest.

the Eastern Bloc countries of Slovakia, Hungary, Romania, and Bulgaria with temperatures reaching 43 C (116 F), poor road engineering and heavy truck traffic left many of the roads lumpy and bumpy. At times I felt like I was mogul-skiing, with each bump reverberating through my entire body. In Turkey, cycling in very soft tar made pedaling twice the amount of work. There were no signs of local long distance cyclists—they must have known something we did not!

In contrast to the concentrated homes in villages of Europe, American homes, particularly in the West, can be many miles from town, making cycling an unrealistic option for commuting. It's very apparent that the American suburban sprawl was built when traveling by car was not considered such a threat to the environment. However, one of the benefits of the vast U.S. roadways was that they were wonderfully wide (nearly 3-foot shoulders) and welcoming to the long-distance cyclist. We also made great use of the many converted rails to trails bike paths—particularly in Oregon, South Dakota, Minnesota, Wisconsin, and New York's Erie Canal. We cycled the Elroy-Sparta bike trail in Wisconsin for 32 miles, which was the first "rails to trails" bike path in the United States (in 1967) converting railroad tracks built in the late 1800s. I really enjoyed the trail riding, not only for its tour through the backwoods, but because the grades were usually less than 3 percent.

City Life

For a long-distance touring cyclist, cities are often avoided at all costs: complexity of city roads, traffic chaos, noise and pollution. In European cities, it was not easy to roll into a hotel and lock up the bike because most hotels are quite old and compact. Furthermore, while

Lois Evans

The touring team of Sue Moyer, Hewes Agnew, Moira Gorman, and Annie O'Grady rest at a sidewalk cafe in Europe.

most of us North Americans love the old-world charm of Europe, within those quaint old city walls was the cyclists' nightmare: the dreaded cobblestone roads. We quickly ditched our bikes and opted for walking!

With most rest days in old pedestrian-friendly European cities, we were spoiled by the varying cultures and local history. Sitting atop Sacre Coure sipping a lovely glass of wine, my mind drifted to the romance and beauty of Paris. Likewise, wandering around so many German university towns and relaxing at one of many bier gardens gave me a sense of timelessness. After a few days of riding, I was left in awe at Vienna's abundance of art museums and music—so much talent in one city! Hidden in an alleyway, we discovered Jazz land, which seemed more or less a group of musicians enjoying some music and we just happened to be some extra guests. Booming Budapest captured the vibrancy of life with streets lined with trams. We ducked down the alley into one of many quiet and secluded coffeehouses.

Moving east, some towns struggled with poor urban planning as we saw farm animals such as horses roaming between apartment blocks. Unfortunately, with the presence of the Ceausescu regime, time has not been so kind to Bucharest. Some claim it's the Paris of Eastern Europe, but I was not so sure. During the Ceausescu regime (up to 1989) great efforts and money were put into building some behemoth buildings of all sorts of designs (gothic, baroque, modern, and anything in between). And while great efforts were put into the buildings, the lack of sidewalks and the street crossings heading into cement walls indicated an appalling lack of city planning. Traffic was chaotic. There was the feeling of a new dawn for the city, but with a hint of being haunted by its recent past (e.g., bullet marks on buildings).

On the outskirts of Istanbul, we began a descent, barreling through an overly planned town called Kemburgez. I wondered if I was in Turkey or perhaps in "Anywhere, USA." I spotted a Starbucks and wondered if this was the same country where I had seen shepherds herding their flock in bare feet. Arriving in Istanbul, with 17 million inhabitants delicately balanced between Eastern and Western cultures, the city pulsated with energy 24/7. Late night, I escaped the bustling streets and markets onto a Bosporus riverboat to drift along enjoying the changing scenes and distant Turkish music emanating from the banks into the early hours of the morning.

In the United States, our tour mostly avoided major cities, so this gave us the opportunity to witness some of America's natural beauty. We quickly passed through Portland, Oregon, as we set our eyes on mammoth Mount Hood, standing at 11,249 feet (3,429 meters). It was simply breathtaking to see it emerging in the distance days before we were worshipping its base. Barreling through old canyons, we were led into Boise, Idaho, whose tranquil yet luscious city emerged out of barren landscape. Wyoming's Grand Tetons were a very challenging cycle ride with inclines of 12 to 18 percent and a hidden gem for the wildlife and outdoor enthusiast. We descended for a beer in the Million Dollar Cowboy Café with its saddle bar stools. The Black Hills of South Dakota had so much to offer with its patriotic Mount Rushmore and impressive soon-to-be Mount Crazy Horse. Very memorable was Mitchell, South Dakota (population 15,000), home to the one and only Corn Palace. I can only think this town will be once again a boomtown if ethanol energy takes off.

Continuing across Minnesota and Wisconsin, we enjoyed pedaling through beautiful rolling hills and pastures. Heading east, as the population picks up, so do the entertainment centers including the Wisconsin Dells. Crossing by ferry, we saw the effects of the auto industry—pockets of poverty were apparent all across Michigan. We crossed into Canada through Port Huron, one of the busiest shipping ports in the world. Before we knew it, we were in Niagara Falls with spectacular Canadian views. Upstate New York has much history with

Annie O'Grady

A covered bridge is part of the bike trail in Vermont.

its heyday of the Erie Canal but most of the small towns were struggling to survive. As we crossed into Vermont, it was looking just like the postcards: this state is pristinely beautiful and quaint. Our trip ended in the beautiful sandy beaches just outside of Portsmouth, New Hampshire, which retains its old New England charm. The natural beauty of North America runs from coast to coast.

A Taste of Local Customs

One of the greatest benefits of long distance cycling is getting in shape. Burning upwards of 8,000 calories not only led to weight loss, but the ability (and sometimes need) to sample extra treats along the way. With an abundance of locally grown produce in both America and Europe, we had endless opportunities to sample a wide selection of delectable choices.

Traveling along, apart from the very arid Wyoming, each state had an extensive variety of fresh fruits and vegetables. In Oregon, we were tempted with succulent fresh nectarines and mouth-watering Bing cherries. With my Irish heritage, I was also enamored with Blackfoot, Idaho, otherwise known as the "Potato Capital of the World." Heading east, there was an abundance of pick-your-own raspberries, blueberries, and apples, as well as commercial crops of soybean, corn, beets, beans, cucumber, carrots, and peas. Canada farms shifted to growing pears, apples, and tomatoes. We joined some locals to pick the remnants left behind from the automated farm equipment. Most inspiring was that many of the old tobacco farms in southern Canada had been converted to ginseng farms.

Likewise, in Europe, we were equally spoiled with fresh locally grown fruits and vegetables as well as tantalizing pastries. With pastry as part of the staple French and German diet, we stopped each morning to enjoy an éclair, croissant, or apple strudel. Vineyards were sprinkled across France and Southern Germany that made champagne, wine, schnapps, and beer. More than once, we were lured into a sample of the local concoction.

And of course, burning 8,000 calories entitles one to a daily dose of ice cream. Early on, I initiated a DQ count. Each day, we scoured the towns for a local Dairy Queen, building my Blizzard blog to a total of 33 (out of 50 days). At one point, I almost landed myself a job serving up Blizzards! As I realized the 'Subway-man' (TV advertisements) was promoting weight loss through Subway sandwiches, I too managed a meager 5 pound weight loss with my daily indulgence of a Blizzard. As an ice cream connoisseur, I can say that it was available across Europe but with a slightly different texture. Some liked it better, but for myself, I will stick to my DQ.

Annie O'Grady

Lois Evans takes time for some fresh raspberries at one of the many "pick-your-own-produce" farms in the United States and Canada.

Historic Waterways

If you want to incorporate a few wonderful stopovers into a cycling adventure, just look for water on your map. Every great city seems to be just a stone's throw from a rampaging river. Whether it is the Thames, tamed by the Greenwich Barrier in London, the sedate

Seine, or the mighty Danube, all seem to flex their muscle during thawing seasons, and with the reported increase in temperatures, are certainly becoming a greater threat. However, the advantage of cycling along a river is two-fold:

1) Water flows downhill (and so does the bike most of the time!)

2) The riverbanks tend to be fairly flat.

The Paris to Istanbul ride covers more than nine hundred miles along the Danube, making use of the old Orient Express rail tracks. This might be one of the best eco-friendly vacation secrets. The combination of cycling, history, and outdoors was both relaxing and inspiring. The Danube changed personalities—some days looking like a stream, peaceful, possibly frail, and quiet; other days, large and lazy; and yet other days, bulging, determined, confident, and controlling. Similarly, the banks adjusted in harmony (or not), as the terrain varied from flat (extremely, very, and nearly) to being sprinkled with modest and mean (challenging) hills. With water markings acting as physical signs, there was plenty of natural history here.

Across America, we ducked and weaved along many different river sources including the Columbia and John Day Rivers in Oregon leading to the long and winding Snake River heading across Idaho and Wyoming into Jackson Lake (in Grand Teton National Park). In the west, much of the power is derived from hydroelectric plants along the many rivers. With very arid land, western U.S. settlements and farming have been economically developed with the use of irrigation. In an effort to develop the Riverton region of Wyoming, Congress passed an act in 1902 ratifying an agreement with the Indians of the Wind River Reservation, which resulted in the building of Bull Lake Dam, Wind River Diversion Dam, and Pilot Butte Dam. Looking about the place today, it appears to remain an extremely dry area and somewhat sparsely populated. There continues to be a thriving American Indian influence with casinos accentuated by local Wal-Marts, Kmarts, and all the American fast food joints. That's progress, eh?

We passed the two largest rivers in the United States (Missouri and Mississippi) both providing hydroelectric power to the local areas. Before we knew it, we had cycled across Canada and could hear the sounds of power. We were overlooking the American Falls/ Bridal Veil Falls (176 feet tall; brink: 1,060 feet) and the Horseshoe Falls (167 feet tall; brink: 2,600 feet) and realized we were staring in awe at one of the greatest natural resources: water. Harnessing the power of Niagara Falls generates about 25 percent of all the power for New York State and Ontario, Canada.

Weathering The Weather

For some, cycling in blistering heat is the kiss of death, but I revel in it. Both trips had insufferable heat, with temperatures consistently hitting 46 C/120 F. At times, it felt like my face was in a pizza oven. Water bottles got hot so quickly it became not just warm, but hot—unbearable to drink. To escape the heat, we enjoyed long afternoon naps in the hard-to-find shade. We found wilted sunflowers and evidence of forest fires in more than a few towns in both United States and Europe. Cycling in these temperatures for me was not only physically very difficult, but also emotionally unbearable to watch locals, with just shovels and picks manually building a highway at high noon! In Romania, we saw families (grandmother, mother, son) working with rudimentary tools (sickles, pitchforks, and handsaws) in the excruciating heat. Seeing this, I realized that as much as I believe modern life has contributed to global warming, automation certainly has its place. While eco-friendly, manual labor in these conditions seemed inhumane. Naturally, as these countries modernize, they too will want or rather, need, air conditioning and automobiles.

Lois Evans (Lost Springs, Blizzard) and Annie O'Grady

Dairy Queen Blizzards helped power the bicycle tour across America's Heartland.

While Europe was prone to daily rain showers, they were most often brief and at night. The locals knew the weather patterns well, as they generally cut down from England. Our cycling was interrupted only once and the locals told us it would take only twenty minutes to pass. Across America, rain was infrequent, but when it came down, Mother Nature showed who was boss. There were tornado shelters across the Midwest. On one particular day, we were given our first clue—it was 6:00 am and the sky was a fiery red! By midmorning a cloud was chasing us, making it as dark as night. The local reporter advised us that the storm would arrive within minutes. Darting to a barn, we were stopped in our tracks as lighting and thunder were upon us. Unlike the fast moving weather of Europe, we were stalled for two hours. With tornadoes and hurricanes, it seemed the weather was far harsher and unpredictable in America, especially on a bike.

Now there is a grand debate among all long-distance cyclists: Is it easier to cycle East to West across America or West to East? Everyone has an opinion. Seems the answer is always the opposite direction of whatever direction you are going. Cycling into the headwinds that hid all across North America was a brutal and emotionally depleting experience. For us, it seemed we had more than our fair share of headwinds that made even the "easy" short-mileage days terribly tough. They say you are in South Dakota when "the wind blows you into the next state." And there were days when I thought perhaps I would end up back in Wyoming. With few windmills in sight, it left me wondering if America was making the most of the wind power. Europe had its fair share of windmills dotted across the landscape.

Our Timely Impact on Nature

It seems to me there are pros / cons and pluses / minuses to everything in life. Man's impact on the environment is no exception. In America, we struggle to offset the impact of our nation growing exponentially after the discovery of the automobile. And with a sprawling suburbia, we are challenged to substitute our necessity to drive. Not only are cars having an affect on the air we breathe, they are a threat to wildlife. Roadkill across America is rampant and includes a variety of species: deer, snakes, raccoons, badgers, skunks, chipmunks, and various birds. Of course, among the roadkill, we all spotted numerous lost action figure toys (usually decapitated). Across the Western United States, we were treated to all sorts of wild animals including a few bears in the Grand Tetons, bison looking dainty and roaming freely in the Black Hills National Forest, antelope near Hell's Half Acre and wild horses thundering by us in Oregon. Prairie dogs popped up all across the northern plains.

In Europe, the environment is challenged by the impact of widespread farming, leaving few wild animals, besides birds, to be found. On one particular morning, I woke to screeching noises and wondered what sort of wild animal was lurking nearby, only to realize we were on the edge of a zoo and the screaming monkeys were safely behind bars. A few days later, I thought I was dreaming, only to realize we were near another zoo and it was now lions roaring in the morning. We passed by a field and did a double take: camels! Where did they come from? Looking a bit forlorn, the circus was in town. Moving toward Eastern Europe, much like every family has a car in America, every family seemed to have a horse, cow, donkey, or mule.

Dogs were the nemesis of Eastern Europe. They ranged from small Romanian dogs chasing our heels to larger 'all night barking' Bulgarian dogs and any combination thereof. Our guidebook warned of wild dogs and I was relieved that they turned out to be mangy and stray. In the USA, only a few dogs occasionally quickened our pace. The good news about being one of the slower cyclists is that after chasing about 50 bike riders, the dogs had no energy left to chase me.

Recycling

With miles and miles of pedaling, I was lost in thought only to have my mind distracted by the sight of bottles and cans, an eyesore amid the beautiful wildflowers in both America and Europe. Then again, it could be worse. Due to a successful "Adopt-a-Highway" campaign, which began in 1985, whereby volunteer groups take responsibility for a section of highway, America's roadways are remarkably clean. And more recently in America, the war against water bottles has just begun!

"Give a hoot, don't pollute" was a wonderful 1970s U.S. campaign that I recalled as I was cycling along the Bulgarian and Turkish roadways. How they could benefit from such a campaign. Unfortunately, the roads were littered with not just water bottles but just about anything and everything including TVs, refrigerators, PCs, ironing boards, and just plain trash. It was heartbreaking to see national parks and campgrounds laden with garbage.

Making Friends

With long-distance cycling, one is not only able to make friends with fellow riders but with locals. In both the United States and Europe, it was not just cycling that made these trips spectacular, but sharing little snippets of experiences with strangers and riders alike.

In a bike group, bonding with forty or so strangers is not always easy. As we were on the trip for different reasons, it all came down to chemistry, respect, a sense of humor, and a little bit of luck. On my U.S. trip, within days, our group broke into little social packs with nicknames. Without any pre-trip training, I fell in with the slowest riders, picking up the tag name "Final Four," as we finished last nearly every day. We soon took to playing practical jokes on the 3 Amigos, the Alumni group, the Wolf pack, and Deadly Duo. Along the way, we encountered many budding and inspirational entrepreneurs, taking their little bit of nature and improving it—whether it be the man making oversized rocking chairs, the guy taking a chance on a rundown gas station, or the lady on a spiritual journey hand-painting Mandelas. It was inspiring.

In Europe, my encounter with the locals made the trip spectacular. Working through language barriers, we were left to manage with hand signals and smiles. It worked every time! In Romania, with a flat tire in front of a garage that seemed to double as a house, the chap saw our dilemma and generously offered his very old repair kit. In Turkey, I was astounded by the generosity—a shepherd in raggedy old clothes and floppy shoes offered me bread. In a small town, the local policeman stopped by with fresh melon on a plate. Despite the language barrier, we shared jokes—a man was watering the fields with a big fire hose while his wife was left weeding—we all carefully noted who was doing all the work! A truck stopped and offered a few of the riders some watermelon and a lift to Istanbul. I was humbled that those who had the least were willing to share the most.

Looking Back

I am still pinching myself as I look at my photo album. I was an ordinary Anglophiled American who dared to live my dreams. Cycling across America and Europe opened my eyes to living life with adventure and in search of my next adrenalin rush. And while it started simply as a means to see the world in an environmentally friendly manner, I have become an addicted cyclist. Hardly a day goes by when my mind does not drift back to a person I met or something I saw. On a personal level, I have understood that life is a journey and not a destination.

I had given very little thought to planning, either training or logistics. With our consumption-driven world, it was quite liberating to realize one needs very little to survive. As for cycling, I am now addicted to a sport that allows me to get fit, see the sights and meet the locals—a wonderful way to build global relations. And while there was evidence of environmental challenges everywhere I went, they certainly were for different reasons: North America developed during the Industrial Age, Europe developed during farming age, and Eastern Europe suffered with some dictatorships and civil unrest. It was, though, refreshing to see the abundance of natural resources either being used (local foods and water) or with great potential (wind). And while Europe retains much of its Old World charm, America's natural beauty is simply breathtaking.

Putting the daily news stories aside, I reflect back that the cycle trips gave me a chance to share experiences that, even on the smallest level, allowed us to build a more peaceful global community. Whether it be sipping French champagne, learning of the 1956 Hungarian revolution with locals, visiting the Mauthaussen Death Camp, or sharing bread with a local shepherd in Turkey, it's these experiences and

Patrick O'Grady

The Final Four finish up with a dip in the Atlantic Ocean in New Hampshire.

acts of friendship that give humanity such meaning. Intellectually, my mind has been awakened to the challenges of the environment. Witnessing much painstaking manual labor and poverty, the frequent sightings of mobile phones in the fields and kids playing video games in dank Internet cafes puzzled me. With such easy access to modern technology, I wonder how it all fits in with Maslow's hierarchy of needs and if these priorities were helping or hindering the people.

These two experiences, show me the world is much smaller than I imagined and perhaps, its people are not so different. After all, life comes down to the simple things: Burger, Brew and Buddies! No matter where I have been on my trips and regardless of the standard of living, this was a common thread. The 'burger' might have been a hotdog, a curry, a baguette, schnitzel, goulash or a kebab. The 'brew' may be English lager, French wine, American beer, a Mexican margarita, raki or just simply cay (that's as in chai tea). And buddies were the friends and family.

On the Home Front

www.indexopen.com

Naturally Green Buildings

by Stephen Collette

As a species, we have been building green and natural buildings, since, well, we began building. Right back in the beginning everything was made out of rocks, trees, sticks, and mud. We've actually forgotten a fair bit of that knowledge, which to some degree is good, but we have also lost some really useful and practical knowledge that, if applied today, would help make our lives more comfortable and healthier—and our homes cheaper to build. Let's look at the various ideas and options and how to apply them to your existing house.

First let's talk about slinging some mud. Not mudslinging talk, but talk of actually slinging mud. This goes back as far as human construction and, for me, back to when I was a toddler. It's that easy and fun, and even more so as an adult when you are allowed to. Mud and its variations of clay, lime, and earth are all really great building materials. They can stand up to a remarkable amount of abuse, and with the right precautions, can even be used outside. Earthen plasters are typically locally found materials that have the ability to turn creamy when wet (like cake icing) so that you can trowel them on a wall, and will dry really hard when you are done. How hard, you ask? Well,

www.indexopen.com

A classically built adobe home can stand the test of time, but tend to hold up better in warmer climates.

hard enough that there are lime plasters on houses in colder climates that are at least a hundred years old, and in Europe, some even older than that.

Adobe homes in the southern, warmer climates are made of mud bricks that dry in the sun. These are good for a couple hundred years if you build them properly and take care of them. Adobe can also be used in cooler climates, but typically indoors, or as part of an insulated wall system (Adobe doesn't offer much insulation for northern climates).If you are building new, your options expand and you can look at interior adobe block walls. The best part about earthen plasters and walls is that if you ding them while moving furniture—and you will—all you have to do is get the spot a little wet and rub it smooth again. It's that easy. For those of you who may not be willing to dig up the back garden to put some mud on your walls, you can purchase clay plasters and clay paints in a range of beautiful colors that you can apply to your existing drywall. Using clay paints instead of conventional ones gives you that softer, natural feeling without having to trowel.

Another benefit of incorporating earthen plasters, finishes, and walls is that it actually make a home a little healthier—the materials regulate indoor humidity levels. The walls actually absorb moisture and then slowly release the moisture later. This reduces the humidity swing in buildings and makes it more comfortable inside. A natural process, these walls do this with no adverse effect upon the wall or your home. Drywall, on the other hand, likes to suck up water, but it doesn't release it as well, which can lead to growing mold instead.

Mud Plus: Variations

From straight mud, adding some straw to the mix can greatly increase the decorative and insulative quality. The type of wall you get depends on how much straw you add. Adding bits of chopped straw to a mud wall creates "cob," which is what you did in kindergarten, in the backyard, mixing mud and anything else you could throw in. Well, it turns out it gets pretty stiff when you add some straw—stiff enough to throw against a frame of sticks in small coblike balls. This method offers tremendous amounts of creativity in creating a wall and works well for sculpturing your favorite gargoyles to sit atop your walls. Cob is slightly more insulative than adobe and works really well on indoor walls and creative, curvy details.

However, if you use just straw and add mud to the outside faces of it, that gives you a straw-bale construction wall. These are super-insulating, in the range of R-35 to R-50, which is very good compared to a typical 1970s home with R-12 in the walls. (R-values are a common measure of insulation in the building industry.) You use regular square bales, stack them like bricks, and plaster the outside surfaces. They're good for a few hundred years if you build them properly. Straw bales are also versatile in terms of design. Big deep window wells (24 inches) and curvy walls that can look Mediterranean or Sante Fe style are quite common looks for these homes. Finishes on the walls can be anything mentioned above. These homes are great in climates that need insulation, and are better suited for more northerly areas. Straw-bale walls are too dense to burn, just like throwing a phone book on a fire. They are hard work for pests, with nothing to eat, so it keeps down the usual rodents and bugs, unlike pink insulation, which is easy to dig through and make a nice nest. The straw is hollow (just like . . . straw) so water wicks through the walls in vapor state and keeps the wall system nice and dry, thus preventing rot and mold. Finally, the big bad wolf will not blow this house down. Remember 24-inch walls are stronger than typical 6-inch walls by a significant margin, especially when covered with plaster on both sides.

It's Old, It's New, It Works

All natural building does is take timeworn standard practices—indigenous local building materials and processes—and apply them to the global home. This can work very well, as these types of homes have been built for thousands of years without a single building inspector complaining. Over time, the bugs have been worked out and the dos and don'ts have been passed down through generations.

New natural builders today have learned from old masters and built a lot using trial and error. It's a very forgiving process as long as you follow good building practices and skills. You don't even have to build your entire house out of natural materials to make a difference. You can use them in renovations and additions or just in the finishing details. If you want your home to blend in with the neighborhood, you can add siding to a straw-bale wall. The options for building green are limited only to your imagination. There are lots of books out there that people can read, and workshops and schools offering training in natural building. It's worth taking a weekend workshop after reading about the method of choice, and seeing if it is a fit for you and your house plans. If it is, do the research, get your hands dirty, and understand as much as you can about how to make it successful before tackling it yourself or hiring a builder.

Green building is the modern take on these processes: natural building techniques such as timber frame, log homes, stackwall or cordwood construction, and numerous others. In your travels (or in your hometown) if you have seen really old homes built prior to manufacturing, you are looking at a natural home. Modern builders and designers have this global palette to work from, and they also have some new materials and products that were not available in the past. Now with the global economy, we can have access to a variety of interesting and green building products.

How Green Do You Mean?

Green building, by definition, is the most ecological and environmentally friendly approach to a building problem that fits the most criteria set out by the owner of the building. Bamboo and concrete are two great examples. Bamboo is a plant that is harder than any North American hardwood, and is basically a weed. It grows inches per day and can be harvested yearly with no damage to the plant. It can be made into beautiful floors, veneers, and now even clothing. This is better than chopping down old growth forests, right? But it is shipped on a boat from across the globe. Is it green? Concrete is healthy, nontoxic, doesn't grow mold, is very strong, will last for years and years, can use recycled fly ash from coal plants (mostly tiny bits of glass and other non-combustible silicon materials that melted), and can be structural and decorative at the same time—from walls to counters, almost anything can be concrete. It is, however, the largest producer of greenhouse gases because it takes a tremendous amount of energy to mine the materials, heat them to extreme temperatures, and ship them. Is it green? Both can be green and cannot be green, depending on your personal ideals, beliefs and criteria. With each product that you look at, you need to define some filters and choose your materials based on that.

Criteria for Green Building

Natural Materials

Natural is where we start. Ideally, the products used in the construction are as natural and close to original state as possible. The more the manufacturing process is involved, the less natural it is. So clay paints, hardwood flooring, solid wood furniture, stone, tile, timbers, and exposed wood all fall into this category. So does twig furniture, wood shelves instead of kitchen cupboards; linoleum (made from linseed oil) rather than vinyl flooring (made from polyvinyl chloride). Timberframe houses are a great example because the timbers have probably been around for a few hundred years and already used on a couple of other buildings. And when your house is finally torn down (hopefully in a really long time), those timbers will be used on another building. All of the natural building types listed above can be used in your home. You can integrate these natural building materials to a point where your neighbors may not even realize you are using straw or adobe or cob. They can completely blend in, if so desired. Or on the contrary, you can flaunt your natural green addition and let the world know how beautiful it can be.

Healthy

Healthy comes next on the list of green building. We would like to see products used that are not off-gassing harmful and toxic chemicals inside the house. Particleboard that is glued with formaldehyde binders falls into this category. Formaldehyde is great if you are a grade 11 frog in a jar, but it isn't any good for you. You have to ask for formaldehyde-free glues on anything with particleboard to be sure. Paints with VOC's (the stinky part of paint) are toxic and can impact brain functions. Low or no VOC paint solves this problem, and now it's available everywhere in hundreds of colors. To understand what goes into products, you need to look up the MSDS (Material Safety Data Sheets) for each of the products. These will tell you what ingredients are in the product, and then you can search online for what those products do to you and your family. That way you can make an educated decision about what you purchase.

Two good rules of thumb: 1) If it is really stinky, don't use it, and 2) If the ingredients have more than twelve syllables, then it's probably bad for you, too.

Local

Local products are important for green building. Having a really great product shipped all the way by boat and truck to you takes a massive amount of energy and can make a green product a bit more dirty brown by the time it gets to you. So bamboo floors may not sit well with you, but local maple or pine might be a better fit—you can even talk to the person who milled the floor if you look hard enough. Find local manufacturers that use recycled materials and make stuff like glass tiles or wood cabinets. Using local materials saves gas, and your local economy, all with one thoughtful purchase. Salvage and reuse stores are great for this too. You can always find cool and quirky stuff to fit your style at reseller stores. Habitat for Humanity stores are in most cities now, and don't forget about the local salvage companies that always take out the good, reusable materials from buildings prior to demolition.

However, try not to reuse old windows or toilets; neither are terribly efficient and you will spend more on water and heating to cover the initial savings. Also remember some old painted items like doors and trim may have lead paint on them, so don't sand them, but use natural-based strippers to remove the paint.

Efficient

The next area is efficiency. This is the cheap part of you rising up and saying, "I want something that isn't going to cost me a lot to use." Great, revel in this inner cheapness because cutting your energy costs helps save your pocketbook and the environment. Take a look at your monthly utility bills and figure where the money is going. If it is electricity, then how do you reduce it? Switching out your bulbs for compact fluorescents (CFLs) will make a huge savings. By changing the five most-used bulbs in your house, you will save $20 to $30/year on utilities. Plus they will last for ten years. So for $3/bulb, you are in fact making money off of this light. Now that's bright. Look for Energy Star qualified products for any electrical purchase, from refrigerators to dishwashers to computers, stereos, windows, and, well, everything. Energy Star rated means they are the most efficient models in their class, which means the cheapest to operate.

Think about total efficiency when integrating green strategies. While you can install solar panels to generate the power you already use, very often purchasing a new Energy Star-rated fridge is more economical than the solar panels for your roof—your old energy hog will require two or three panels, while the new fridge would only need one. That makes sense.

Integrate Ongoing Green Strategies

Green building design doesn't end the first day you sleep in your new home. Once installed, you need to remember to use those easy-to-adjust electrical and heating systems. A programmable thermostat can save loads of energy, or you can simply set your thermostat back 4–6 degrees when you are in bed or not at home so that you are saving money and not heating/cooling the house when you don't need it. Put everything possible on timers and power bars and turn them off when not in use. Some new TVs consume more electricity off than the old style TV when on. Hit the power bar when done—and kill those "phantom loads" that are stealing money. Finally, insulate and air-seal your house so that the money you are putting in to heat and cool stays inside. Have an energy audit done on your house and see where you are losing money, literally. Energy audits show you the invisible loss of energy using a blower door test, and are the best bang for your buck for energy savings.

Durable products need to be looked at in a green home. If you buy a super warm-and-fuzzy feeling product and it lasts for a couple weeks or a couple of years, instead of a lifetime, then you have wasted your money, and now you are sending that product to the landfill. Durability is key to a green house and all products need to stand up to the abuse you are going to give them.

The partner to durability is sustainability. Is the product sustainably made, built, harvested? Did the wood you are using come from a clear cut logging process or was is certified by a third party like Forest Stewardship Council to be sustainably harvested? Were workers exposed to toxic chemicals and poor pay to make your product and were worker conditions safe and fair? Is the main component of the material easily renewable, like straw-board panels, where straw can be harvested a couple times a year, versus a particleboard panel from wood that takes several years to grow before harvest? Once you know what questions to ask and certifications to look for, you can purchase with confidence.

If you have the opportunity to pick a location or add an addition to your house, then you really want to consider passive solar design. This is the lowest of the low-hanging fruit for you, so missing out on this is missing the whole boat. The sun is a pretty amazing thing: it comes up every day and warms us up. There is more energy from the sun that hits one square yard of your house in one hour than you could consume in a day. It's crazy. What we want to do with the sun in a passive way is let it come into our home when we want it to, and warm us up, like in winter. In the summer time we want to keep it out of the house so that things stay nice and cool. Passive solar design takes this into consideration so that overhangs and window design allow the winter sun to penetrate as deep as possible and shade and protect the house from the hot summer sun. It's as easy as a bit of overhang and some thought. Taking this into your design will reduce your requirements for heating and cooling significantly. It will also reduce your lighting needs.

There are many choices and decisions that you can make and consider when thinking about green building. Take the time to do some research and then talk to your builder about your goals. If your builder isn't interested in building better, then consider a better builder. It's your money, your mortgage, and your family living in the home. There are lots of builders out there who are eager to learn more about green building or who are doing it. Find dealers who sell green building products and ask for tradespeople who use their products. There are green building consultants out there as well, who can source the people and products that meet your needs and can make the process easier. The more legwork you do up front, the more satisfaction and pleasure you will have in your new green and natural space.

The Residential Rain Garden

by Roslyn Reid

Rain gardens are one of the hot new topics in the ecological approach to everyday problems. A rain garden is a residential, landscaped garden in a shallow depression that receives runoff from nearby impervious surfaces. This concept is not really new—for decades, corporations have been employing a similar technique called bioretention technology (commonly known as retention basins) to handle their runoff and capture pollutants. Rain gardens differ from these basins, not only in scale, but by the inclusion of vegetation specifically intended to return water vapor to the atmosphere via transpiration—a process in which plants draw water up by their roots, then let it evaporate into the air via their leaves.

Interest in the residential use of rain gardens began overseas in the 1980s. By the 1990s, the concept had reached the United States, where landscape architects and universities started to experiment with them as part of an approach called IMP, or Integrated Management Practice. (Other mysterious acronyms you will commonly find in the pertinent material, and which are worth remembering, are BMP, for Best Management Practices; and LID, for Low-Impact Development.)

Estimates show that about 12 percent of the world's soils may experience flooding; in the United States, it's closer to 16 percent. Studies by the Environmental Protection Agency (EPA) indicate that a typical city block can generate as much as nine times more runoff than a comparably-sized wooded lot. According to the agency, stormwater runoff is the leading environmental threat to estuaries in the United States.

As residential land becomes scarcer and housing becomes denser, the rain garden has emerged as an inexpensive—not to mention delightful—method of handling common runoff from houses, such as that from gutters, driveways, and patios.

Similar Use, Smaller Scale

Employing plants to handle water runoff has been practiced down on the farm for many years. Called "vegetative filters" in agricultural terms, these types of vapor-returning plants are still used by farmers along their stream banks today. Such plants limit the amount of runoff as part of measures to control toxic algae, which could otherwise form in the water and be fatal to cattle and pets.

Residential rain gardens were first conceived of in the United States in 1990 by a team of Maryland stormwater specialists working under Larry Coffman, the assistant director of Programs and Planning, Environmental Resources, in Prince Georges County. Because no real guidelines for the construction and use of rain gardens existed at that time, the team basically had to invent them. The intent was to mirror the natural way in which forests or meadows process heavy rainfall. In 1993, the team published the Maryland bioretention guidelines for rain gardens, which is now available online in its entirety. Two years later, landscape architects at the University of

Michigan began retrofitting experimental "rainwater gardens" across two blocks of existing residential properties in Maplewood, Minnesota (a suburb of Minneapolis).

A few years after the Michigan team completed its project, Coffman was contacted by the designers of the Prince Georges County community of Somerset, Maryland. To his delight, they said they wished to incorporate the IMP guidelines his department had developed for handling water runoff into their formal residential proposal. As a result, the final design for Somerset included a 300- to 400-square-foot rain garden on each of the nearly 200 lots in the community, along with some other innovative overall techniques intended to deal with total water runoff.

It looked like rain gardens' time had arrived. Since those early days, several other states—notably those around the Great Lakes—have launched rain garden projects. Both the Brooklyn Botanic Gardens and Temple University have installed functioning rain gardens as models for their communities, with the rain garden at BBG handling 20,000 gallons of rainwater from its roof each year. And the Clean Water Campaign in the city of Alpharetta, Georgia, has even produced a how-to video!

Planning and Construction

Because workshops on rain garden construction are cropping up all over the country, and a great deal of information is available on the Internet now (see Resources section), this article focuses on the basics so you can decide if you wish to tackle this kind of project. Much of the available material on building rain gardens is intended for entire communities, but the principles are the same for individual home gardens—you'll just have to do it on a smaller scale.

First, find out if any construction permits are necessary in your area. Then walk around your property during and after a rainstorm to observe how water runs off. This is the best way to determine an appropriate location for your rain garden. Look for low areas where water pools after the rain stops or places where a lot of water is running off the property from impervious surfaces. If you discover that the optimum spot for a rain garden is too close to structures or inconvenient for some reason, the water will need to be diverted to the rain garden via a pipe or ditch. This will result in added construction time, materials, and cost.

Because expansion is easier to accomplish than downsizing, it is better to start off with a smaller rain garden and observe its effectiveness for some time. If the water remains in the rain garden for too long (more than a couple of days), the garden needs to be enlarged to accommodate more runoff. A calculation tool for your roof is available on the Web site of the Brooklyn Botanic Gardens at the bottom of

Courtesy of city of Maplewood

Rain gardens are becoming more common in Maplewood, Minnesota as the city provides some support for homeowners.

this page: www.bbg.org/gar2/topics/design/2004sp_raingardens1 .html (In short, it's the square footage of your roof × 0.623 × annual inches of rainfall. This means a 1,000-square-foot roof produces about 6,230 gallons of runoff for every 10 inches of rain.) The BBG site is an excellent source for all kinds of pertinent information on rain gardens and other sustainable gardening techniques, such as rain barrels. Even so, decisions should be based on personal observation of your specific situation, not just "official" procedures.

Now, it may sound obvious, but it's worth mentioning that a rain garden should be built downhill from any structures! Also, if you're planting trees in your rain garden, you should take into consideration any damage the roots might do to nearby foundations, walls, or underground pipes. Plan your garden for the available space, then consider aesthetics and scale. (Although it's unusual, some small rain gardens have even been built on rooftops!)

A typical rain garden consists of three strata: a root zone, a highly conducive middle storage layer, and a subsoil lower layer. (This particular model does not employ auxiliary piping and is not intended to handle snowmelt.) The size of the proposed rain garden should be 10 to 20 percent of the area of impervious surface whose runoff the garden is intended to process.

As a finishing touch, add a three-inch layer of hardwood mulch after all the planting is done—this will suppress weeds and help filter the water as it percolates into the ground. Maintenance of a rain garden is fairly minimal. It does not require fertilizer, so upkeep usually consists of pruning, weeding, and replacing plants.

Before initiating any construction, you should conduct a soil percolation test for your property. Your county extension agent can help with this procedure (see Resources). Depending on the test results, a good mix for starting your rain garden might be one part topsoil (not clay), one part compost or peat, and two parts sand. Please note that not all sand is appropriate for this kind of project—be sure to use garden sand, which does not contain weed seeds. You can begin building your rain garden by applying this mix in several layers.

There are several incidental factors to consider. A deeper rain garden decreases the evaporation rate, which affects plant survival. Water loss through leaves also varies from day to day according to sun and wind exposure. For a rain garden to be feasible, the subsoil should have good permeability—more so than rock, but not as much as sand. In areas with less permeable soil, it may be necessary to construct a trench-and-pipe system beneath the rain garden to carry off excess water. For good information, clear graphics, and easy to follow diagrams on this technique, check out the Web site of the British company Interpave. (www.paving.org.uk)

There are also a few safety concerns. If you have small children, you might consider installing a fence around your rain garden. Some municipalities might even require this—again, check with yours before you start the project. In any event, it is a good idea to somehow alert visitors of a rain garden's presence, perhaps by the use of decorative garden markers. And, of course, do not place your rain garden in a location where you might accidentally drive your car or lawn mower into it!

In some climates, the prospect of increasing the mosquito population comes into play when making a decision about having a rain garden. While the insect's reputation as a nuisance and carrier of the West Nile virus are real concerns, rain gardens are designed to process water rather than retain it like a basin or pond—the gardens at Somerset allow water to pool for no more than forty-eight hours. Therefore, there is less potential for standing water, which is what mosquitoes prefer as breeding grounds for their larvae.

Types of Plants

In this section, we shall refer to rain garden plants by their appropriate British term, *air drainers*. One reliable technique for determining which air drainers would be suitable for your particular rain garden would be to check out your local swamp, if you can find one. Swamps are very efficient at returning water vapor to the atmosphere via transpiration. Your plants can also do double duty by serving as a "living fence" between yourself and the neighbors!

Trees

Because trees would most likely be the tallest plants in the rain garden, they should be placed in the rear or in places where they will allow the most sun to reach the smaller plants. Weeping willows are the classic wetlands tree—a mature willow can give off a great deal of water in a day. (Most broad-leafed trees will have the same effect, but willows love water.) Bear in mind, however, that a weeping willow's typical lifespan is only about thirty years. And also be aware that your rain garden will need to be larger to accommodate trees of this size.

If you prefer conifers, consider the swamp cypress and dawn redwood, which are popular choices for marshy gardens. You should realize, though, that these are both deciduous trees—they shed bark as well as needles and leaves—so they can be somewhat messy.

If you prefer more color in the garden, you might want to look into the flowering air drainer trees, such as dogwoods. Even in wintery locations, you can still have color in your rain garden by choosing the proper plants.

Shrubs

In addition to weeping willows, there are quite a few types of shrub willows available—including the pussy willow, which can have either gray or white catkins. These diminutive willows are excellent for smaller rain gardens and can also be planted alongside the trees in larger ones. They are vigorous growers and can be pruned back hard. Shrubs are also a good way to add more color to the garden, as various combinations of leaves, flowers, and even fruit are available.

Smaller Plants

The perimeter of the rain garden is ideal for smaller air drainers. This category includes water irises, marsh marigold, and various rushes. Skunk cabbage can also be used if it is kept under control—these plants can grow as large as four feet tall!

You can finish off the drier edges of the garden with typical swamp flowers like the viola, phlox, meadowsweet, astilbe, hosta, and ferns. These plants are especially good for shadier rain gardens.

Wildlife

If your rain garden handles a considerable amount of runoff, you may be tempted to stock it with a few fish—maybe even the edible kind! However, this is not a good idea, at least as far as the fish are concerned. Besides water vapor, plant transpiration also sends oxygen into the atmosphere. Because the cooling effect of a rain garden is minimal, this removal of oxygen from the water can cause the fish to die, especially during the hot summer months. Even though fish eat mosquito larvae, which would seem like the perfect "green" way to control mosquitoes, the fish wouldn't last long in such an environment. It's best to restrict animal life to whatever volunteers wish to live in your rain garden—toads, peepers, salamanders, as well as butterflies and hummingbirds.

Costs and Savings

Quite a few rain gardens have been started with grant funding. This can be obtained anywhere from the federal level right on down to your own town. Check your local county extension service for possible seed money (so to speak).

In the United States, many rain gardens are still pilot projects, so costs have not yet been fully assessed. However, we do have some idea of how to save money by using this environmentally friendly approach to handling runoff. The greatest cost saving realized so far appears to be in communities where rain gardens are integrated into the initial planning stage. Cost savings at this scale result from the design, such as the ability to reduce gutters, curbs, and trees and other landscaping along the streets. Decreasing these infrastructure expenditures (anywhere from 15 to 50 percent on a given site) can reduce taxes and special assessments for homeowners. In addition, some municipalities are willing to waive wetland impact fees for new communities that make wide use of rain gardens to control their runoff. And in some places, there can be tax savings for homeowners because of reduced need for infrastructure repair or repaving due to water damage.

Because rain gardens are considered a long-term solution for runoff, it's hard to project cost savings at this early stage. Aside from fewer assessments, direct savings for individual homeowners is generally difficult to estimate. However, when used instead of extensive landscaping such as retaining walls and conduits to prevent runoff damage, a rain garden is definitely more cost effective. Also, if you need to install a sump pump into an existing basement, draining into a garden is much cheaper than connecting it to municipal sewers. (In most places, it's illegal to drain sump pumps into storm sewers.) Rain garden studies are ongoing and should provide more information on this aspect of their use in future years.

The typical cost for the construction of a single residential rain garden is less than $1,000, with about one-third going toward excavation and the rest being spent on plants and other material. Of course, the final cost depends on how much piping and other incidentals is needed on your particular property, as well as who does the excavating—the homeowner or a contractor. In Somerset, some homeowners consider their rain gardens to be an "added value" to their houses, a feature that increases the resale price of the property.

In using eco-friendly technology such as rain gardens, we are striving, as Larry Coffman says, to "use nature to protect nature, and make things prettier, too."

Resources

The first and foremost resource available to any kind of home gardener is the office of your local county extension agent. They are in the blue pages of the phone book under "County Government—Extension Services." The invaluable advice and help of this service can smooth the way during unfamiliar procedures such as percolation tests, and the agency can also suggest appropriate rain garden plants that will grow well in your area.

Web Sites

Highly recommended is *The Bioretention Manual of Prince Georges County, Maryland,* the guide written by the people who initiated the rain garden trend in the United States. This document is available for downloading at www.co.pg.md.us/Government/AgencyIndex/DER/ESD/Bioretention/bioretention.asp

As previously mentioned, another useful resource for design purposes—as well as interesting reading on a range of other gardening topics—is the Brooklyn Botanic Garden Web site at www.bbg.org Plan to spend considerable time surfing this information-rich site.

And rounding out our top three is the Web site of the British company Interpave, the Precast Concrete Paving & Kerb Association, at www.paving.org.uk (Click on "Domestic," then "Responsible Rainwater Management" to find their section on constructing rain gardens.)

Two other Web sites of note are www.raingardens.org maintained by Rain Gardens of West Michigan; and the Clean Water Campaign of Georgia www.cleanwatercampaign.com

Books

Dunnett, Nigel; and Clayden, Andy. *Rain Gardens: Bringing Water to Life in the Designed Landscape*. Portland, OR: Timber Press, 2007.

Stephenson, Ashley, ed. *The Garden Planner.* New York: St. Martin's Press, 1981.

Articles

Dietz, Michael; and Clausen, John. "Saturation to Improve Pollutant Retention in a Rain Garden." *Environmental Science & Technology*, Vol. 40 No. 4, 2006, pp. 1335–1340.

Dussaillant, Alejandro; Wu, Chin; and Potter, Kenneth. "Richards Equation Model of a Rain Garden." *Journal of Hydrologic Engineering*, Vol. 9 No. 3, May/June 2004, pp. 219–225.

Goldsby, Terry. "The Good Pond Plants." *Progressive Farmer*, Sept. 2007, p. 20.

Hager, Mary Catherine. "Low-Impact Development." *Stormwater*, Jan./Feb. 2003.

U.S. Environmental Protection Agency. "Maryland Developer Grows 'Rain Gardens' to Control Residential Runoff." *Urban Runoff Notes*, Aug./Sept. 1995, Issue #42.

"Water Algae Can Kill Livestock." *Progressive Farmer*, Aug. 2007, p. 75.

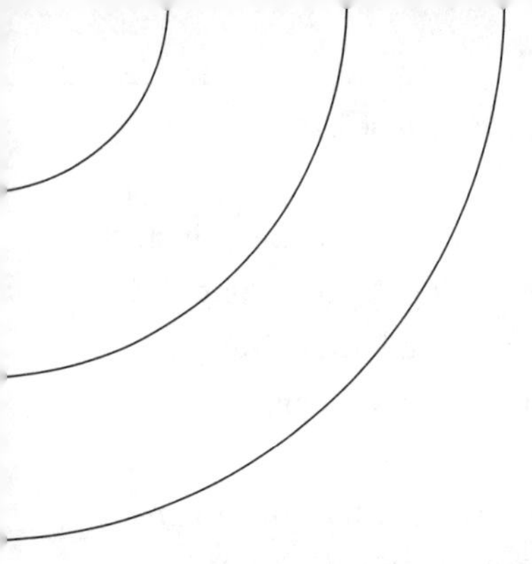

Vermicomposting: A Sustainable Solution at Your Disposal

by Ken Perry

Every year, millions of tons of organic refuse finds its way to landfills, incinerators, municipal sewer systems, and septic systems via trash pickup or garbage disposals. The Environmental Protection Agency estimates that, on average, each American generates 4.3 pounds of trash each day. On a yearly basis, this is equivalent to burying 82,000 football fields six feet deep in compacted garbage. However, about 47 percent of this trash is organic in nature (12 percent is food waste; 35 percent is paper or paperboard) and could be disposed of in better ways. The environmental and financial implications of this are huge. The best way to mitigate the resultant environmental problems might well lie in dealing with it before it enters the waste stream.

Most people are familiar with the process of composting whereby the natural breakdown (decomposition) of organic materials results in a dark soil-like material (humus), which has great value as a soil amendment. Composting is a natural occurrence that we have recognized can be utilized in a managed way to dispose of refuse. One step beyond this, and a complement to it, is the utilization of worms to compost organic matter. This is known as vermicomposting, *vermi* being the Latin name for "worm."

Worms, or No Worms!

There are several advantages of vermicomposting. Regular composting is a thermophilic process, relying on heat generated by the decomposition process to work effectively. This requires a deep pile and varied composition of material. The optimum pile temperature for composting to occur ranges from 90 to 150 degrees F. Pile temperature below this range will result in little or no composting activity.

Vermicomposting, on the other hand, is a mesophilic process, taking place at ambient temperatures. The optimum temperature for the vermicomposting process is from 55 to 80 degrees F. This process involves the worms eating and excreting the organic matter. There is no need to turn or layer a pile (a routine part of regular composting) to achieve the proper temperature.

Regular composting must take place outdoors and the recommended pile size is a minimum of one cubic yard. Vermicomposting can take place in a bin as small as one square foot of surface area that is six inches deep. These temperature and space factors allow for the indoor use of worms. Vermicomposting can easily be done in cold climates and urban settings. Many urban dwellers are happily feeding their kitchen scraps to their composting worms. However, not all worms are suitable for use in a compost bin.

The Right Worm for the Job

Several thousand species of earthworms have been identified by researchers. These many species have been grouped into three categories. The categories are anecic, endogeic, and epigeic worms.

Worm-Enhanced Compost

Vermicompost is enhanced by the digestive process of the worm. It is very high in phosphorus, potassium, calcium, magnesium, and nitrogen compared to thermophilically produced compost (from a regular outdoor bin).

Anecic worms are large worms that live deep in the soil. They may tunnel down as deep as ten feet, establishing permanent burrows. They come to the surface in order to pull organic matter into their tunnels, where it is stored until they are ready to consume it as food. The most familiar worm in this category is the night crawler. When the anecic worm is taken from this environment, it will not grow or reproduce.

Endogeic worms rarely come to the soil surface. They build horizontal burrows and feed on mineral particles and decayed organic matter. These worms are often found around the roots of plants, where they feed on soil rich with decaying matter and bacteria and fungi.

Epigeic worms live in decaying organic matter on the surface of the soil, not in soil. This is the category of worm that can be utilized in vermicomposting. Because it is a surface-dwelling worm, it is possible to replicate its environment in a bin. The earthworm most commonly used in bin systems is the redworm, whose Latin name is *Eisenia fetida*. This worm is found throughout the world. It is the preferred worm for composting systems because of its tolerance for handling any changes in environment. These worms are raised on earthworm farms located throughout the country and can readily be obtained via Internet sales or a visit to a local farm. A vermicomposting system utilizing redworms is feasible on an individual level or on a large-scale municipal or institutional scale. This article will deal mainly with how an individual or family can get started in vermicomposting.

Initial Considerations

Several factors should be taken into consideration when undertaking a vermicomposting venture. Redworms can survive in temperatures ranging from about 35 to 88 degrees F, but are most productive between 65 to 80 degrees F. Temperatures at the extremes will stress the worms—below 50 degrees F, the worms will slow down and become less productive; above 90 degrees F, the worms may well be too hot to survive in a closed bin.

The worms also have a need to live in an aerobic environment; in other words, they need to live in a bin that has a good oxygen flow. It is also important that moisture drains readily out of the system to prevent it from becoming anaerobic, or deprived of oxygen. The ideal moisture level in the system would be in the 60 to 70 percent range. This is roughly equivalent to a damp sponge, which gives off a few drops of water when squeezed. Once you have decided on the proper location for your system, it is time to either make or buy a bin.

Obviously, buying a bin is easier than making one. There are many bins available commercially that are designed specifically for worm composting, some of which facilitate the worms separating from the finished compost as the process evolves. On the other hand, a homemade bin may be customized to fit your needs. A worm bin can be made from many materials. Scrap lumber or an old plastic tote can be used. When building a bin out of wood, make sure not to use pressure-treated lumber. The materials used in the process of pressure treating are harmful to worms. In general, a homemade worm bin should be longer and wider that it is deep. Holes should be drilled on the sides and the cover of the bin to ensure adequate oxygen supply. To allow for drainage, use a quarter-inch bit and drill fifteen holes per square foot on the bottom of the bin. The bin should be elevated so that the moisture that percolates through the system can be collected.

This can also be used as a liquid fertilizer for houseplants or gardens. Some commercial bins are designed to optimize aeration and drainage. Once you have your bin constructed and a location picked out, it is time to obtain your redworms and prepare the bin.

Preparing the Bin

There are some basic steps to take to ensure that your vermicomposting venture is successful. Plastic totes being used to build bins should be washed and exposed to sunlight before worms are placed in the bin.

The bin will need to be prepared for the arrival of the worms. Initially, the bin is lined with a layer of bedding. This is where the worms will live. The food waste is buried in the bedding. Shredded newspaper is a convenient and widely used bedding material. Avoid glossy, colored paper as it has a metallic content that produces toxins harmful to the worms. The shredded newspaper should be fluffed up to a depth of six inches and moistened to the consistency of a damp sponge. Some commercially made bins come with a block of coconut fiber, which can be soaked in a pail of water. This will absorb eight times its weight in moisture and can be spread out in the bin as bedding.

Worms are customarily sold by the pound. When starting out, it is probably a good idea to begin with one or two pounds of worms, keeping in mind that given proper conditions, the worm population will grow over time. The general rule of thumb is redworms will eat half their weight in decomposing material every day. It is a matter of personal choice as to how many worms you want to start your system. To buy worms, you can contact any number of worm farms on the Internet. If you want to stay local, many nurseries and garden centers have connections with worm farms. County extension agents are another great resource.

In any case, once the worms are at home in the bedding, it is time to start feeding them.

A Healthy Lifestyle

Worms like a vegetarian diet. Fruit and vegetable scraps and peels are good food for them. Any number of organic items that would usually be discarded can be fed to them: coffee grounds and filter papers, tea bags, crushed egg shells, pasta and rice, bread and cereal, houseplant clippings and dead flowers, shredded paper, paper towels, and napkins. (However, large amounts of paper are better handled in large-scale vermicomposting operations). The worms do not start to eat until the waste starts to decompose because they have no teeth and thus cannot eat until the food is broken down—they are actually eating the aerobic microorganisms that cause the decomposition. Some people chop up the waste or even puree it to speed up the decomposition process so that the worms can get at the food more quickly.

Unlike traditional composting, which can involve adding selected animal products into the mix, meats and dairy products should not be put into the worm bin to avoid the odor associated with decaying

The Healthy Worm Diet

Technically, anything that can be composted is safe for vermicomposting, though yard waste and coarse items such as twigs and branches should be left outside. Grass clippings that may have been sprayed with chemicals will harm the worms. Pet manure should be avoided because it can contain toxins that cannot be mitigated by the worms' digestive process (and thereby eventually harm your garden). The manure of swine and cattle is OK, but is best left to large commercial operations.

protein products. And while most other compostable items can theoretically go into the worm bin, anything that decomposes slowly should be composted in an outdoor pile.

As the worms settle in to their new bin environment, the population will begin to grow. The rate at which the worm population increases is the variable that determines how much waste can be composted. Given the proper temperature, aeration, food, and space, the worms will multiply rapidly. A mature redworm can produce two to three cocoons per week. Each cocoon will average three hatchlings, which will become mature worms in two to three months. When mature, they will begin to produce cocoons. When the population of the bin exceeds one and a half pounds of worms per square foot of surface area, the worms will slow their reproduction because of space constraints. It is not unusual to start a bin with one pound of worms and have three to five pounds of worms a year later.

Mature worms are characterized by a swollen ring about one-third of the way down their body. This is called the clitellum, which produces the mucus needed for cocoon production. Worms are hermaphrodites, having both male and female sexual organs. However, the worms need a partner to reproduce. Two worms of approximately the same size will come together at the clitellum and exchange sperm. Mucus then hardens and each worm will slough off a cocoon after being joined together for up to three hours. The cocoons look like grape seeds and turn from light to dark as the time to hatch approaches. Redworms can produce many such cocoons during the course of a year.

An Added Benefit

Once the bin has been established and the worm population has begun to grow, the consumption of organic waste by the worms will have noticeably increased. After three or four months, there will be a layer of fine dark material building up on the bottom of the bin. This is the vermicompost or as some call it, the worm castings. This material constitutes the second benefit of feeding your garbage to worms. The first benefit is achieved by taking the organic material out of the waste stream. The second benefit is the production of a wonderful soil amendment for gardens and houseplants. This material is highly valued by those who wish to garden organically and reduce reliance on chemical fertilizers. While not everyone gardens or tends houseplants, there is a good chance they may know someone who does. A gift of vermicompost is sure to be well received.

Harvesting the vermicompost can be done in different ways, depending upon the size and type of bin being used. A commercially made bin with a system of stacking trays makes it quite a simple process. The worms start eating on the bottom level. When the tray is full of vermicompost , another tray is stacked on top of it. These trays have hundreds of holes in them, which the worms can crawl through. As food is added to the new tray, the worms begin to crawl upward through the holes, following the food and leaving behind the finished vermicompost. This process is repeated with a third tray. By the time this tray is full, the worms will have left the bottom tray following their food upward. The vermicompost can now be emptied out of this tray. The empty tray is then placed on top and the process continues.

Harvesting the vermicompost from a single layer bin can be somewhat more labor intensive.

Does the Worm Bin Smell?

In a properly balanced worm bin, there is very little odor. A slight earthy smell might be noticed when opening the bin. However, the worms are actually eating the microbes that cause the obnoxious odors as food decomposes.

One method for separating the worms and compost in a single layer system is to put the food on one side of the bin. Over time, as the worms exhaust the nutrients on the unfed side, they will migrate to the side being supplied with food. It is then possible to take the compost and remaining worms and make a pyramid-shaped pile on a flat surface. Over this pile place a strong light. Because the worms do not like light, they will move to the middle and bottom of the pile. The worms that have congregated at the bottom can be scooped up and put back in the bin.

A more mechanical means of harvesting would involve building two frames. Build one frame 2 × 3 feet long. Then build a 2 × 2-foot frame. Place the 2 × 3-foot frame on top of a tarp laid on a flat surface. Attach ¼-inch hardware cloth to the bottom of the 2 × 2-foot frame so it becomes a sifter, and place it cloth-side down on top of the larger frame. Fill the smaller frame with the compost and worms. Slide it back and forth over the bottom frame. The vermicompost will fall through the hardware cloth and the worms will remain on top. Place the worms back in the bin and collect the vermicompost from the tarp.

Great for the Garden

The vermicompost is a most valuable commodity for anyone who is an indoor or outdoor gardener. When used as a soil amendment in place of chemical fertilize, quite amazing results can be achieved in terms of plant growth. The vermicompost is a superior product when compared to regular compost. Testing has shown it to be significantly higher in phosphorus, calcium, magnesium, potassium and nitrogen. It also has superior moisture-retention properties. Passing through the worm's digestive system, the organic matter acquires enzymes not found in regular thermophilic compost.

Vermicompost is a wonderful medium for starting seedlings in the spring. A mixture of 80 percent potting soil to 20 percent vermi-

Can the Worms Escape?

If stressed in some way, such as by temperatures that are too hot or too cold, the worms may try to escape from the bin. They are capable of going through incredibly small spaces. Leaving a light on for a while will keep the worms in the bin while you correct whatever is causing the stress.

compost will produce strong and healthy seedlings at a very high germination rate. Seeds sewn in rows in a vegetable garden will benefit greatly from vermicompost sprinkled in the bottom of the seed row. Vermicompost placed in the bottom of the hole when transplanting plants will help the plant achieve strong root growth.

A True Partnership

Once your worm bin is in operation and you have begun to harvest vermicompost, you have completed the circle of sustainability. Remember, you are dealing with an ecosystem, not a machine. The worms have turned your garbage into a product that can be used to grow plants and enrich the soil.

Awareness of the implications of behavior on the quality of our environment is growing all the time. While it is important for government and business to strive to improve the environment, it is equally important for individuals to take positive action in this area. The decision to handle your garbage in a sustainable way can only be made by you. Once you have made this decision, there is an army of redworms waiting to be your partner.

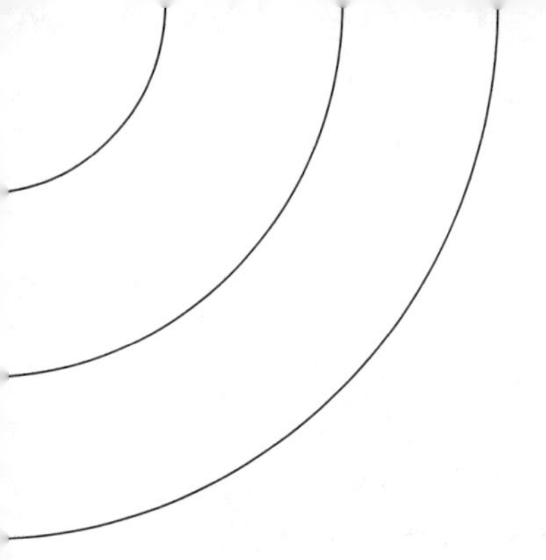

Healthy Homes

by Stephen Collette

So here we are worried about the health of our children, our family members, and the entire world all at the same time. How can we possibly save the world and our children, both within a budget and still have dinner on the table by 5:00? Luckily it's actually easier than you think, cheaper than you think, and you can wear your cape when you are done—and feel like the super hero you are.

Our homes are our sanctuaries, the places we create, maintain, and nurture our families and ourselves. The time and effort we spend on our homes reflects who we are and our values. Having a healthy home is something we all assume that we actually have—never having reason to believe otherwise. This article is going to walk through your house and show you what you are doing right, what you might not be doing so well, and how to make things healthier for your entire family. So take this book and let's start walking around your house together.

First let's start outside, right at the front door. This is the point of entry for almost everyone that comes to your house. Look down, what do you see? A mat hopefully, and if not, this is where we begin.

Mats, especially the really scrubby, rough kinds do one amazing thing—they stop dirt from getting into your house—and they do it really well. Why clean more than necessary? Once inside, that dirt can travel far and deep into a house—right to the farthest corners! This dirt can bring bugs, molds, bacteria, fecal matter, and pesticides into your home, none of which sounds particularly pleasing. So install a good mat, and get people to take their shoes off at the door, at all the doors, and you have just made a major air-quality improvement in your house, and you haven't even stepped inside. A pretty good return for a $25 mat.

Once inside your house, let's go to the kitchen, as it's always a fun place to be. Look up at the range hood on your stove. Do you have one? If you do, does it exhaust outside or inside? Turn it on and put your hand over the top to see if you feel air. It should exhaust outside, especially if you have a gas appliance. Why you ask? Have you ever lit a fire in a fireplace without opening the flue on the chimney? No, of course not, because that would put smoke and combustion products into the house and be dangerous and toxic to my family. So ensure that the range does exhaust outside—this is absolutely critical if you have a gas appliance. However, even if you have an electric range, it is still important because the moisture generated from cooking needs to be removed from the house to prevent the excessive moisture that fosters the growth of mold. Until you can get it exhausted outside, try cracking a kitchen window when cooking. Kitchen range hoods vary in price, but it's a good idea to shop for the quietest one you can afford so you won't turn it off because "it's too noisy."

Drinking water is a big deal in a lot of places, whether municipal water is safe enough or well water is potable. A lot of people buy bottled water. Did you know that the bottlers have fewer guidelines than municipal water has to follow? Just because it comes in nice bottles doesn't make is safer. In fact, we now know that the phthalates (chemical compounds that make plastics more flexible) leaching out of those bottles are hormone disruptors that can affect your health. If you are on municipal water, I recommend filtering the water for chemicals as the bare minimum. This can be a tap or pitcher type carbon filter, taking out the chlorine and such. Remember to change the filter when required, because if it sits too long, it can adversely impact water quality, not improve it. If you want more filtration, you can spend as much as you want, but carbon filter will do the brunt of the work for you. For well water, have it tested—ideally every three months. If you are concerned about runoff or contamination, spend the money and have it tested for those concerns to ensure the safety of your water. Inspect your well annually, or have a professional do it for you. With a thorough analysis completed, you will know exactly which contaminants you want to filter out and buy the most suitable filtration method.

Now let's walk into your living room. Look down again. Carpet or solid surface? Well if the answer is carpet, then we need to look at your vacuum. We usually buy vacuums based on sucking power, but have you ever looked at the other end of the vacuum, the part that exhausts? Think about this: for all the air coming in, at the other end it blows it back out, and depending on the quality of your filter, that air might be seriously dirty. Vacuum filters are critical to air quality—the better the filter, the better the air. HEPA (High Efficiency Particulate Air) filters are the best out there. They trap the smallest bits possible. Nothing beats HEPA. Ensure you purchase a true HEPA, as you will see lots of knock-offs out there. There are variations in quality even among HEPA machines. Inexpensive ones have small filters and allow the air to bypass them, while the more expensive units are better built, have bigger filters, and are airtight, which shut off when the filter is clogged, ensuring you get the filtered air—and only the filtered air—coming out. These are worthwhile investments that you will pass down to your grandkids.

www.indexopen.com

The indoor-air quality of homes with hardwood floors and area rugs that can be cleaned outdoors is often better than that of carpeted homes. Carpet can trap allergens and particulates.

The very best vacuum is one that exhausts outside, like central vacuums should. To make sure a central vacuum is working properly, run to your central vac canister now and see if there is an exhaust pipe coming off of it and going outside (I said outside, not into the garage). If not, then it's exhausting in your house or garage, and that isn't very effective, now is it? Ideally they exhaust outside to get rid of the particulates.

Regardless of what type of vacuum you have, it helps to vacuum, so keep doing it. Go to a vacuum shop and see if you can get a better filter/bag for your unit, improving its filtering ability. Then save up and get a HEPA vacuum when you can. The best option however is to get rid of the carpet completely.

Dust Bunny: Friend or Foe?

Getting rid of carpet is a big deal; we love that warm fuzzy feeling of carpet, especially in the cold winter. But have you ever seen a dust bunny on a carpet? How about on a solid surface floor? Sure on a solid floor, all the time. Well dust bunnies, contrary to popular beliefs, are our friends (I tell my wife that every day). The house's natural convective currents corral the dust for easy collection every day, creating the bunnies, which are too heavy to be airborne. This single fact makes them, and the solid surface flooring better for your health—you don't breathe in a dust bunny! Carpets don't have dust bunnies as the ultrafine particles are scattered all over the carpet until you walk across them and stir them up, sending them into the air where you breathe them in and they lodge deep in our lungs. Area rugs are better, as you can take them outside, hang them over the fence and beat them with a tennis racket. It's cheaper than therapy and is a great, healthy alternative. Sweeping solid surface floors is just as effective as vacuuming, so use one or the other. Just avoid using a chemical disposable floor sweeper, as they happen to contain a fair number of chemicals, which leave a film on your floor for your crawling kids and pets to absorb. Stay natural with soap and water if you need to wash, or a microfiber sweeper that can be washed and reused hundreds of times.

Since you are already down looking at the dust and dust bunnies, go ahead and take a look at your ductwork. Can't get your head in? Try sticking a digital camera down your ducts and take a picture. You'll be pretty amazed. Ductwork is a great place for dust to hang out, along with toys and bugs and dog food. You should really try to keep them clean because ducts are the lungs of your house. Dirty ducts moving dirty air equals coughing kids. So stick that fancy vacuum you have down there and clean them out. All of them. Try to do this regularly since most of the debris in ductwork is in the first few feet anyway. Every couple of years have a company come in and clean them thoroughly—more frequently if you have lots of kids/carpets/pets/allergies.

Now down to the basement to see the bottom half of those ducts and the furnace. If you can tape up the ductwork joints, then you have done two amazing things: First, you have improved the air quality of the house, as the duct joints allow dirty, dusty air from basements, attics, walls, and other yucky places to be drawn into the duct through the Venturi effect (air gets sucked in as the furnace air passes by). Second, because the air pulled into the duct is cooler that the heated air, you are paying lots to have dirty air delivered to your room, so taping the joints makes things both cleaner and more energy efficient. Nice. Be sure to use aluminum tape and not duct tape, because duct tape is not designed to work on ducts—it's temperature sensitive.

The furnace is the last bit of this breathing house portion. Look at your furnace—and more importantly—look at what you have stored around the furnace. Any paints, solvents, glues, gardening sprays, pesticides, etc. near the really large air sucking machine that brings this air to you and your family? Right. We store our junk in the furnace room, but really that isn't as smart as you would think. All those cans of paint are leaking VOC's (Volatile Organic Compounds), which are the toxic stink in paint. Pesticides are designed to kill living creatures, and don't discern between a stinkbug and you. These are all leaking and being drawn through your house. Don't believe me? Then try opening a can of paint, the one with an inch of paint left for just in case a wall needs a touch-up. Is it gone, and dried up? That's because the volatile chemicals escaped, leaving the film. Send that stuff to your hazardous waste depot and improve your air quality dramatically.

Now pull out the furnace filter. Let's assume you have the fiberglass furnace filter that comes standard for everyone. This filter is designed to stop your cat from getting wedged in the furnace fan, and not much else. It doesn't do a thing for air quality and is reducing the life of your furnace. Filters are rated 1 to 20 on the MERV

(Minimum Efficiency Reporting Value) scale and fiberglass filters score a 1. HEPA filters (like those in vacuums are the best) score a 17 out of 20. Great, but they are pretty expensive and can cost around $1,000. Some people really need this type of filtration, but not all of us. A one-inch paper-pleated filter will cost about $25 and will give you a 12 out of 20. That is a great return on investment. These filters should be changed every three months. These filters will dramatically improve the air quality in your home.

Since we are down in the basement now, let's look at your dehumidifier. Dehumidifiers are critical to basements. Basements are dark, damp, and musty, and have been since they were cold cellars and we stored rutabagas in them, hoping they would grow mold so we wouldn't have to eat them. Nothing has changed; we still don't eat rutabagas. Whenever the heat is not on, you need to dehumidify, period. Relative humidity levels should be around 40 to 50 percent in the basement. If your basement smells musty, that is caused by excessive moisture. Dehumidifiers are sized for square footage, so make sure you get one that can do the job. The old brown models from your grandparent's place will suck as much electricity as water and cost you a fortune to operate. Switch it out for an Energy Star rated model, so you are using the least amount of electricity. Buy one with a built-in hygrometer so you can set it to the proper humidity level—the new ones have built-in hose bibs so you can drain it into the floor drain or tub and you never have to think about it again.

OK, now let's find your cleaning closet. Take a good long smell of your cleaning products. Did you cough? Does it smell like April showers, fresh mountain, dewberry springtime, or whatever stink they put in the product? Let's sit back and think about a few things. First, cleaning products that we buy at the grocery store are made with petroleum products—lots of them. Since gasoline is stinky, they add more petroleum based products to make them smell better. These chemicals are seriously toxic to your family. Carcinogens (cancer causing), hormone disrupters, blood disrupters, neurological toxins, and poisons are just a few of the issues with these cleaners. They are doing more damage to your family than if you didn't clean your house. Honestly. So let's get simple. Do you remember Grandma using baking soda and vinegar? Grandma wasn't dumb, you know, she knew how to clean. These two work amazingly well and there are lots of recipes online that you can find to make your own cleaners. Get the kids to make them for science class. If you don't want to make your own, try going to your local health food store and switch out your current cleaning product for a more natural based product. How can you tell if it's natural based? A good rule of thumb is if the ingredient list has words with more than six syllables, then it's probably bad for you. Changing your cleaning products will make the single biggest difference in air quality and health to your family that you can do for little or no cost. This one is paramount above all others.

Finally let's go to your bedroom, hopefully the healthiest place in your house, since it's the one room you spend the most time in. So already we know that solid surface is better, we have stopped with the air fresheners, and switched to beeswax candles instead of paraffin (paraffin is a petroleum product too) to set the mood. Let's get the clothes off the floor, which makes it difficult to clean, so try adding some more shelves to the closet, getting some more hangers, or just making the laundry bin easier to hit. Your bed itself is the focus here, so let's finish up with it.

Dust mites live with us and are part of our lives. They eat our skin cells, hair follicles, and other stuff. They live in our beds lots, since there happens to be those sources for them, plus nice warm and moist conditions to make for very happy dust mites. The first thing we do when we get up in the morning is tuck the little guys in for the day by making our bed. This gives them all the food, the warmth, and the moisture from all that sweating in the night to make for a great party. So the dust mites drink, eat and be merry while you are at work. Now we are not actually allergic to dust mites—but to their excrement, unfortunately. We need to reduce both to be healthy. The easiest way to deal with dust mites, is to take away the ideal breeding conditions. That would mean, airing out your bed, by folding the sheets back and not making it right away. (Note, if this page is folded down, your teenager has been reading this.) It is however absolutely true, since dust mites don't like sunlight (ultraviolet) and will shrivel up and die, thereby reducing your allergen load. Now for pillows. After 10 years your pillow is half original material and half dust mite and dust mite feces, according to a University of Manchester study, so change your pillows every few years, and hang them outside to bleach in the sun. Do the same for your mattress and give the neighbors something to talk about. So by just airing out your bed, which costs absolutely nothing, you will make things significantly better for health and wellness.

There are many more things that you can do, most are just as easy as these points. Try finding a building biologist or healthy home inspector near you to help find more ways to make your family healthier and identify the things that may be more serious. Taking steps like these will ensure that you and your family will have many years enjoying your healthy house.

An Introduction to Green Roofs and Walls

by Scott D. Appell

As a native New Yorker and professional horticulturist, I needed living plants surrounding me at all times. Having had no outdoor in-ground space around my former SoHo artists' loft apartment building, I earnestly cultivated window-boxes on every window ledge, developed an extensive fire-escape garden (though short lived as it was illegal to block the fire escape), and created an astonishing interior landscape with enormous houseplants, twelve-foot-tall potted tropical trees (illuminated by commercial hydroponic lighting fixtures), and a stocked goldfish pool complete with re-cycling fountain. And before moving to the Caribbean—where I now reside—the last building-wide endeavor was to create a typical urban rooftop garden of containerized trees, shrubs, flowers, and vegetables. Although modest, it was a lovely and magical setting for all of my neighbors to commune among the flora—even though it was hot, smoggy, and oddly claustrophobic.

For decades, the general conception of rooftop gardens, whether humble or vast, amateur or professional, were restricted to terra cotta or plastic flower pots (great and small), fiberglass containers of every imaginable design, or astronomically pricey, custom-made, cedar or teak planters; all acquired for the cultivation of an infinitely diverse world of plants.

But recently there has been a dramatic and involved evolution of the perception of a "roof garden." Innovations in design and implementation as well as breakthroughs in horticulture, combined with a deep need to cultivate and nurture the Earth as living entity (not solely flora or fauna or, indeed, ourselves) has produced a groundbreaking outcome: the "green roof." Now entire elevated, horizontal, and pitched rooftop surfaces may be landscaped—in the truest sense of the word—with vast, verdant areas of perennials, trees, shrubs, and even lawns enhanced with birdsong, the whir of hummingbirds, the buzz of bees, and the flutter of butterflies. The sterile roofs of apartment buildings, banks, parking garages, factories, schools (a great eco-wise student project), hospitals (rehabilitating, to say the least), and private homes can become a microcosm of an unfettered, fertile Garden of Eden. Utopian, eco-friendly parks in the sky have arrived; and from that concept, the idea has migrated over the cornice and downward to transforming the walls of the edifice itself with the emergence of "green walls," also called vertical gardens.

Green Roofs

What are green roofs? As the name suggests, they are intentionally vegetated (planted) roofs—not ones that have just gone wild and weedy through neglect. In reality, anything from the aforementioned rooftop garden through extensive, lush landscapes to mowed turf grass (a rooftop *petite déjeuner sur l'herbe* or round of croquet, perhaps?) to even a smattering of living mosses and lichens qualify under the description. Also known as brown roofs or eco-roofs when used for conservation purposes, the basic maxim for green roofs is that

Bill Shank

The ficus plants growing on the walls and roof of this house makes the indoor temperature several degrees cooler each summer.

nature doesn't just live in the countryside: buildings (of all types) can provide fantastic habitats for wildlife—and humans—too.

What are the benefits of green roofs? They are an attractive roofing option that can reduce urban heat islands by providing shade and transpiration (the release of water from plants which cools the surrounding air). They also reduce sewage system loads by assimilating large amounts of rainwater, absorbing air pollution, collecting airborne particulates, and storing carbon. A green roof also protects the underlying roof material by eliminating exposure to the sun's ultraviolet (UV) radiation and extreme daily temperature fluctuations—the ambient exterior temperature of a green roof is 20 to 80 Fahrenheit degrees cooler than that of surrounding unplanted roofs. They also serve as living environments that provide habitats for birds and other small animals while addressing growing concerns about urban quality of life. They reduce decibel levels transmitting from the exterior surroundings and insulate the building from extreme temperatures, mainly by keeping the building interior cooler in the summer.

Furthermore, green roofs actually reduce stormwater runoff. As impermeable surfaces like buildings and pavement replace open space and vegetation, green roofs can play an increasingly important role in stormwater management. During rainstorms, green roofs act as a sponge, absorbing much of the water that would otherwise run off. Researchers estimate that three to five inches of soil or growing medium absorbs 75 percent of one-half inch or less of rainfall. Green roofs also filter and break down pollution from rainwater. This is achieved by the root systems' bacteria and fungi, which utilize the natural filtering processes. As a result, nitrogen and phosphorous are broken down and detoxified. The beneficial process increases over time as rooftop plants and root systems mature.

Critical Decision: What Type of Green Roof?

To complicate matters, there are two types of green roofs: intensive and extensive.

An **intensive green roof** requires a minimum of one foot of soil depth and can accommodate fairly large trees and shrubs, perennials, and comparatively complex landscapes. It adds between 80 to 150 pounds per square foot of load to building structure depending on the plant selection, soil characteristics, or type of substrate (the planting medium). Regular foot traffic is not only accommodated, but also encouraged. Walkways, garden structures, benches, and water features can complete the overall design. There is significant, regular maintenance required to keep the planting tidy and weed-free. A complex irrigation and drainage system is also required.

Conversely, **extensive green roofs** require only one to five inches of soil depth and are capable of including many kinds of perennials, ground covers, dwarf shrubs, and grasses. It adds only 12 to 50 pounds per square foot depending on soil characteristics and the type of substrate. However, extensive green roofs are not usually designed for public accessibility, they are intended, rather, to be viewed from observation areas around the perimeter, although a simple walkway of pavers (flat rock blocks) used for annual maintenance is highly desirable because it limits the trodding upon sensitive or brittle plant material and the compaction of the soil. Alternately, planted "green islands" can be created with the actual roof surface acting as paths between them; the actual roof surface may be ornamented with a layer of lightweight pumice stone, lava rock or attractive mulch and irrigation systems are relatively simple.

Both styles of green roofs require a slope of at least 1.5 percent to ensure proper drainage. Aside from this minimal slope for drainage, these gardens are created on flat rooftops.

For the average homeowner, the extensive green roof is more feasible to afford, build, plant, and ultimately maintain by virtue of its more shallow soil depth. If large trees are desired, it probably would be easier to have appropriate planter boxes designed and installed than to have to deal with the extra overall added substrate, additional weight, upkeep, etc. Pitched roofs are not exempt from being "greened," but they'll need an additional specialized support system to hold the planting in place, a modified irrigation system—administering water and nutrients from the apex of the slope to trickle downward over the planting and perhaps a gray-water runoff system installed at the roof's gutter or at ground level to be translocated and utilized at an in-ground planting elsewhere. This will increase the initial installation costs, but drainage will never be an issue. Pitched roofs should be designed as extensive green roofs, using perhaps an inch of planting medium, as well as the appropriate plants. Cacti, succulents (fleshy plants that store water in specially adapted organs), alpine plants, and some Mediterranean herbs are particularly well-suited for angled culture, being "sure-footed" growers and requiring far less frequent watering to flourish.

Assembling the Roof

A green roofing system can consist of a series of assembled layers within a containing frame of pressure-treated wood or a galvanized metal. The six layers from bottom to top are as follows.

The **waterproofing layer** is applied to the roof surface itself because asphalt and bitumen are very susceptible to damage by roots, which may lead to leaks. The next layer, the **root membrane** may consist of a commercial pond liner, butyl lining, or 300-micron damp-proof polythene sheet spread upon the roof's surface. The next layer is called the **filter sheet**, which allows water to drain off the roof, but stops the escape of ultra-fine particles from the planting medium. The **moisture blanket** is used for extensive green roofs, and will ensure the soil retains enough moisture to support plant life. Industrial ones that do not disintegrate can be procured, , but recycled cardboard boxes or old blankets achieve the same (though temporary) effect. As the name implies, the **drainage layer** facilitates the channeling-off of liquid. Commercial products can store water as well and are made of plastic or geotextile materials. They often resemble egg cartons or the textured walling in recording studios. The last layer is the **soil or substrate layer**, which is the actual growing medium into which the plants are set. You have two options here: a true soil mixture (which is very fertile but heavy) or a "soilless mixture" (which is not naturally fertile but very light-weight) composed of peatmoss, perlite, vermiculite, crushed porous pumice stone, or lava rock. In either case, the addition of horticultural or aquarium charcoal to the substrate proves beneficial in keeping water-soaked soils "sweet" by avoiding anaerobic bacteria, root rot, and plant death.

Alternatively, I have seen intensive green roofs made of custom-made galvanized steel planters, two inches deep with drainage holes drilled into them. They must be brought up in the freight elevator in segments or hauled up the exterior of the building with pulleys, fit into place like a giant jigsaw puzzle upon the waterproofed roof surface, filled with substrate, and planted. This is probably an easier method, but extremely costly.

Currently, the upfront cost of an extensive green roof in the United States starts at about $8 per square foot, which includes materials, preparation work, and installation. In comparison, the cost of a traditional roof starts at about $1.25, while cool roof membranes start at approximately $1.50 per square foot. In addition, extensive green roofs cost more than traditional roofs because they require more material and labor for installation, in part, because of the scarcity of green roof contractors. As the demand for green rooftop gardens increases, upfront costs will likely decrease. However, if you take into account the future summertime energy savings, the price of a green roof over its lifetime is closer to that of a traditional roof. In fact, the vegetation can extend the life of a roof, because less solar energy reaches the roof substrate, limiting damage from UV radiation as well as daily temperature fluctuations, both of which cause repeated contraction and expansion. Furthermore, depending on local codes, it might be possible to do without stormwater infrastructure investments.

Getting Help

In October 2001, the American Society for the Testing of Materials (ASTM) established a Green Roof Standards Task Group, and their focus is to provide national standards for green roof technologies. Members have defined and reviewed green roofs and provide guidelines for further study. This Task Group has been set up under the E06.71 Subcommittee on Sustainability in Buildings, part of the 1946 ASTM Committee E06 on Performance of Buildings. For more information, access the WK575 Practice for Assessment of Green Roofs dated February 7, 2003.

In addition, design professionals can offer a great deal of help in establishing a green roof or wall. They can provide you with essential information and creative expertise. What kinds of consultants will you need to hire and what can you expect them to do?

Basically, **architects** and **engineers** can evaluate the strength of a building. **Landscape architects** can design a horizontal or vertical garden and select the necessary plant material for it within your budget. They can also design decking, paving, garden structures (lath houses, gazebos, and such) as well as lighting and irrigation systems. **Contractors** build things from the designs of qualified professionals.

The level of skill you need and the number of consultants required will vary with the complexity of your project. How do you find your consultant(s)? Check with local professional associations—New York City, for example, has an organization of horticultural specialists known as Metro-Hort. Ask a potential consultant for a client list (including contact numbers) and get in touch with those people to ask their opinion and ask to visit former installations to see for yourself. Don't be bashful about scrutinizing a prospective candidate; the extra legwork works for your advantage.

Green Walls

If the thought of a cooling, verdant, vegetal rooftop sounds remarkable, imagine the sight of a growing wall. The overall effect is that of a gargantuan tapestry of innumerable floral textures and colors, depending on the plants selected; foliage in infinite shades of greens, blues, grays, burgundies, and the various tones of chartreuse and yellow from variegated leaves. Many appropriate perennial plants have a season of flowering as well, adding to the visual splendor. Of course, the vertical landscape will attract a variety of bird and insect life, and in the southern states, small reptiles as well.

Fabrication is remarkably cutting-edge and requires 10-millimeter-thick (about 0.39-inch) waterproof PVC sheeting covered with two layers of polyamide felt (a nonfabric polymer material that acts like a capillary to transport moisture), which is attached with construction staples. Holes (which can snuggly accommodate a small root ball) are strategically cut into the felt for the plants in the desired vertical landscape design. Imagine a gigantic slice of Swiss cheese with artfully arranged holes. A narrow hose, punctured every 4 inches with a 2-millimeter (about 0.0787-inch) hole, will be attached horizontally to the length of the top of the wall above the planting. An electric timing device makes it easy to ensure regular, light administrations of a diluted nutrient solution. This requires a proportioner, or "commercial greenhouse hose-attached feeder" to mix water and nutrients—to be affixed between the water source and hose (visit www.charleysgreenhouse.com). This will emulate a slow trickle coursing its way down a mossy rock face. The mixture should be dispensed at least twice daily initially or more frequently if the wall faces south or west—both very hot and drying exposures. It should be noted that when using cacti and succulents as well as other drought-resistant plants, watering can be cut down to a seven-day cycle (or longer) depending on how long the felt stays moist—making sure the layers of felt have become thoroughly saturated before turning off the water pressure. A ground-level gutter can divert the nutritional runoff liquid to other gardens as needed in the form of gray water.

The structure is then attached to a metal skeleton (PVC side towards the wall) that stands two to three inches out from the supporting waterproofed wall. The space traps a cushion of air, which acts as insulation both for the building and for the plants' roots. Young vegetation in small containers (or even seedlings) straight from the nursery is employed. The existing root ball is pushed through the snug hole in the felt and the roots will grow in between the moist felt and PVC sheeting to intermesh with its neighbors, creating a solid mass of roots. It weighs about 30 pounds per square yard. A wall can last at least 30 years with minimum care: although depending on the ultimate height of the wall, ladders, scaffolding or pulleys and hoists will be needed for the annual spring-cleaning (removing dead growth, possible plant replacement, pruning, etc.). Because there is no soil, weeds are practically nonexistent.

This technique is highly adaptable for home use: from a 20 × 23-foot wall of a single story private residence to fair-sized apartments or office buildings. The Musée du Quai Branly in Paris boasts a lush, internationally renowned 8,600-square-foot, three-story-tall façade lodging 15,000 individual plants!

A far less ambitious system is being developed by Elevated Landscape Technologies in Canada. It consists of modular, interlocked rectangular planting containers—sort of angled window-boxes—composed of a high-density polyethylene, a stable plastic resistant to ultraviolet rays, temperatures, and chemicals in fertilizers. They may be attached to the wall and filled with a standard planting medium. Utilizing a "true" soil, slow-release, timed fertilizer granules can be added to the mixture and will alleviate the need for any additional fertilizing. Once again, a gutter can catch and divert runoff as gray water. When the plant material has filled in, the effect is a true vertical garden.

The Hardiness Zone Chart

Before collecting or cultivating plants, be aware of the United States Department of Agriculture (USDA) Hardiness Zones. The USDA has set up an easy-to-follow, fundamental guideline for potential gardeners. The various categories, called Zones—which range from USDA Zone 1 to USDA Zone 11—reflect the annual winter low temperature for a typical year in a specific geographical location within Canada, the United States, and points south. Basically, the higher the number of a Zone, the warmer the winters. For example, USDA Zone 1 lies in midcentral Canada, and USDA Zone 11 falls in the Florida Keys, Hawaii, and the Caribbean. Sadly, with global warming, this chart will ultimately have to be reworked by the USDA as the winters are becoming noticeably warmer in the boreal states; horticulturists nationwide are reporting the successful cultivation of flora which would not survive the ambient hibernal temperatures a decade ago.

USDA Zone 1: Below -50°F
USDA Zone 2: -50°F to -40°F
USDA Zone 3: -40°F to -30°F
USDA Zone 4: -30°F to -20°F

USDA Zone 5: -20°F to -10°F
USDA Zone 6: -10°F to 0°F
USDA Zone 7: 0°F to 10°F
USDA Zone 8: 10°F to 20°F
USDA Zone 9: 20°F to 30°F
USDA Zone 10: 30°F to 40°F
USDA Zone 11: Above 40°F

Some Thoughts on Planting, Care and Culture

By virtue of its large expanse, planting a green roof may prove to be a little tedious—you will need plenty of time and elbow grease as well as sunscreen, a wide-brimmed hat, and kneepads for rooftop plantings or tall ladders, pulleys, and scaffolding for vertical gardens. Don't forget an array of gardening tools—you'll need the same types as for the typical in-ground landscape. Of course, a water source is critical—many have forgotten to check if there is a rooftop spigot! What will you do with garden refuse—weeds, leaves, dead plants, and other organic debris? Will you compost on the roof? Lug waste downstairs to an allocated ground-level area? Pest control: organic or otherwise?

Intensive green roofs are relatively easy to plant by virtue of the deeper soil—it is pretty much like planting flora in the ground. However, extensive styles with as little as one inch of substrate, may need modified planting techniques. For example, cutting the root ball from the bottom upward, creating halves or thirds that can be gently pried apart (without breakage) to facilitate sitting comfortably into the allotted depth. Purchasing plants in sufficient quantities grown in small containers—2 to 3 inches wide—means there is a smaller root ball to contend with, which translates as minimized root damage. Or utilize seedlings. Bare rooted plants work well, too. Be sure to water them thoroughly after transplanting (the addition of SUPERthrive™ [see below] to the water truly does reduce transplant shock). Conversely, when planting cacti and succulents, the opposite rule applies: do not water the newly planted flora for a week to ten days after installment. This allows the damaged roots to callous over and will avoid root rot and plant death. In addition, never mix succulent plants with those that need frequent watering.

Because of the limited, often lean or non-nutritive qualities of the planting medium of green roofs—or the complete lack of soil in green walls, a continuous fertilizing regimen is hypercritical for success. Having a removable proportioner attached to the irrigation system makes application easy. Liquid seaweed and fish emulsion are excellent organic, liquid, water-soluble fertilizers, as are compost or manure tea when it is possible to make them. Although granular commercial fertilizers have their merits, the runoff from continuous use can negatively effect water tables and ground water and burn roots or foliage during dry conditions. The absolute best (in my far-from-humble-opinion) supplement to be employed in conjunction with fertilizers is a trademarked product called SUPERthrive™. It is an extremely concentrated—1 or 2 drops per gallon of water or 3 liquid ounces per 100 gallons of water—mixture of micronutrients and vitamins that produces absolutely astonishing results in plant growth without root burn or buildup of soluble mineral salts or any of other negative byproducts of chemical plant foods. It is available at most upscale nurseries.

Suggested Plants for Green Roofs and Green Walls

There are no hard-and-fast rules for planting on a green roof or wall, other than it's practical to use climate appropriate species that increase in width (but not necessarily height), grow quickly for immediate coverage, and do not require semiannual division or pruning. This includes clumping, spreading or prostrate, herbaceous perennials, alpine plants, herbs, cacti, succulents, and dwarf shrubs.

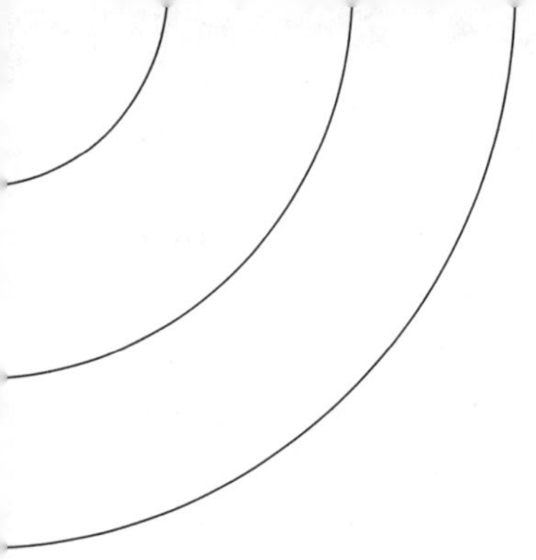

A Guide for Carbon-Free Living

by John Ivanko

Weird weather. Extreme storms. Apple trees blooming in the fall, not spring. Longer growing seasons, by weeks, not days.

There's mounting evidence that our climate is changing and most of the leading researchers around the world are pinning the dramatic changes on human activities. While some political leaders, corporations, and individuals prefer to stay on the sidelines in addressing the potentially catastrophic impacts brought about by climate change—also called global warming—a growing number of people, companies, and organizations are aggressively pursuing ways to head off the most severe impacts of an overheating planet. They're choosing to live a carbon negative or carbon-free life.

The Greenhouse Effect and Global Warming

When sunlight penetrates Earth's insulating atmosphere of greenhouse gases, gases which include carbon dioxide, water vapor, methane, and nitrous oxide, it's converted to infrared energy and emitted back into space. Greenhouse gases, or GHG, in the atmosphere absorb some of the heat creating the so-called greenhouse effect, stabilizing climate and making it suitable for life.

By burning fossil fuels like coal, natural gas, and oil to power our machines, heat buildings, or generate electricity, we're increasing the concentration of carbon dioxide and other greenhouse gases, thus trapping more heat that would otherwise escape into space. The more potent greenhouse gases, like methane, come from the expanding agricultural practices related to livestock and growing human populations. Nitrous oxides are most prevalent from industrial factories in increasingly industrialized economies. While there's been naturally occurring cycles of warm and cool periods on Earth, present carbon dioxide levels already are far above anything measured in the previous 650,000-year period.

Global warming is not just about the rising average planetary temperature, but its effect on weather patterns, atmospheric conditions, and ocean currents, creating increased variability and unpredictability in weather. Global warming fosters increasingly severe weather events and far-reaching impacts like rising oceans or receding freshwater lake levels. Most of the scientific community agree that the impacts of global warming—increased intensity of storms, increased frequency of hurricanes and tornadoes, extended periods of drought, extreme heat waves, torrential rain downfalls—are likely to get more pronounced as we move further into this century, contributing to other weather-related events like prolific wildfires, widespread outbreaks of disease, loss of food security, or extreme water shortages.

According to the planet's leading scientists authoring the latest 2007 report from the Intergovernmental Panel on Climate Change (IPCC), global warming has rocketed to "very likely" being due to humans' increase in greenhouse gas emissions. On a planet where the average American contributes 15,000 pounds (7.5 tons) of carbon dioxide per year—enough to fill up the Goodyear Blimp—a sense of urgency is growing, thanks to increased public awareness, media attention, and scientific validity. According to the IPCC, the goal is to reduce greenhouse gas emissions below 1990 levels—about 60 to 80 percent—just to stabilize our planet's already elevated greenhouse gas levels.

Going on a Carbon Diet

There are numerous ways to go on a carbon diet and begin living a net zero, carbon-neutral or -negative life. This can be accomplished by both reducing our carbon dioxide emissions (and, if possible, methane emissions) from our lifestyle and livelihood as well as paying for carbon offsets from organizations that invest in projects that counteract our emissions that are hard to avoid, like airline travel for business or heating a home with natural gas.

To help guide your reduction of carbon emissions, Godo Stoyke, author of *Carbon Buster's Home Energy Handbook*, details numerous ways to optimize and prioritize your investment in energy-saving appliances and technologies that offer the highest returns for reducing your carbon dioxide emissions. He calls it carbon busting: Employing the most cost-effective methods to drastically lower greenhouse gas emissions. Of course, there's plenty of behavioral and lifestyle decisions that help cut your carbon emissions without spending any money at all. In *Stormy Weather: 101 Solutions to Global Climate Change*, Guy Dauncey lays out various practical options that address your work, community, and lifestyle.

The following are various facets where you can go carbon free, sometimes incorporating carbon-busting strategies while other times just making simple changes in the way you live, work, shop, travel, and eat. For those aspects of your lifestyle and livelihood where you cannot reduce your emissions, purchase carbon offsets.

Inventory Your Carbon Footprint

Not including business activities, an average household in the United States living in a 2,000- to 2,500-square-foot home with one sedan car and one SUV (or light truck) emits 57,000 pounds of carbon dioxide each year. This can be broken down as air travel (1,080 pounds), gasoline (26,920 pounds), natural gas (9,027 pounds), water (697 pounds), and electricity (19,323 pounds), writes Stoyke in *Carbon Buster's Handbook*. How do you compare?

A wide assortment of carbon dioxide calculators are available online to assist you in determining your emissions from transportation (i.e., automobile and airline travel), heating and cooling, and various other aspects of how you live and work. Before going on a low-carbon diet, see how much electricity, natural gas, heating oil, and gasoline or diesel fuel you're already using. Tallying a year's worth of utility statements and gas station bills provides a clearer picture of your energy usage patterns and carbon emissions. Plus, when faced with an estimate for a new appliance or renewable energy system, you'll be better equipped to factor in the energy costs.

Stoyke shares analyses that explore options for transportation, appliances, lighting, and heating/cooling. Some items, like a fifteen-year-old refrigerator, should be replaced immediately, while other appliances can be replaced after they're worn out. It turns out that investing in reducing carbon emissions provides a better yield than stashing away your savings in government bonds yielding 5 percent or investing in mutual funds earning a 10 percent annualized return.

Carbon-Free: On the Road

Transportation accounts for the largest source of greenhouse gas emissions, so exhausting ways to eliminate or minimize vehicle use goes a long way.

Walk, Bicycle, or Use Public Transportation

Walk or bicycle to your job, store, and community activities, since every gallon of gasoline you avoid burning is one less pound of carbon dioxide released into the air. About 40 percent of all vehicle trips in the United States are within 2 miles of home. Small efforts can add up—instead of using a car that gets 25 mpg for a 10-mile round trip, regular commuting by bicycle can prevent about a ton of CO_2 from entering the atmosphere each year (50 miles per week times 50 weeks divided by 25 MPG).

Choose High-MPG Vehicles and Try Biofuels

Vehicle use and liquid fuel choice are perhaps the most important and cost-effective ways to reduce your carbon emissions.

• Select the most fuel-efficient car that meets your needs, with the highest miles per gallon, or MPG, rating. (see www.fueleconomy.gov) By replacing every automobile getting 25 MPG—approximately the U.S. average—with a vehicle that gets 45 MPG, emissions would be cut by almost a billion tons a year if the vehicle is driven the U. S. average of 10,000 miles a year.

• Switch to a fuel-efficient gas-electric hybrid car like the Toyota Prius or Honda Insight.

• Diesel automobiles like the Volkswagen Jetta TDI that operate at least part of the year on a blend of biodiesel, can reduce emissions significantly. Select a diesel vehicle and fill it with as high a blend of biodiesel as you can get that's appropriate for your climate. Biodiesel does have a high jell point, so it's not ideal for cold weather use.

• You can also select a vehicle that you can fill up with widely available corn-based ethanol, a fuel made from corn and blended with gas with ratios as high as 85 percent (E85). According to Argonne National Lab, an ethanol blend of just 10 percent can reduce GHG emissions by more than 12 percent when compared to unleaded gasoline. But there's debate as to whether you're actually coming out ahead at the pump based on the energy value of the corn-based ethanol; you might end up using just as much, just filling up more. So-called cellulosic ethanol made from biomass like paper pulp or fast-growing switchgrass is better for the environment and provides more energy per unit of input; however, cellulosic ethanol is still under development.

• Better yet, avoid car ownership by renting one when needed through car-sharing programs that feature hybrid vehicle fleets.

Carbon-Free: In the Home

Select Energy Efficient Appliances and Lighting

Energy efficiency and conservation remain the most cost-effective ways to reduce your expenses and cut your carbon dioxide emissions. Money saved on your energy bill can be set aside for additional replacements or appliance upgrades. Electricity is the most expensive form of energy and mostly produced with coal-fired power plants in most parts of the country, so shifting to natural gas for cooking and heating needs may be a more cost-effective and carbon-reducing solution if putting in your own renewable energy system is not viable. For every kilowatt hour of energy saved, your CO_2 emissions will fall by 1.6 pounds, depending on how electricity is generated locally, according to Dauncey in *Stormy Weather.*

• Replacing incandescent lights with compact-fluorescent bulbs provides a guaranteed 120 percent return on your investment while immediately reducing your energy needs and carbon emissions.

• Put power strips on any appliances like televisions or DVD players, so you can easily cut "phantom loads," electrical currents flowing to appliances 24/7, even when the appliance is off.

• If you use lighted holiday decorations, switch to LED (light emitting diodes) lights.

• For cooking in the home, consider replacing an electric stove with a natural gas one.

• When cooking, use energy-efficient cookware like the Swiss double-walled Kuhn Rikon Durotherm cook pan, Crock-Pots, and pressure cookers.

• Search out Energy Star-certified appliances that are more energy efficient and therefore, result in fewer carbon dioxide emissions. Replacing hard-duty machines like clothes washers, refrigerators, and air conditioners makes the greatest impact. Visit www.energystar.gov

• If outdoor lighting is necessary, consider using motion sensor-controlled lighting with LED floodlights or high-intensity discharge (HID) lamps: either metal halide, high-pressure, or sodium and low-pressure sodium lamps, which provide the most output per watt.

Carbon-Free: For Shelter Construction

Green Design and Natural Building

Your home can be a huge energy drain and require a lot of material and energy to construct. There are plenty of relatively low-cost ways to help reduce heat loss or gain that will make your home more comfortable while whittling down carbon emissions.

• Seal air leaks around windows and doors.

• Add R-40 insulation to attic spaces and R-12 insulation to basement walls.

• Install shrink-foil window kits on at least half your windows if you do not have low-emissivity, gas-filled, double-pane windows.

• Install a solar tube—relatively easy-to-install devices that permit daylight into rooms without heat loss or gain commonly associated with traditional skylights—in one of the more frequently used rooms.

• For new construction or remodeling, select sustainably harvested materials, natural materials sourced locally, and materials made with recycled content. Also examine various site considerations to optimize solar gain, and consider landscaping options to reduce heating and cooling needs.

• Remodel, build, and live in a home that is appropriately sized for your needs rather than a grandiose mansion.

Carbon-Free: Power Generation

There are many ways for homeowners to be free from utility expenses while completely breaking your addiction to fossil fuel. While limited by your site, many homeowners generate their own electricity with a residential-sized wind turbine or solar electric photovoltaic system, a solar thermal system to heat hot water or for in-floor radiant heating, use a geothermal system to heat or cool their home, and, where downed wood is readily available, use a wood stove for heat. People living in or near cities can collect waste fryer oil from area restaurants and convert it to biodiesel to use in oil-burning furnaces.

Each of these renewable energy systems takes huge carbon emission bites out of your contribution to global warming. According to the American Solar Energy Society's landmark report, "Tackling Climate Change in the U.S." concentrating on solar power, photovoltaics, wind power, biomass, biofuels, and geothermal power, combined with energy efficiency measures, can displace approximately 1.2 billion tons of carbon emissions annually by the year 2030—the magnitude of reduction that scientists believe is necessary to prevent the most dangerous consequences of climate change.

Carbon-Free: At Work

Making Your Livelihood Have a Triple Bottom Line

• Explore options to telecommute or work on flexible time arrangements to avoid hours idling in traffic. Companies adopting telecommuting have found savings related to equipment and office space needs, a reduction in emissions, and, in some states, actually received tax credits. See www.tjobs.com/hiresavings.shtml

• Help your company adopt a "triple bottom line" approach to business that considers the community, environment, and the economy in how it operates and in the types of products or services it sells. Adopt the same carbon-reducing practices on the job as you employ at home.

• Car-pool with colleagues or use mass transit if you're unable to walk or bicycle to work.

• Better yet, work from home and avoid commuting all together; perhaps start a small business. See www.ecopreneuring.biz

Carbon-Free: On Vacation

• Pursue ecotourism-related travel experiences in which travel helps restore or preserve the cultural areas you visit while enriching the local community. See ecotourism.org.

• Support carbon-negative businesses or organizations that have made a commitment to both reduce their carbon emissions and purchase carbon offsets for their operations.

• Since airline travel, especially long-distance trips, result in huge CO_2 emissions, travel closer to home.

• Rather than numerous weekend trips, try to travel for a week-long getaway since it can reduce your emissions (depending on how far you travel) and cut down on the fuel you end up using compared to taking multiple weekend jaunts.

Carbon-Free: Lifestyle

• There are always ways to further reduce the frequency of trips into town by piggy-backing shopping with a trip to an evening concert or church. Combining errands or picking something up for a neighbor can whittle away the amount of driving you do.

• Eliminate junk mail. Every year, 100 million trees' worth of direct mail is sent to U.S. homes, consuming more energy than 3 million cars on the road. Over 5 million tons of unwanted mail ends up in dumps, according to the Center for a New American Dream.

• Buy used, local, or get it for free. When securing something used, perhaps through Craigslist, eBay, Freecycle, secondhand stores and flea markets, you're reducing the energy and resources that would otherwise go into making something new.

• Dump the clothes dryer and line dry your laundry.

• Use warm/cold instead of hot/hot wash mode for washing your clothes.

• Run a dishwasher only when it's full.

• If you have a computer, make sure the computer is on sleep-mode or turned off when not in use.

• Adhere to annual furnace and vehicle tune-ups, try to reuse or recycle products, and find other ways to creatively reduce your consumption and waste.

• If you cannot generate your own energy from renewable sources, buy "green power," electricity that comes from renewable energy sources, from your utility if it's offered.

Carbon-Free: In Your Community

A growing number of communities are starting to re-create themselves with an emphasis on building local relationships and a more interconnected local economy where products or services can be secured locally, purchased directly from neighbors. Some communities are embarking on plans to produce some or most of their fuels from non-fossil-fuel sources, like processing soybean oils into biodiesel.

The explosive growth in the "buy local" movement parallels the direct-to-customer growth of local farmers' markets and community supported agriculture, or CSA, whereby shareholders buy shares in a farm for boxes of produce delivered during the growing season and local farmers' markets. Many farmers serve regional customers through buyer clubs or ship directly to their customers from the farm at competitive pricing. Instead of shipping products thousands of miles, you can focus sales in what has been called your foodshed. The implication for these new approaches to business distribution is the reduction of transportation costs, fuel use, and therefore greenhouse gas emissions.

Carbon-Free: At the Supermarket

Agriculture as currently practiced uses myriad forms of fossil-fuel-based chemicals and pesticides and large tractors for cultivation of the fields. Along with an American dietary emphasis on meat products for nourishment, eating lower on the food chain by consuming fruits, vegetables, and herbs can result in a precipitous drop in CO_2 emissions. For every pound of meat you decline to eat, summarizes Dauncey, your GHG emissions fall by 10.5 pounds of CO_2 equivalent (accounting for methane generated by livestock).

- Shopping closer to home at farmers' markets or supporting a CSA cuts down on the distance food must be transported.
- Eating seasonally reduces the distance food is shipped around the country, presently averaging between 1,200 to 2,500 miles.
- Stock up the pantry and eat through your cupboard each year. It will help you avoid wasting the U.S. average of 474 pounds of food each year.
- Where possible, select organic, pasture-raised, or sustainably grown products, since stewardship and organic approaches to agriculture actually help sequester CO_2, according to studies by the Rodale Institute. It also eliminates the amount of chemicals used on crops.
- Better yet, start growing some of your own food in your backyard, patio, or in a rooftop garden.

Offsetting the Carbon Emissions You Can't Avoid

Thanks to carbon-offset programs, within minutes on the Internet or over the telephone, you can completely offset your carbon dioxide emissions. Purchasing carbon offsets are one way to quickly become carbon negative, especially related to those aspects of our carbon diet that are hard to avoid, like airline travel.

Trees absorb carbon dioxide from the atmosphere, storing the carbon in the wood for the life of the tree (and beyond). Renewable energy credits, or RECs, reduce the amount of carbon dioxide and other greenhouse gas emissions when fossil fuels like oil, gas, or coal would have been otherwise burned, emitting greenhouse gases into the atmosphere. For every kilowatt hour of electricity generated from renewable energy sources like wind turbines, photovoltaic systems, or from methane captured on farms, one kilowatt hour less of energy needs to be generated by burning fossil fuels.

Among some of the many purveyors of such carbon sequestering programs include:

Carbonfund.org Foundation: A nonprofit organization offering easy and affordable ways to eliminate your climate impact, hastening the transformation to a clean energy and technology future through various carbon-offset programs. www.carbonfund.org

Trees for the Future: A nonprofit organization that assists in planting trees in developing countries around the world, helping restore ecological integrity, fostering community enterprises, and providing carbon offsetting certificate programs for businesses like Global Cooling and Trees for Travel. www.treesftf.org

Native Energy: A nonprofit organization offering renewable energy credits with WindBuilders or RemooableEnergy (100 percent farm methane). www.nativeenergy.com

Solar Electric Light Fund (SELF): A nonprofit organization promoting, developing, and facilitating solar rural electrification and energy self-sufficiency in developing countries, installing photovoltaic (solar electric) systems that displace the use of kerosene or diesel fuel, thus helping reduce carbon dioxide emissions. www.self.org

TerraPass Inc.: A for-profit company that develops and markets economically viable products that combat global warming by mitigating human-made environmental emissions, investing in renewable energy systems to offset carbon emissions. www.terrapass.com

Further Resources to Turn Down the Heat

• *The Carbon Buster's Home Energy Handbook* by Godo Stoyke (New Society). Reduce your carbon emissions while cutting your home energy costs and save over $17,000 in just five years.

• *Rural Renaissance: Renewing the Quest for the Good Life*, by John Ivanko and Lisa Kivirist (New Society). Covering everything from energy efficiency and managing a kitchen garden to renewable energy, *Rural Renaissance* describes how to transform your farm into a carbon-neutral operation.

• *Stormy Weather: 101 Solutions to Global Cimate Change*, by Guy Dauncey with Patrick Mazza (New Society) . Providing 101 solutions to cutting your carbon emission by reducing fossil fuel use, buying carbon offsets, and selecting green energy options with your utility if you can't generate your own energy.

Funding Your Renewable Energy Systems

Visit the Database of State Incentives for Renewables and Efficiency (DSIRE) at www.dsireusa.org for the latest state and federal financial resources, grants, and tax credit information for renewable energy and energy conservation.

About the Authors

Scott D. Appell is a garden writer, horticultural taxonomist, ethnobotanist, and botanical tutor. He is the author of four books, *Tulips*, *Pansies*, *Orchids*, and *Lilies*. He is a regular contributor to publications of the Brooklyn Botanic Garden, was a contributing author for Llewellyn's *Herbal Almanac* from 2002 to 2004, and appears regularly in the award-winning publication *Plants & Garden News*. His work has been featured in *Martha Stewart Living, American Homestyle, The Journal News,* and *The New York Daily News*. He has identified the floral motifs in Impressionist art for the Metropolitan Museum of Art and in archival textiles for the Cooper Hewitt Museum. Scott lives, writes, gardens, and teaches horticulture on Vieques, Puerto Rico. His consultation company is called The Green Man©.

Lisa Barnes is the founder of Petit Appetit, a culinary service devoted to the palates and health of infants and toddlers. She teaches parents how to provide fresh, healthy, organic foods to their children through private in-home cooking classes, mother's groups, cooking demonstrations, and parenting workshops throughout northern California. She is the author of the iParenting Media Award winning book, *The Petit Appetit Cookbook: Easy, Organic Recipes to Nurture Your Baby and Toddler*. Lisa is currently writing a baby-food cookbook for Williams-Sonoma, and also contributes her blogs, writings, and recipes to various online parenting and organic Web sites (OrganicToBe, iVillage, Mommy Track'd, Chic Blvd). She is on the board of directors of Leah's Pantry, a nonprofit organization that provides nutrition workshops to families, children, and seniors living in transitional and affordable housing. Lisa lives in Sausalito, California, with her husband Lee, son Jonas, and daughter, Ellery. Visit Lisa's Web site at www.petitappetit.com

Dave Boehnlein hails from southeastern Wisconsin, where he would love to return someday and have his own permaculture site. For now, however, he is learning everything he can as the education director and intern coordinator for the Bullock's Permaculture Homestead (www.permacultureportal.com) in Washington State. He also works as research coordinator for Exos Design, an international environmental design company.

Mark Field Bruland was born and raised in the city of Detroit until he left to attend Michigan State University in the mid 1970s. Growing up in Detroit, he developed a romanticized notion of farming from his parents. His father, a dentist, regaled the family with youthful escapades on a relative's farm in Edmore, Michigan. While in college, Mark met and fell in love with Nancy, his wife of over thirty years, before graduating with a bachelor's degree in dairy science. This kicked off a career working for food manufacturing companies, beginning with Kraft Foods in Wausau, Wisconsin. After a 23-year-stint working in southern California, Mark, Nancy and their daughters Emma and Chloe moved back to southwest Wisconsin where they bought the forty-six-acre parcel now known as Appley Ever After Farm. Mark recently constructed an on-farm market building from which to sell their farm products, along with some of their Amish neighbors' crafts and food products. Mark and his wife have taught two organic farming classes at Wisconsin Technical College and Mark continues to write and record new age and neo-classical music. Contact Mark at omschloe@frontiernet.net or by writing him at Appley Ever After Farm, E7439 Getter Road, Viroqua, WI 54665.

Stephen Collette is principal of Your Healthy House, which focuses on indoor environmental inspections and building consulting. Stephen is a certified building biologist environmental consultant and LEED-accredited (Leadership in Energy and Environmental Design) professional. Stephen works to make homes and buildings healthier and greener through the knowledge of building science and environmental health fields.

Paige Doughty is a freelance writer and environmental educator. She graduated with a master's of science in environmental education from Lesley University and the Audubon Expedition Institute in May 2007. Her current activities include working for The Green Streets Initiative, a grassroots organization in Cambridge, Massachusetts; teaching for the Massachusetts Audubon Society, and writing. She hopes someday to live permanently in Western New York and start a farm, but her husband isn't quite ready for rural life! She sees her life's work as helping people reconnect with the natural world, in order to act and care for the Earth and all the beings who live here. For more information visit www.paigedoughty.typepad.com

Laura Gardiner is a Montessori teacher, community activist and vegan milk shake enthusiast. She is a co-founder of the Chicago-based Allium Collective, an intentional community promoting sustainable alternatives in urban living and connecting activist communities across the animal rights, environmental, and peace and justice movements. For more information see www.alliumcollective.org. Laura can be reached at alliumcollective@gmail.com

Graham Hill is a lifetime Boulder, Colorado, resident who has always had a thirst for entrepreneurship and the environment. A University of Colorado graduate, Hill has continued sinking his teeth into the fabric of the Boulder community. He has directed, sold, lobbied, and marketed several operations for diverse electric-vehicle companies including Trans2, Daimler Chrysler, Currie Technologies, and Dynasty Motorcars. In 1997, he founded 21 Wheels, which offers consulting, product placement, and a general methodology toward evolved or modern mobility. His involvement with other cutting-edge advancements in mobility include Carshare, Electric Bikes and Segways, and founding his EcoPass (transit) Program in his neighborhood. His work in the Intermodalism field includes work at Denver Union Station, neighborhood centers, and large commercial developments. He currently is the President of Boulder Carshare amd the Denver Electric Vehicle Council, co-chair of the Boulder County Clean Air Consortium, and sits on the Community Cycles Board. As a principal with Zenn Motorcars, they launched a public company in 2006. He is currently engaged in developing a miniature excursion train in the Missouri Ozarks and recently started a pedicab company called Swift Turtle. In April 2004, he founded the public-private nonprofit company Boulder Breeze, a community effort to bring back the streetcar. He is married and lives in Boulder with his wife Cathy. They have two girls, Peyton, 7; and Lexie Bowe, 5.

Joshua Houdek works on the land use campaign for the Sierra Club and focuses on transportation issues. He began organizing with the North Star Chapter early in 2005. While living in western Colorado for three years, Joshua was active with the Colorado Environmental Coalition, the Rocky Mountain Chapter of the Sierra Club, and the Western Colorado Congress, a grassroots alliance that empowers people to protect their environment. Joshua has a bachelor's degree in geography from the University of Iowa and holds a master's in outdoor education and recreation from the University of Minnesota. When he is not working with an incredible committee of volunteers and dedicated staff, he can be found bicycling, climbing, hiking, and traveling internationally.

Megan Holm lives in Minneapolis, where she bikes year-round, and tries to take at least one bike trip a year. She has ridden across the United States, down the East Coast, throughout the Midwest, into Canada, and also around Ireland and into Scotland. Megan spent the last five years working in a cooperative bicycle shop in Minneapolis where she learned how to actually fix the bicycles she was traveling on. She has presented numerous workshops and presentations about bicycle touring and related topics, including bike commuting, winter riding, and basic bike maintenance. She strives to empower more women to ride their bikes. Megan also loves baking, reading, *Democracy Now!*, and choral music.

John Ivanko and Lisa Kivirist are national speakers, innkeepers of the award-winning Inn Serendipity, widely published journalists and photographers, marketing consultants, and co-authors or contributors to ten books, including *Rural Renaissance, ECOpreneuring, To Be a Kid* and *Be My Neighbor*. Traveling to thirty-five countries on five continents, John has written about or researched numerous ecotourism, green business and sustainable development projects or operations. They've been published in *Mother Earth News, Hobby Farms, E Magazine,* and *Natural Home* as well as contributing to numerous projects for the nonprofit organization, Renewing the Countryside. Inn Serendipity—recognized as one of the "Top 10 Eco-Destinations in North America"—and the home-based marketing consulting company are completely powered by the wind and sun, with net negative carbon emissions. They share the farm with their son, a colony of honeybees, and millions of ladybugs. For more information, see www.ruralrenaissance.org and www.innserendipity.com

Laura E. Kreger grew up in the Minnesota Heartland where she learned how to ride a bicycle, climb a tree, and host a proper potluck. After earning a technical communications degree with an emphasis on health sciences from the University of Wisconsin-Stout, she moved to Portland, Oregon. Much of Laura's time is spent writing, rock climbing, garage saling, acquiring large stacks of library books, trying to grow a vegetable garden on a concrete balcony, participating in the Imago Dei Community, and making lists. Recent projects include embroidering T-shirts for her sister's make-believe band, compiling her six-year-old niece's letters into a comprehensive encyclopedia about unicorns, and trying to convince her roommate that having a worm compost bin inside their apartment is indeed a good idea.

Elizabeth Laskar, one of the United Kingdom's first ethical image and style consultants, is the co-founder of the Ethical Fashion Forum™, works as an independent ethical-fashion consultant worldwide, and is the in-house image consultant in London's first ethical boutique. Her international development involvement includes projects in Ghana, South Africa, and the Commonwealth. She has successful helped women in Ghana increase their earnings from $2 to up to $10 a day by linking them with the fashion sector in the UK. Other campaigns have included working with BBC, London Fashion Week, Paris Prêt a Porter, Paris Ethical Fashion Show, The Ecologist, British Bengali Chambers of Commerce, and NGOs. Raising awareness of ethical fashion is an ongoing task for Elizabeth, who founded SARIDRESS to raise awareness about sustainability issues among young people while creating bespoke dress designs from secondhand saris. She also sat on a roundtable discussion led by Coventry University at the House of Lords in London on Sustainable Enterprise and is on the steering committee for the Young Leaders Integrity Alliance. For more, visit www.ethicalfashionforum.com

Annie O'Grady is an American who has lived and worked for fifteen years in London, England. She has a career in technology and has recently relocated back to the United States with her dog, Sir George. She has a lifelong passion for writing, traveling, adventure and the outdoors. In 2006, she cycled across America (www.anniesbigbikeadventure.blogspot.com) and in 2007 she cycled across Europe (www.annieseuropeanbikeadventure.blogspot.com) and walked the El Camino from St. Jean Pied de Port, France, to Santiago, Spain.

Ken Perry is now living his lifelong dream of worm farming, contracting, and running a book-fair business after varied careers in social work. He lives in an old New England farmhouse, located in the rolling hills of Rollinsford, New Hampshire, with his wife and two cats. His millions of worms are housed in the basement of an attached nineteenth-century post-and-beam dairy barn. You can visit his Web site at www.redworms-greenearth.com

Roslyn Reid is a longtime gardener and contributor of art and articles to Llewellyn publications. Her work has also appeared in magazines such as *Tightwad Living* and *Thrifty Times*, and many of her letters have been published in *Time, Newsweek, Horse Illustrated, The Old-House Journal*, and other general interest magazines. She is one of the contributors to Susun Weed's book, *Breast Cancer? Breast Health!* and to various Web sites. Her ongoing project is to rejuvenate the former fruit farm where she lives in New Jersey with her husband and two Pembroke Welsh Corgis, Bonny and Molly. Currently growing on the grounds around her home are a fruit tree grove, a couple of hazelnut trees, several kiwi vines, a stand of black raspberries, a fig tree, and some blueberry bushes.

Anne Sala considers herself lucky to have grown up in the Connecticut River Valley of rural New Hampshire. There, she learned to appreciate the tastes associated with farm-fresh foods. Although she left the region before the whole "local foods" movement caught on, she loves visiting all the artisans that have set up shop around her hometown. Currently, Anne is a freelance journalist living in Minnesota. She works hard to create as many opportunities for herself to appreciate the hard work chefs go through to bring local foods to the table in restaurants all over the Twin Cities.

Kari C. Tauring, an author, educator, and performance artist, got her first taste of political activism in 1978 when state representatives visited her school to hear the children's pleas for clean water and air—and her sixth-grade class pumped out "Save The Boundary Waters" bumper stickers. That concern for the environment has continued into her adulthood as both a teacher and citizen. Kari has served on the greening committees for the Longfellow Community Council and Minneapolis Public Schools. In 2005, her green curriculum for children was featured in the national conference of the American Community Gardening Association. "Ms. Kari's Summer Green Thumbs" made a convincing argument against calling any plant a "weed." She also teaches the importance of diversity and sustainability on every level in an urban setting through her writing, performance art, and the example of her life.